Lecture Notes in Computer Science 6863

Commenced Publication in 1973
Founding and Former Series Edit
Gerhard Goos, Juris Hartmanis, a

Steven Furnell Costas Lambrinoudakis
Günther Pernul (Eds.)

Trust, Privacy and Security in Digital Business

8th International Conference, TrustBus 2011
Toulouse, France, August 29 – September 2, 2011
Proceedings

 Springer

Volume Editors

Steven Furnell
University of Plymouth, School of Computing, Communications and Electronics
Plymouth, PL4 8AA, UK
E-mail: sfurnell@plymouth.ac.uk

Costas Lambrinoudakis
University of Piraeus, Department of Digital Systems
18532 Piraeus, Greece
E-mail: clam@unipi.gr

Günther Pernul
University of Regensburg, Department of Management Information Systems
Universitätsstraße 31, 93053 Regensburg, Germany
E-mail: guenther.pernul@wiwi.uni-regensburg.de

ISSN 0302-9743   e-ISSN 1611-3349
ISBN 978-3-642-22889-6   e-ISBN 978-3-642-22890-2
DOI 10.1007/978-3-642-22890-2
Springer Heidelberg Dordrecht London New York

Library of Congress Control Number: 2011933586

CR Subject Classification (1998): C.2, K.6.5, D.4.6, E.3, H.4, J.1

LNCS Sublibrary: SL 4 – Security and Cryptology

Typesetting: Camera-ready by author, data conversion by Scientific Publishing Services, Chennai, India

Printed on acid-free paper

Springer is part of Springer Science+Business Media (www.springer.com)

Preface

This book presents the proceedings of the 8th International Conference on Trust, Privacy and Security in Digital Business (TrustBus 2011), held in Toulouse, France, during September 1–2, 2011. The conference continues from previous events held in Zaragoza (2004), Copenhagen (2005), Krakow (2006), Regensburg (2007), Turin (2008), Linz (2009) and Bilbao (2010).

The recent advances in the information and communication technologies (ICT) have raised new opportunities for the implementation of novel applications and the provision of high-quality services over global networks. The aim is to utilize this 'information society era' to improve the quality of life for all citizens, disseminating knowledge, strengthening social cohesion, generating earnings and finally ensuring that organizations and public bodies remain competitive in the global electronic marketplace. Unfortunately, such a rapid technological evolution cannot be problem-free. Concerns are raised regarding the 'lack of trust' in electronic procedures and the extent to which 'information security' and 'user privacy' can be ensured.

TrustBus 2011 brought together academic researchers and industry developers who discussed the state of the art in technology for establishing trust, privacy and security in digital business. We thank the attendees for coming to Toulouse to participate and debate the new emerging advances in this area.

The conference program included one keynote presentation and seven technical papers sessions. The keynote speech entitled "The Shifting Security Perimeter and the Computer in Your Pocket" was delivered by Ram Herkanaidu, Kaspersky Lab (UK). The reviewed paper sessions covered a broad range of topics, from authentication and authorization in digital business to security usability and risk management, and from privacy and identity management to reliability and security of content and data. The conference attracted many high-quality submissions, each of which was assigned to four referees for review, and the final acceptance rate was 35%.

We would like to express our thanks to the various people who assisted us in organizing the event and formulating the program. We are very grateful to the Program Committee members and the external reviewers, for their timely and rigorous reviews of the papers. Thanks are also due to the DEXA Organizing Committee for supporting our event, and in particular to Gabriela Wagner for her help with the administrative aspects.

Finally, we would like to thank all of the authors that submitted papers for the event and contributed to an interesting set of conference proceedings.

September 2011

Steven Furnell
Costas Lambrinoudakis
Günther Pernul

Organization

General Chair

Günther Pernul   University of Regensburg, Germany

Program Co-chairs

Steven Furnell   University of Plymouth , UK
Costas Lambrinoudakis   University of Piraeus, Greece

International Program Committee

Alessandro Acquisti   Carnegie Mellon University, USA
Isaac Agudo   University of Malaga, Spain
Marco Casassa Mont   HP Labs Bristol, UK
David Chadwick   University of Kent, UK
Cheng-Kang Chu   I2R, Singapore
Nathan Clarke   University of Plymouth, UK
Frederic Cuppens   TELECOM Bretagne, France
Ernesto Damiani   Università degli Studi di Milano, Italy
Sabrina De Capitani
   di Vimercati   Università degli Studi di Milano, Italy
Jan Eloff   University of Pretoria / SAP Research,
                                      South Africa
Carmen Fernandez-Gago   University of Malaga, Spain
Eduardo B. Fernandez   Florida Atlantic University, USA
Simone Fischer-Huebner   Karlstad University, Sweden
Sara Foresti   Università degli Studi di Milano, Italy
Jürgen Fuß   Upper Austria University of Applied Sciences,
                                      Campus Hagenberg, Austria
Dimitris Geneiatakis   Columbia University, USA
Juan M. Gonzalez-Nieto   Queensland University of Technology, Australia
Dimitris Gritzalis   Athens University of Economics and Business,
                                      Greece
Stefanos Gritzalis   University of the Aegean, Greece
Marit Hansen   Independent Centre for Privacy Protection
                                      Schleswig-Holstein, Germany
Audun Jøsang   Oslo University, Norway
Christos Kalloniatis   University of the Aegean, Greece

External Reviewers

Bastian Braun	Institute of IT Security and Security Law, Passau, Germany
Vit Bukac	Masaryk University, Czech Republic
Jaromir Dobias	Masaryk University, Czech Republic
Mariki Eloff	University of South Africa, South Africa
Stefan Fenz	SBA Research, Austria
Safaa Hachana	SWID, France
Al-Sinani Haitham	Royal Holloway, University of London, UK
Markus Huber	SBA Research, Austria
Ravi Jhawar	Università degli Studi di Milano, Italy
Peter Kieseberg	SBA Research, Austria
Jiri Kur	Masaryk University, Czech Republic
Andreas Leicher	Novalyst IT AG, Germany
Manuel Leithner	SBA Research, Austria
Hsiao-Ying Lin	National Chiao Tung University, Taiwan
Giovanni Livraga	Università degli Studi di Milano, Italy
Martin Mulazzani	SBA Research, Austria
Alexios Mylonas	Athens University of Economics and Business, Greece
Kenneth Radke	Queensland University of Technology, Australia
Ahmad Sabouri	Goethe University Frankfurt, Germany
Daniel Schreckling	Institute of IT Security and Security Law, Passau, Germany
Sebastian Schrittwieser	SBA Research, Austria
Tobias Smolka	Masaryk University, Czech Republic
Andriy Stetsko	Masaryk University, Czech Republic
Petr Svenda	Masaryk University, Czech Republic
Lorenz Zechner	SBA Research, Austria

Table of Contents

Intrusion Detection and Information Filtering

Management of Privacy and Confidentiality

Cryptographic Protocols/ Usability of Security

Electrostatic Force Method:
Trust Management Method Inspired by the Laws of Physics

Konrad Leszczyński and Maciej Zakrzewicz

Poznań University of Technology,
Piotrowo 2, 60-965 Poznań, Poland
{konrad.leszczynski,maciej.zakrzewicz}@cs.put.poznan.pl

Abstract. Online auctions are among the most important e-commerce services. Unfortunately it is very difficult to assure trust in such customer-to-customer environment. Most auction sites utilize a very simple participation counts system for reputation rating. This feedback-based reputation systems do not differentiate between sellers who trade in luxury goods and those who sell worthless trinkets. A fraudster can easily gain reputation by selling hundreds of cheap books and then cheat while selling a few expensive TV sets which are not as good as described on item page.

In this paper we present a novel trust management method called *Electrostatic Force Method* (EFM) which calculates *Personal Subjective Trust* instead of overall reputation value. The trust value depends on price and category of an item one wants to buy. In this method a seller could have high trust value for someone who wants to buy a book and at the same time this seller may not be trustworthy for someone who wants to buy a TV set. Furthermore our method can be applied in addition to the system currently used by eBay-like online auction sites because it does not require any additional information other than positive, negative or neutral feedback on transactions.

Keywords: online auction sites, reputation system, trust management method.

1 Introduction

Statistics (see [18,15]) show that hundreds of millions of people are using online auction sites like eBay[17], Taobao[19] and Allegro[16]. Obviously these sites give a great opportunity to traders who can choose from a vast number of offers and meet millions of potential customers. Online transactions, however, are a bit more dangerous than traditional ones due to the anonymity of portal users. Furthermore, the majority of popular auction sites use the same very simple trust mechanism in which the credibility of a user is the number of positive feedbacks minus the number of negative ones. This mechanism is insufficient in many aspects. Firstly, reputation of a buyer and reputation of a seller is treated equally.

S. Furnell, C. Lambrinoudakis, and G. Pernul (Eds.): TrustBus 2011, LNCS 6863, pp. 1–12, 2011.
© Springer-Verlag Berlin Heidelberg 2011

Overall reputation score combines information of feedbacks gained after buys and sells, so one needs to study detailed information about potential traders to check if she/he has gained reputation by buying or selling[1]. Secondly, buyers are often hesitant to give negative feedback for fear of retaliation if the seller is a huge online store (on which a single feedback has virtually no effect) and occasional buyer (with only a few reputation scores) does not want to get any negative feedback. Thirdly, in existing reputation system it is impossible to check what kind of sold item is represented by a feedback and how expensive it was. Existing reputation systems create some kind of Simpson's paradox[11], because information about a seller who trades with luxury goods and worthless trinkets is aggregated into a single reputation value. It is unlikely for anyone to buy a TV in a grocery shop in non-virtual environment, whereas it is rather common situation in online auctions. Let us consider a hypothetical seller *Cut-Me-Own-Throat Dibbler* who has gained high reputation score by selling 400 *"lucky amulets that bring good health"* for 3 euros each and then starts acting dishonestly. After selling every four or five cheap amulets he sells one expensive TV set which is not exactly *"new and in good condition"* for 500 euros. This so called "accumulation" fraud is an increasing problem (see [7,3] for example). In the existing system, *Dibbler* will constantly gain increasing reputation score as long as he gets positive feedback for more than half of transactions.

We argue that the best solution for the problems discussed above is to replace the overall reputation value with Personal Subjective Trust (PST) evaluated by Electrostatic Force Method. The trust for a seller should by different depending on what a buyer wants to buy. In the above example *Dibbler* is trustworthy from the point of view of someone who wants to buy a lucky amulet but at the same time Dibbler is not trustworthy for someone who wants to buy a TV set.

Moreover we do not have to change the way users rate each other. A great advantage of the trust system currently used by eBay, Taobao, Allegro and other auction sites is the simplicity of use. We do not intend to confuse users with sophisticated method of rating but we want the item page to show PST evaluated by EFM in addition to overall score currently used. That solution will allow buyers to quickly and easily asses credibility of sellers, most importantly their credibility in contex of selling the particular kind of item.

2 Related Work

The Feedback Forum used by most auction sites (like [17,16,19]) is perhaps best known example of rating system. It is impossible for a buyer to read all the textual comments associated with all potential sellers' previous transactions, therefore auction sites sum up all positive comments and substract all negative ones and present it as a single reputation score. This system has many drawbacks (see also [5,12,2]). Many researchers presented trust algorithms and metrics

---

[1] Overall reputation score is shown next to user's name on every item page so it is visible at a glance, whereas details about feedbacks are visible only on user's information pages.

based on more sophisticated reputation functions to quantify trust, for example classic algorithm SPORAS [13] and PeerTrust model [12]. These algorithms use a *consensus-based function* i.e. all system's users agree how trustworthy is every particular user. Our previously presented Asymptotic Trust Algorithm (ATA) [4] can be implemented along with the commonly used trust system and provide some useful information about user's reputation history but it is also consensus-based.

Some scientists (e.g. [1]) suggest that the trust of a user cannot be presented as a single global value and depends on who is asking for the trust value. Algorithms like HISTOS [13] or RRM [14] based on the principle: *If A trust B and B trust C, then A should trust C to some extend.* However others (like for example Marsh [6]) pointed out that trust is not transitive.

Unfortunately above methods do not deal with the Simpson's paradox mention in the Introduction, because they aggregate user's reputation to a value/score regardless of the situation in which one is asking for trust. Furthermore most of these solutions are difficult to introduce into existing auction systems because they change the way user interact.

Most scholars realised that negative feedbacks are very rare (see [4,10,9]). Mainly because buyers are often hesitant to give negative feedback for fear of retaliation. [8] presented an interesting idea how to deal with *implicit feedbacks* but a simpler way is to treat sellers' reputation differently and more carefully.

3   Electrostatic Force Method (EFM)

3.1   Definitions and Metaphor Based on the Laws of Physics

EFM is inspired by *Coulomb's Law* describing the electrostatic interaction between charged particles. In EFM feedbacks gained by a seller are represented by *Feedback's Charges* q in 3-dimensional Euclidean space, called *Reputation Space* – Figure 1. Positive electric charges q^+ represent positive feedbacks, negative electric charges q^- represent negative feedbacks and neutral feedbacks do not change reputation therefore are not represented by charges. When a transaction is made and a feedback is given, a new Feedback's Charge is located in the Reputation Space. Price and category of sold item determine the position of the charge. Once put particles can not move, they are fixed in the Reputation Space. Coordinates of Feedback's Charge are:

- The z coordinate is constant $q_i z = 0$, charges are placed only on the xy plane.
- The x coordinate represents the price of the sold item $q_i x = \log_2(price_i)$. We use $\log_2$ to "smoothly" differentiate items by their prices. We have assumed that when feedbacks are compared the distance between feedbacks related to an item for 10€ and an item for 20€ should by the same as the distance between feedbacks related to an item for 100€ and an item for 200€.
- The y coordinate represents the category of the sold item. There is a certain distance between each pair of categories, for example *Computers* and *Electronics* are similar therefore these categories are relatively close to each

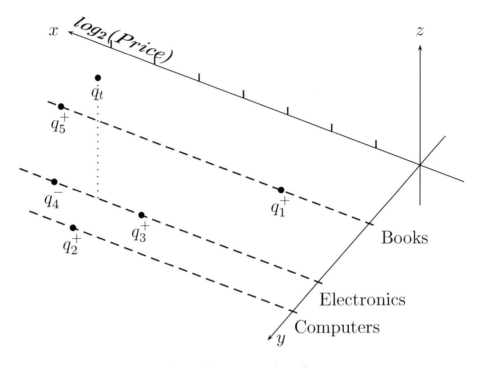

Fig. 1. Reputation of a seller

other. Auction portal administrators may freely define distances between categories, so it may be impossible to arrange a lot of categories on one axis but this is only a metaphor and EFM does not need the position in y-dimension to evaluate trust but only requires distances Δy_{ab} between each pair of (a, b) categories. In particular the distance between categories may be defined as

$$\Delta y_{ab} = \begin{cases} 0 & \text{if } a = b \\ constant > 0 & \text{if } a \neq b \end{cases}$$

Instead of a single reputation value a buyer evaluates an item dependent trust value. To evaluate seller's trust a *Trust Test Charge* q_t (a negatively charged particle $q_t = -1C$) is placed in the Reputation Space and Coulomb force is calculated. The location of the Trust Test Charge is determined by price ($q_t x$) and category ($q_t y$) of the item the buyer wants to buy and certain (arbitrarily chosen) location in z-dimension $q_t z$. The z-component of Coulomb force vector represents the seller's trust, i.e. the stronger the Test Charge is pulled toward the xy plane (plane with all charges representing feedbacks) the more trustworthy is the seller.

The electrostatic force is inversely proportional to the square of the distance between charged particles. Due to this property the item dependent trust value is highly influenced by feedbacks related to items from the same or similar category and similar price.

In the simplest implementation each particle has the unit charge (for example one coulomb $q^+ = 1C$ and $q^- = -1C$). However it may be desired to treat old feedbacks as less important – this can by easily achieved by decreasing the charge in time. Every feedback puts a new particle with a maximum charge and then the charge starts "fading" slowly until it disappears completely after a long time. It is also possible to build a system with more options for feedback provider by allowing users to use charges of different strength to indicate different levels of satisfaction or dissatisfaction. For example, we can easily adopt EFM to 5-star rating system[2].

3.2 Example

Figure 1 show an example of a seller's reputation. The seller sold the following items:

- A cheap book for 4€ and gets positive feedback for this transaction (q_1^+).
- A computer part for 32€, gets positive feedback (q_2^+).
- A piece of electronics for 16€, gets positive feedback (q_3^+).
- A piece of electronics for 64€, gets negative feedback (q_4^-).
- A very rare and expensive book for 128€, gets positive feedback (q_5^+).

Assume that a buyer wants to buy an MP3 Player for 32€ from the seller. The Figure 1 shows Trust Test Charge q_t over the Electronics category over the place on the xy plane where potentially a Feedback's Charge would be located for this transaction if the feedback will by given.

3.3 Formulas

According to the Coulomb's Law, the force exerted on Trust Test Charge q_t by charged particle q_i is defined as:

$$\vec{F} = kq_t \frac{q_i}{r_i^2} \hat{r}_i$$

where r_i is the distance (between q_t and Feedback's Charge q_i) and $\hat{r}_i$ is a unit vector pointing along the line from q_i to q_t. k is called "Coulomb force constant" (or "the electric force constant") and in real physical world is defined to be $k = 8.99 * 10^9 \frac{Nm^2}{C^2}$ but in our system it is just a scaling factor.

The principle of linear superposition may be used to calculate the force on the Trust Test Charge due to a set of n Feedback's Charges:

$$\vec{F} = \sum_{i=1}^{n} \vec{F}_i$$

---

[2] 5-star rating system is used by eBay as Detailed Seller Ratings. A buyer can rate: accuracy of item description, communication, delivery time and postage & packaging charges.

The unit vector $\hat{r}_i$ may be calculated using simple geometry:

$$\hat{r}_i = \frac{\Delta x_{it}\hat{x} + \Delta y_{it}\hat{y} + \Delta z_{it}\hat{z}}{r_i}$$

where $\hat{x}$, $\hat{y}$ and $\hat{z}$ are unit vectors directed along the positive axes a, y and z respectively. Δx_{it} is the difference of positions in the x-dimension between the i-th Feedback's Charge and the Trust Test Charge, defined as $\Delta x_{it} = (q_i x - q_t x) = (\log_2(price_i) - \log_2(price_t))$. Δy_{it} is the distance between category of Trust Test Charge and category of i-th Feedback's Charge (distances between each pair of categories are defined arbitrarily). Δz_{it} is the difference of positions in the z-dimension $\Delta z_{it} = q_i z - q_t z$. All the Feedback's Charges are placed on the xy plane (always $q_i z = 0$) and $q_t z = constant > 0$, therefore $\Delta z_{it} = -q_t z$. And the distance between Trust Test Charge and i-th Feedback's Charge is defined as:

$$r_i = \sqrt{{\Delta x_{it}}^2 + {\Delta y_{it}}^2 + {\Delta z_{it}}^2}$$

We defined the Personal Subjective Trust of a seller as the force that pulls toward the xy plane therefore to calculate trust PST we need only the magnitude of the z-component of the force vector:

$$|\hat{z}_i| = \frac{\Delta z_{it}}{r_i}$$

EFM defines Personal Subjective Trust of a seller as:

$$PST = kq_t \sum_{i=1}^{n} \frac{q_i}{r_i^2}|\hat{z}_i|$$

$\Delta z_{it} = -q_t z$ and q_t is a negative charge $q_t = -1$ so we do not need to use vectors to calculate trust and instead use the formula:

$$PST = kq_t z \sum_{i=1}^{n} \frac{q_i}{r_i^3} \tag{1}$$

PST needs to be calculated in three cases: when an auction is started, in case of new bid (change of price) and when the seller gets a new feedback (in this case the whole sum do not need to be calculated again, only one component is added to previous PST value). Time complexity of this algorithm is O(n) (where n is the number of feedbacks received by the seller). We implemented PST method in C#, and observe that standard desktop computer with Pentium 4 processor needs less than 0.01s to calculate PST for a seller with more than 100000 feedbacks therefore our method will not overload auction portals' servers.

4 Experimental Evaluation

To verify if EFM meets our expectations we performed a series of experiments. We used synthetic datasets to observe how the calculated trust value will differ in certain circumstances. Gathering real data from auction site allows us to make sure that EFM is useful.

4.1 Verifying the Principles

Firstly let us test the behaviour of EFM in case of extremely simple situation to demonstrate and verify the principles. Figure 2a shows a Reputation Space of a seller who sold one item for 4€ and one item for 1024€ and got positive feedbacks for this transactions. Figure 2b shows a Reputation Space of a different seller who also sold one item for 4€ and one item for 1024€, but this seller got negative feedback for the expensive item. A buyer wants to buy an item for 64€ (also from the same category) so Trust Test Charge is placed in both Reputation Spaces to evaluate and compare sellers credibility. For the sake of clarity every item belongs to the same category and Figure 2 does not present the y-dimension. In this experiments we used the following parameters: $q_t z = 4$ and

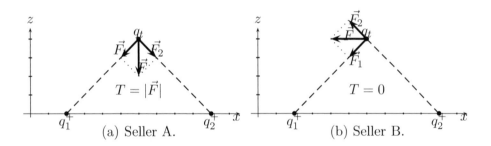

(a) Seller A. (b) Seller B.

Fig. 2. Evaluating credibility of sellers with only 2 feedbacks in only one category

$k = 32$ (with this parameter's values length of vectors on the figures represents their magnitude). We can use Formula (1) to calculate Personal Subjective Trust: For seller A: $PST = 32 * 4 * (\frac{1}{\sqrt{4^2+0^2+4^2}^3} + \frac{1}{\sqrt{4^2+0^2+4^2}^3}) = \frac{2}{\sqrt{2}} \approx 1.414$ And for seller B: $PST = 32 * 4 * (\frac{1}{\sqrt{4^2+0^2+4^2}^3} + \frac{-1}{\sqrt{4^2+0^2+4^2}^3}) = 0$ As we can see negative and positive feedbacks neutralise each other and positive ones adds up so the basic requirement is met.

Let us use the same sellers to demonstrate how the trust looks from different points of view. Imagine buyers who wants to buy 7 different items (in particular it might by a single buyer who wants to buy 7 items at once). When a buyer enters an item page he/she sees trust value of the item's seller. With EFM presented trust value will be also different for different items. Figure 3 and related Table 1 show 7 different evaluations (7 different Trust Test Charges)

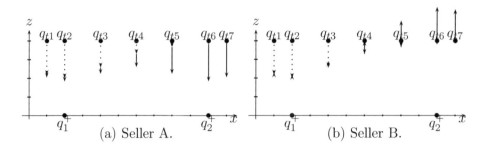

Fig. 3. Evaluating credibility in cases of 7 different items to buy

Table 1. Values of trust from the perspective of 7 different items

	q_{t1}	q_{t2}	q_{t3}	q_{t4}	q_{t5}	q_{t6}	q_{t7}
Item price	2	4	16	64	256	1024	2048
PST: seller A	1.960	2.179	1.772	1.414	1.772	2.179	1.960
PST: seller B	1.692	1.821	1.090	0.000	-1.090	-1.821	-1.692

Table 2. Δy distances between categories

	Computers	Electronics	Phones	Books	Others
Computers	0	2	4	6	10
Electronics	2	0	2	4	8
Phones	4	2	0	4	6
Books	6	4	4	0	4
Others	10	8	6	4	0

related to 7 items with different prices (again items are from the same category for the sake of clarity).

Figure 3 shows only z-component of forces. Sum of the z-component of forces between the Trust Test Charge and Feedbacks' Charges is the Personal Subjective Trust evaluated by EFM whereas x and y components of Coulomb's force do not influence trust value. Dotted lines represent the z-component of forces between Test Charge and feedback q_1 and solid lines represent the z-component of forces between Test Charge and feedback q_2. This simple experiment demonstrates that credibility of a seller depends not only on the number of gained positive and negative feedbacks but also depends on the kind of sold items related to these feedbacks. Ignoring the fact that history containing only two feedbacks is insufficient to asses seller in any case, we can see that seller B is quite reliable (has good history) in case of unexpensive item but is untrustworthy in case of expensive ones.

To perform further experiments we had to define distance (Δy) between each pair of categories. Table 2 presents distance we have chosen to perform our experiments. These values are based on our intuition (for example phones are similar to electronics so distance between this categories is small) but of course they may be defined differently. Now we can calculate PST for the example presented in subsection 3.2 (and Figure 1): $PST = 32 * 4 * (\frac{1}{\sqrt{3^2+4^2+4^2}^3} + \frac{1}{\sqrt{0^2+2^2+4^2}^3} + \frac{1}{\sqrt{1^2+0^2+4^2}^3} + \frac{-1}{\sqrt{1^2+0^2+4^2}^3} + \frac{1}{\sqrt{2^2+4^2+4^2}^3}) \approx 2.511$

4.2 Real Dataset

To examine real life use case we used transaction history of certain Allegro users. Figure 4 presents feedbacks gained by two sellers between 20th February and 1st March 2011[3]. Let us consider a buyer who wants to buy a certain phone accessory,

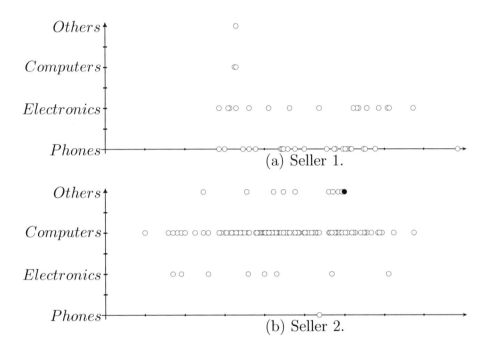

Fig. 4. Reputation Space of two sellers from the point of view of someone who wants to buy from Phones category

both sellers offered it for 41.25€ [4]. The y-axes on both Figure 4a and Figure 4b represent Feedback's Charges distances from Phones category i.e. figures show Reputation Spaces of these two sellers from the point of view of someone who wants to buy an item from category *Phones*. The x-axes is related to sold items

---

[3] On Allegro detailed information are available only for recent transaction, so we will consider only small part of sellers history. To perform this experiment we chose sellers who sold a lot of items in that short period of time.

[4] Assuming exchange rate in March 2011: 1€ = 4PLN.

prices ($q_i x = \log_2(price_i)$). Each empty circle on the figure represents one positive feedback. In our dataset there is only one negative feedback – the black circle on Figure 4b in category "Others".

Seller 1 gained 87 positive feedbacks and Seller 2 gained 198 positive feedbacks and 1 negative so in the currently used reputation system during chosen time they score 87 and 197 respectively. As we can see the Seller 2 gets over twice the points as the Seller 1 but most of Seller's 2 feedbacks are related to Computers category. He/she sells a lot of computers, computer parts and accessories but only occasionally something from Phones category. Seller 2 on the other hand is specialised in Phones and Electronics.

Using the same parameters as before, i.e. $q_t z = 4$, $k = 32$ and distances from Phone category from Table 2 we can calculate Personal Subjective Trust for both sellers:

– Seller 1: $PST = 121.1$
– Seller 2: $PST = 126.5$

As we can see, in this case sellers are almost equally trustworthy. We would like to point out that values of parameters that we have chosen assure that PST value is in the same scale as currently used reputation score. This experiment shows that buyer will be able to easily compare PST value with reputation score currently used. PST slightly greater (like in case of Seller 1) indicates that the seller trades mostly in items similar to the item the buyer wants to buy. In case of Seller 2 PST is smaller than simple feedback count because he/she sells a lot of items from different categories. Auction sites users may accept new measure easier if its values will be similar to the one currently used.

4.3   Impact of Parameter Settings

Let us now examine how the trust value evaluated by EFM will differ if we change Trust Test Charge position in z-dimension. Table 3 presents PST value of the same two sellers from the point of view of a buyer who wants to buy the same phone accessory for 41.25€ but in case of differently defined $q_t z$ parameter. For better illustration we have adjusted the k scaling factors in such a way that

Table 3. PST value for different $q_t z$ parameter

$q_t z$	1	2	4	8	32	100
PST: Seller 1	587.385	297.897	121.115	38.591	2.695	0.278
PST: Seller 2	113.562	132.933	126.537	66.818	5.985	0.629

PST of Seller 1 is equal to his/her feedback count, Table 4 presents the results. As we expected the lower the values of $q_t z$ the more favoured will be the sellers who trade in items very similar to the item the buyer wants to buy. If $q_t z$ value is very height, EFM produces results similar to simple feedback count systems used currently.

Table 4. PST value for different $q_t z$ and k parameters

$q_t z$	1	2	4	8	32	100
k	4.740	9.346	22.986	72.142	1032.865	10008.923
PST: Seller 1	87	87	87	87	87	87
PST: Seller 2	16.820	38.823	90.894	150.637	193.185	196.602

5 Conclusion

In this paper we have presented a novel approach to trust management in online auctions. Feedback-based reputation systems currently used by auction sites and algorithms presented in literature aggregate trust and ignore the context of item's price and category. This creates kind of Simpson's paradox. Many of these algorithms of course take price into account when calculating reputation score but they simply treat expensive items as more important (which is not always the case) and "flatten" trust to a single value. One can easily imagine a seller who is very thorough and helpful when selling a TV and does not care when selling small potatoes. We believe that Electrostatic Force Method is the first method that deals with this Simpson's paradox and is still easy to use and understand from users' point of view. The presented method shows sellers in different light depending on what kind and how expensive item one wants to buy because one seller may be more trustworthy when one wants to buy a TV and other may be better in case of book sales.

EFM is focused on sellers' reputation because the success of a transaction depends mostly on seller's honesty. A buyer who usually sends money before getting the product takes a great risk, whereas a seller might easily cheat by selling items which have some hidden failures or are second-hand instead of new. A buyer simply does not get the product if she/he does not pay, so it is very unlikely that a buyer will cheat. Treating sellers differently assures that buyers will not hesitate to submit a negative feedback when necessary, which may be the case in currently used system, because of buyers' fear of retaliation.

In our opinion the best complex solution for reputation system in auction sites is to combine our previous ATA algorithm [4] and EFM with existing feedback-based reputation system. Both ATA and EFM were designed to utilize feedback information currently available on auction sites, we do not need to confuse users with different methods of rating transactions. An item page may present the value calculated by EFM which describes sellers trust in context of this particular item.

In our future work we consider extending this mechanism to buyers' reputation. We want also to adapt our method to work with 5-star rating system used by eBay and similar auction sites as Detailed Seller Ratings. Even more promising seems to be the version of EFM where ratings decrease gradually to make old transactions less important, i.e. new rating puts a maximum (positive or negative) charge and then the charge starts "fading" slowly until it disappears completely. We would like also to find different applications for

EFM not only in e-commerce but also other multi-agent systems. Such reputation mechanism may be useful in all kinds of discussion forums and recommendation systems.

References

1. DeFigueiredo, D., Barr, E.T., Wu, S.F.: Trust Is in the Eye of the Beholder. In: CSE, vol. (3), pp. 100–108 (2009)
2. Houser, D., Wooders, J.: Reputation in Auctions: Theory, and Evidence from eBay. Journal of Economics & Management Strategy 15(2), 353–369 (2006)
3. Kwan, M.Y.K., Overill, R.E., Chow, K.P., Silomon, J.A.M., Tse, H., Law, F.Y.W., Lai, P.K.Y.: Evaluation of Evidence in Internet Auction Fraud Investigations. In: IFIP Int. Conf. Digital Forensics, pp. 121–132 (2010)
4. Leszczyński, K.: Asymptotic Trust Algorithm: Extension for reputation systems in online auctions. In: KKNTPD 2010 - III Krajowa Konferencja Naukowa Technologie Przetwarzania Danych (2010)
5. Malaga, R.A.: Web-Based Reputation Management Systems: Problems and Suggested Solutions. Electronic Commerce Research 1, 403–417 (2001)
6. Marsh, S.P.: Formalising Trust as a Computational Concept. Ph.D. thesis, Department of Mathematics and Computer Science, University of Stirling (1994)
7. Morzy, M.: New algorithms for mining the reputation of participants of online auctions. Algorithmica 52(1), 95–112 (2008)
8. Morzy, M., Wierzbicki, A.: The Sound of Silence: Mining Implicit Feedbacks to Compute Reputation. In: Spirakis, P.G., Mavronicolas, M., Kontogiannis, S.C. (eds.) WINE 2006. LNCS, vol. 4286, pp. 365–376. Springer, Heidelberg (2006)
9. O'Donovan, J., Evrim, V., Smyth, B., McLeod, D., Nixon, P.: Personalizing Trust in Online Auctions. In: STAIRS, pp. 72–83 (2006)
10. Resnick, P., Zeckhauser, R.: Trust Among Strangers in Internet Transactions: Empirical Analysis of eBay's Reputation System. The Economics of the Internet and E-Commerce 11(2), 23–25 (2002)
11. Simpson, E.H.: The Interpretation of Interaction in Contingency Tables. Journal of the Royal Statistical Society, Ser. B 13 (1951)
12. Xiong, L., Liu, L.: A Reputation-Based Trust Model for Peer-to-Peer eCommerce Communities. In: IEEE International Conference on E-Commerce Technology, p. 275 (2003)
13. Zacharia, G., Maes, P.: Trust management through reputation mechanisms. Applied Artificial Intelligence 14(7), 881–907 (2000)
14. Zhang, H., Duan, H.X., Liu, W.: RRM: An incentive reputation model for promoting good behaviors in distributed systems. Science in China Series F: Information Sciences 51(11), 1871–1882 (2008)
15. Alexa Top 500 Global Web Sites, top 500 sites by alexa traffic ranking, http://www.alexa.com/topsites/global/
16. Allegro, the leading Polish provider of online auctions, http://allegro.pl/
17. ebay, the worldwide online auctions, http://www.ebay.com/
18. Ranking of sites. The 1000 most-visited sites on the web, http://www.google.com/adplanner/static/top1000/
19. Taobao, chinese auction portal with over 100 million users, http://taobao.com

Exploiting Proxy-Based Federated Identity Management in Wireless Roaming Access

Diana Berbecaru, Antonio Lioy, and Marco Domenico Aime

Politecnico di Torino, Dip. di Automatica e Informatica
Corso Duca degli Abruzzi 24, 10129, Torino, Italy

Abstract. Federated Identity Management technologies are exploited
for user authentication in a number of network services but their usage may conflict with security restrictions imposed in a specific domain.
We considered a specific case (roaming wireless access for guests) and
extended the Stork SAML-based identity federation to cope with this
problem by adding dynamic data, called meta-attributes, to be used for
authorization even before the user authentication is completed. This concept may be easily extended to other data needed for trust verification
and complex authorization decisions in a federated environment.

1 Introduction

Federated identity management (FIM) is a set of technologies and processes that
let computer systems dynamically distribute identity information and delegate
identity tasks across security domains [1]. By using FIM, web applications can
offer cross-domain single sign-on (SSO), so that a user can authenticate once
at the so-called Identity Provider (IDP) and then gain access to protected resources and services at a Service Provider (SP), provided the two organizations
established a so-called "Circle of Trust". In SSO, data about identification, authentication and user attributes flow from the IDP to the SP, where it can be
used in complex authorization decisions.

In a proxy-based FIM infrastructure [2], a network of *federation bridges* or
proxies is built, where the authentication and attribute flow from the IDP to the
SP through the proxies in the corresponding domains. This improves scalability
because to add a new security domain only the proxies must be reconfigured
with the location of the new foreign proxy, and to add a new IDP only the proxy
in its domain must be reconfigured.

Problem Statement. In a proxy-based FIM scenario, we consider the case of
a user and SP both placed inside a company network protected by a border
firewall, whereas the user's IDP is in a foreign network domain. To let this user
reach his IDP, the firewall must be configured with appropriate permissions: if
the IDP is known "a priori" (or is not subject to frequent change) then it can
be statically configured at the firewall, but if the IDP is unknown, or changes
frequently then we have a configuration problem at the firewall.

Our Contribution. We propose a method for dynamic firewall reconfiguration based on data (meta-attributes and user attributes) retrieved through a

S. Furnell, C. Lambrinoudakis, and G. Pernul (Eds.): TrustBus 2011, LNCS 6863, pp. 13–23, 2011.
© Springer-Verlag Berlin Heidelberg 2011

proxy-based FIM infrastructure. In particular, we used the Stork infrastructure created in the frame of the homonym European project. Stork uses national proxies (one per country) that act as a bridge for user authentication and also retrieve, filter, and map user attributes, which are *certified* by the national electronic identity authorities.

We generalise this firewall configuration problem to investigating how a proxy-based FIM infrastructure can support a wireless roaming access (WIRA) service and, in general, an attribute-based access control (ABAC) process. In the ABAC model [3,4], attributes are used for classifying every party, and access control policies specify the attributes that requesters need to have in order to gain access to data and services. Normally, authorization decisions are taken *after* the user has been authenticated and user attributes have been retrieved. However, when a proxy-based FIM is in place, some authorization decisions must be taken on the SP side *before* the authentication of the users has completed. We call this "authorization-for-authentication", i.e. the problem of validating access to entities and operations of the FIM infrastructure itself. We solve this problem by allowing proxies to dynamically retrieve, validate and distribute a set of "meta-attributes": data concerning the FIM entities and operations rather than the users.

Organisation. Section 2 briefly describes the Stork architecture, along with its main components involved in the authentication process and attribute transfer. In Section 3, we propose meta-attributes as a Stork-based solution to the "authorization-for-authentication" problem, while Section 4 presents the design and implementation of a Stork-based WIRA service integrated with Shibboleth [5]. Conclusions are in Section 6.

2   The Stork Infrastructure

Stork (Secure Identity Across Borders Linked) is a EU-funded project [6] that has defined a pan-european proxy-based FIM infrastructure integrating the various national e-identity approaches. Stork offers a set of identity-related services, like authentication request/response handling and user attribute retrieval and transfer. These services are implemented either by a national proxy server, named PEPS (Pan-European Proxy Service), or by a dedicated software, named *middleware* [7]. Each EU Member State (MS) can freely decide which approach to support. A country adopting the proxy approach runs a PEPS, which is part of a distributed EU infrastructure connecting the national identity infrastructures (Fig. 1). Each PEPS has two interfaces: the one used for communicating with SPs and IDPs is MS-specific, whereas the one communicating with the other proxies uses SAML 2.0 [8] and is specified in the project [7,9]. The SP contacts its national proxy (called S-PEPS) to ask for user authentication, while an IDP responds to user authentication requests originating from its own proxy (called C-PEPS).

To access a web-based service, the user is first asked to authenticate by the SP (step 1) that, when recognizes a Stork user, creates an authentication request

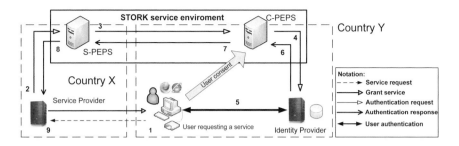

Fig. 1. The Stork PEPS-based approach

and sends it to the S-PEPS through the UA (step 2). Next, the S-PEPS asks the user where is he from, or more precisely in which country his authentication credentials were issued. Upon country selection, the S-PEPS constructs a signed SAML request, which is sent (through the user's browser) to the C-PEPS (step 3). This request is based on the one received from the SP and lists the required user attributes. The C-PEPS selects the appropriate national IDP for user authentication and creates an authentication request which is sent to the IDP (step 4). In step 5, the IDP performs the authentication exchange with the user and returns the appropriate response to the C-PEPS (step 6). After validating the response, the C-PEPS maps the received attributes to the Stork format, and (if necessary) derives additional attributes (e.g. "ageOver" derived from birthdate) for privacy protection purposes. In addition, the C-PEPS requires also the user's consent to forward his attributes to the S-PEPS. Finally, the C-PEPS creates a signed SAML response (containing the user attributes values) and sends it response to the S-PEPS, through the UA with the HTTP POST method (step 7). The S-PEPS performs similar operations as the C-PEPS, and sends subsequently the newly created SAML response to the SP (step 8), where the certified attributes are extracted and verified to eventually grant access to the requested service (step 9).

3   Meta-attributes Support in Stork

The proxy-based FIM in Fig. 1 assumes the following pre-defined trust relationships: all proxies trust each other, SPs and IDPs trust their national proxies, each user trusts its IDP and its national proxy. Establishing trust relationships consists in exchanging authentication credentials and associated metadata. Proxies, SPs and IDPs often exchange credentials in the form of X.509 certificates, while IDPs may decide to use different types of credentials for their users. The prime goal of FIM operations is establishing dynamic trust relationships between users and SPs by controlled retrieval and disclosure of user's identity attributes.

As introduced in Section 1, we extend the basic operations of the proxy-based FIM infrastructure to exchange a set of *meta-attributes*, i.e. data concerning some FIM entity or operation rather than the user. Meta-attributes help in taking access control decisions at the SP, and in mitigating various security threats, like man-in-the-middle attacks or attacks against platform integrity. The purpose of meta-attributes is easily explained in relation to the SAML metadata [10]. In fact, they both describe SAML endpoints and their supported operations. In the basic FIM model, SP and IDP typically exchange their SAML metadata out-of-band, when establishing a mutual trust relationship. SAML metadata may be published also at well-known URLs or in the DNS, as this information is assumed to be rather static. In proxy-based FIM, an alternative way to distribute information on FIM entities and operations is through the proxy infrastructure itself. Meta-attributes allow taking full advantage of proxies' scalability and their pre-defined trust relationships to disseminate and authenticate even highly dynamic metadata.

Based on the needs of the case "authorization-for-authentication", we have extended the Stork's PEPS component to resolve and transfer several meta-attributes: "Address" transfers PEPS and IDP location information to be used in IP-level access control decisions, "Credential" distributes FIM entities' credentials (like certificates), and "IntegrityMeasures" carry data useful to validate the PEPS operational integrity.

The Address Meta-attribute. In a WIRA service, the SP needs to know the IP address and TCP port of the IDP to configure dynamic network access control rules that permit the UA to connect to its IDP, but it may also obtain the C-PEPS location as well (in our experiments in Section 4, the C-PEPS location is known to the SP). In this scenario, the SP initially authorises the UA to connect only to the S-PEPS. The S-PEPS asserts the appropriate C-PEPS address as Address meta-attribute in its first response to the SP, so that the SP can grant the UA access to its C-PEPS as described in Section 2. In turn, the C-PEPS asserts the IDP address in its response to the S-PEPS, that forwards it in its second response to the SP. The SP now grants access to the IDP to allow user authentication and the Stork workflow to conclude. At this point, the SP may decide to grant "unrestricted" network access to the UA.

The Credential Meta-attributes. In Fig. 1, the UA sets up TLS channels with the other FIM entities it is contacting. Assuming that the user directly trusts the C-PEPS but not the S-PEPS, the UA needs to acquire the S-PEPS's certificate in a secure manner (e.g. out-of-band), otherwise either the user should decide directly to trust the S-PEPS certificate or the S-PEPS should have a certificate issued by one of the trusted CAs embedded in the browser. Similar considerations hold for the SP's certificate. All the options above are open to threats against the UA's trusted certificate store, including compromising the store itself, compromising anyone of the trusted (child) CAs, or misleading the user to add untrustworthy certificates to the store.

The Credential meta-attributes allow asserting information about PEPS and SP certificates. The SP and S-PEPS insert their own credentials inside their SAML requests, while the C-PEPS asserts in its response the certificates of the S-PEPS (known by a pre-defined trust relationship) and the SP (received in the request from the S-PEPS). If the UA is a dedicated SAML-enabled component, it can extract these certificates and verify "a posteriori" that the servers to which it connected were authentic (or abort the session otherwise). Implementing the same capability with web browsers is trickier since browsers do not expose TLS sessions and stored certificates through the APIs accessible to client-side web applications. In this case, the C-PEPS, upon extraction and validation, shows the SP and S-PEPS certificates to the user for manual inspection and confirmation. However, the user must compare the certificates' fingerprints with those in the connections with the SP and S-PEPS. The usability of this solution is clearly unsatisfactory and its improvement requires an extension in the browser. For example, VeriKey [11] performs certificate verification with an automated process by means of dedicated verification servers and an extension or a plug-in for common web browsers (on the user side), while no modification is required on the web server to which the user connects to.

Credential meta-attributes are also useful at the SP. In the WIRA service, in addition to the IP address, the SP could retrieve the C-PEPS and IDP certificates and compare them against the ones presented by the servers connecting with the UA. The SP could even establish VPNs with the C-PEPS and IDP to enforce network access control beyond the IP-level.

Credential meta-attributes can also identify UA-owned credentials to help ensuring that the same UA participates in each step of the FIM workflow. In fact, SAML assertions are known to be vulnerable to attacks in browser-based implementations [12]: since SAML assertions are not strictly bound to the browser that originally acquired them from the IDP, attackers could impersonate the user by stealing valid SAML assertions from the browser. SAML 2.0 defines the "Holder-of-Key" (HoK) element [13] as a confirmation method to prevent attackers using stolen SAML assertions. It allows specifying one or more credentials an entity should use to prove its entitlement to spend a given SAML assertion. These confirmation credentials generally differ from the long-term ones shared between the user and the IDP: in [14], they are certificates used by browser-based UAs to connect to IDPs and SPs via TLS with client-authentication. The Credential meta-attributes extend the HoK capability in the proxy-based FIM: the PEPS requires TLS client-authentication and compares the certificate presented by the UA with the Credential meta-attribute in the SAML assertions received from another PEPS or IDP; the PEPS reasserts UA's confirmation credential in its SAML assertions. To support this capability, browser-based UAs should be able to generate volatile certificates to use with all the servers in the same FIM workflow session. Using a static self-signed certificate [15] requires no modification to common browsers, but the user must generate a new certificate for each session to achieve pseudonimity.

The IntegrityMeasures Meta-attributes. These attributes allow asserting data useful to validate the integrity of the PEPS. They are a natural extension of the other meta-attributes as they provide further information for authenticating the PEPS as trustworthy. For example, if TCG techniques [16] are used at PEPS, this information can include reference integrity measures of the PEPS platform.

The UA may then compare this information with fresh integrity measures on the S-PEPS, collected via TCG's remote attestation services. Similarly, the SP may check integrity measures when connecting to the C-PEPS.

Embedding Meta-attributes in SAML Assertions. A straightforward way to embed meta-attributes in SAML requests and assertions is defining new SAML attributes. This is the solution we adopted in our experiments for the Address meta-attribute. An alternative is overloading standard features of SAML 2.0 to provide equivalent semantics: for example, the Subject field allows identifying entities by URIs, which could include IP and port, while the HoK element could transport entity credentials. In this case, the PEPS would not add additional attributes to its assertions about the user, but it would return additional assertions on the entities involved in the FIM workflow (IDP, other PEPS, SP). The various assertions can be linked together just by asserting the role of the subject of each assertion. This approach would improve the flexibility of the solution based on specific SAML attributes.

4   WIRA Service Based on Stork Architecture

Well-known technologies, like Radius, IEEE 802.1X, or VPN, enable *known users* to dock to wireless and wired networks [17]. However, these techniques do not scale easily to the case of *visiting users*. For example, the Eduroam project [18] set up a network of Radius servers using EAP-TTLS to allow visiting users to authenticate with their home credentials. However, changing the authentication method requires upgrading the client application, and Radius/EAP do not offer the rich handling of certified user attributes supported by FIM technology. The ABFAB IETF WG is also working at the application of federated authentication for non-web services, essentially using EAP and Radius in place of SAML. A Shibboleth-based proposal for wireless roaming access in FIM scenario is described in [19], but it assumes that the IDP's location (DNS name and IP address) is known and pre-configured at the SP. We propose a proxy-based FIM solution to gain service scalability and flexibility via the retrieval of IDP attributes and the mapping of user attributes.

Based on Stork, we designed a flexible and scalable SAML-based service for wireless roaming access. The user is connected to a VPN and each connecting user is assigned a private IP address. The network access in the SP domain is protected by a captive portal, hosting a SAML-enabled module, the Access Control Decision Point (ACDP) and the Access Control Enforcement Point (ACEP) modules, as shown in Fig. 2.

The SP machine hosts also the gateway used for connecting the roaming user to the Internet. The packet filtering engine (resident at the ACEP) is driven by the ACDP module, which in turn is triggered by the SAML-enabled SP module, which constructs the SAML authentication requests, processes the responses received from the S-PEPS, and exports the attributes to the ACDP module. The ACDP retrieves the necessary meta-attributes and user attributes and triggers the enforcing firewall scripts of the ACEP module.

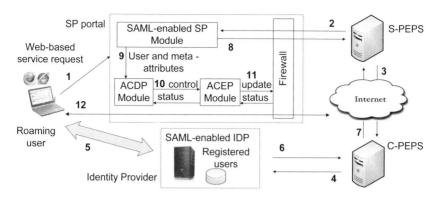

Fig. 2. WIRA service architecture exploiting Stork and Shibboleth 2

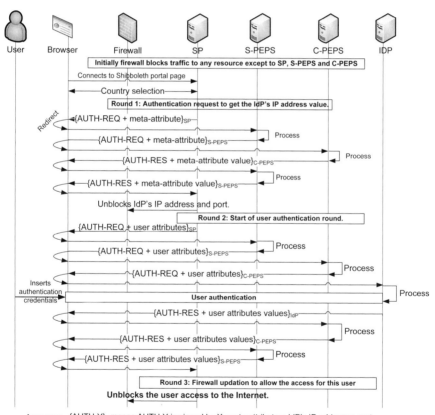

Fig. 3. WIRA Service functionality and messages exchanged

IDP Location Issue. In our service, the IDP location is not known in advance to the SP, but it is maintained at the C-PEPS. Thus, the IDP can freely move its location without notifying all potential SPs. Since the roaming user must connect to his IDP, the SP must selectively grant user access towards the IDP even though the user has not been authenticated yet. The SP enforces this access decision based on the SAML assertion contained in the response from the S-PEPS, which contains the IDP's location: basically, if the response received is valid then the IDP's location is transmitted to the ACDP module, which triggers the firewall scripts (residing at the ACEP module) to permit user network access towards the IDP (step 5 in Fig. 2) and later towards the Internet (step 12).

The WIRA service is composed of three rounds (Fig. 3). In the first one the IDP's Address meta-attribute is resolved at the C-PEPS, transmitted to the S-PEPS, and then forwarded to the SP as part of the authentication response. In the second round, the SP firewall allows the user to authenticate with his home IDP. On successful user authentication, the IDP creates a response with the requested user attributes values and sends it back to the SP, passing through the PEPS proxies. In the third round, the SP takes its authorization decision by allowing user partial or complete network access based on the user attributes received and its internal authorization policy.

5   Experimental Setup for the WIRA Service

The experimental setup consists of a wireless access point, the SP, IDP, PEPS and user's machines as shown in Fig. 4. The SP machine has two network interfaces, one with a public IP address and one with a private IP address in the same subnet as the roaming users. Iptables is used at the SP to permit or deny the IP traffic from roaming users towards the external world. The PEPS and the IDP hosts have public IP addresses. The SP machine runs Ubuntu (v9.04), Shibboleth SP (v2.0), PHP (v5.2.6) and Iptables (v1.4.1.1). The PEPS machine runs the PEPS package developed in the Stork project, which incorporates a SAML engine based on OpenSAML [20], whereas the SP and IDP run the Shibboleth software (v2.0). We chose Shibboleth because it incorporates a SAML 2.0 engine and allows to manage easily IDP and SP functionality through dedicated configuration files. The PEPS functionality is implemented by four Java servlets, two handling the SAML requests from the SPs and other PEPS respectively, and two handling the SAML responses from the IDPs and other PEPS. To create the Address meta-attribute on the C-PEPS, we implemented the IPResolver servlet. The S-PEPS, C-PEPS and Shibboleth IDP servlets run on an Apache Tomcat (v6.0.26) application server. To support user authentication with X.509v3 certificates stored in the browser or on user's smart-cards, we extended the Shibboleth IDP as by default it supports only password-based authentication.

By accessing the SP captive portal, the user is redirected to a PHP script page displaying the countries supporting Stork (step 1 in Fig. 4). Upon country selection, the script redirects the UA to the WIRAstart URL, whose handler is configured in the Shibboleth SP's shibboleth2.xml file indicating to the

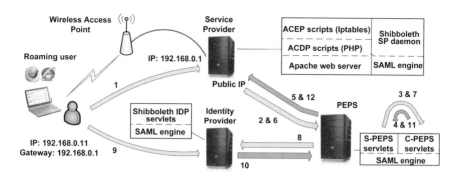

Fig. 4. Experimental setup configuration

Shibboleth SP daemon to generate a SAML request containing the `Address` meta-attribute. The request is sent through the user browser to the S-PEPS proxy servlet (step 2). To support the `Address` meta-attribute, we extended the SAML request with an additional Stork attribute (besides the ones described in [9]) and modified accordingly the Shibboleth SP's configuration and the original PEPS code. The S-PEPS validates the request, re-signs it, and forwards it to the `IPResolver` servlet on C-PEPS, which resolves the IDP's address and TCP port (step 3). Next, a SAML response containing the `Address` meta-attributed is constructed and is sent to the S-PEPS servlet (step 4), which verifies it, re-signs it, and sends it back to the `AssertionConsumerServiceURL` indicated in the `shibboleth2.xml` file (step 5).

The Shibboleth SP daemon validates the response and exports the `Address` value in the environment variable `idpaddr`. This mapping is configured in the Shibboleth SP file `attribute-map.xml`. Next, the UA is redirected to the SP portal's page `index.php`, configured as `homeId` in the `shibboleth2.xml` file. This page extracts the `idpaddr` value and calls a script containing Iptables rules to allow traffic from the UA (whose IP address is read from Apache server's environment variables) to `idpaddr`.

Subsequently, the UA is redirected to another URL configured in the Shibboleth SP's configuration file, so that the daemon generates another SAML request containing the needed user attributes. This request is sent to the S-PEPS proxy servlet (step 6) and then to C-PEPS proxy servlet (step 7), and finally to the Shibboleth IDP (step 8). On the Shibboleth IDP, the user can authenticate either with username and password, the X.509 certificate stored in the browser or a RSA-based smart card. Upon authentication, the Shibboleth IDP generates a SAML authentication response containing the user attribute values extracted from the database of registered users. In case the user authenticates with a smart-card, the national identification number in the certificate on the smart card is used as search key in the registered users database. The authentication response is sent back to the corresponding C-PEPS servlet, which will also filter the attributes that have not been requested and maps the requested ones to the Stork format. After being re-signed, the SAML response is sent to the S-PEPS servlet, which performs similar operations as the C-PEPS and sends finally the response back to the SP handler URL, i.e. the `AssertionConsumerServiceURL`.

If the response `StatusCode` is success, the SP daemon exports the requested attribute values in the environment variables. This ends the second round of user authentication. In the third round, the user is again redirected to the portal page `index.php`, the environment variables are read, and the script containing the Iptables rules for this round is called, granting access to the network based on the user attributes received.

6   Conclusions and Future Work

We have shown that dynamic firewall reconfiguration is needed for guest users to be authenticated via a proxy-based FIM infrastructure (as in the case of wireless roaming access) and proposed a practical solution based on addtional SAML meta-attributes and the Stork infrastructure. By generalising this approach, we could also distribute additional data for dynamic certificate validation and server integrity measurement. Future work will focus on extending our WIRA service to implement additional controls based on this dynamic data, and on best embedding this data in standard SAML syntax and operations.

Acknowledgements. This work was developed in the framework of the EU co-funded project STORK (INFSO-ICT-PSP-224993, http://www.eid-stork.eu). We also thank Hafeez HafeezurRehman for his help in implementing some features of the WIRA service.

References

1. Maler, E., Reed, D.: The Venn of Identity: Options and Issues in Federated Identity Management. IEEE Security & Privacy, 16–23 (March/April 2008)
2. Makoto, H.: Federation proxy for cross domain identity federation. In: Proc. of ACM DIM 2009, pp. 53–62 (2009)
3. Bonatti, P., Samarati, P.: Regulating service access and information release on the web. In: ACM CCS 2000, pp. 130–145 (November 2000)
4. Yuan, E., Tong, J.: Attribute Based Access Control (ABAC) for Web Services. In: Proc. of ICWS 2005, pp. 561–569 (July 2005)
5. Cantor, S. (ed.): Shibboleth architecture - Protocols and Profiles (September 2005), http://shibboleth.internet2.edu
6. Secure Identity Across Borders Linked (STORK) project - Towards pan-European recognition of electronic IDs (eIDs) (2008-2011), http://www.eid-stork.eu
7. Berbecaru, D., Jorquera, E., Alcalde-Moraño, J., Portela, R., Bauer, W., Zwattendorfer, B., Eichholz, J., Schneider, T.: Software architecture design. STORK Deliverable D5.8.2a (October 2010), https://www.eid-stork.eu/
8. OASIS: Assertions and Protocols for the OASIS Security Assertion Markup Language (SAML) V2.0. OASIS Standard (March 2005)
9. Alcalde-Moraño, J., Hernández-Ardieta, J.L., Johnston, A., Martinez, D., Zwattendorfer, B., Stern, M., Heppe, J.: Interface specification. STORK Deliverable D5.8.2b (October 2010), https://www.eid-stork.eu/

10. OASIS: Metadata for the OASIS Security Assertion Markup Language (SAML) V2.0. OASIS Standard (March 2005)
11. Stone-Gross, B., Sigal, D., Cohn, R., Morse, J., Almeroth, K., Kruegel, C.: VeriKey: A dynamic certificate verification system for public key exchanges. In: Zamboni, D. (ed.) DIMVA 2008. LNCS, vol. 5137, pp. 44–63. Springer, Heidelberg (2008)
12. OASIS: Security and Privacy Considerations for the OASIS Security Assertion Markup Language (SAML) V2.0. OASIS Standard (March 2005)
13. OASIS: Profiles for the OASIS Security Assertion Markup Language (SAML) V2.0. OASIS Standard (March 2005)
14. OASIS: SAML V2.0 Holder-of-Key Web Browser SSO Profile Version 1.0. OASIS Committee Specification (August 2010)
15. Gajek, S., Liao, L., Schwenk, J.: Stronger TLS bindings for SAML assertions and SAML artifacts. In: Proc. of ACM SWS 2008, pp. 11–19 (October 2008)
16. Trusted Computing Group, https://www.trustedcomputinggroup.org
17. Manulis, M., Leroy, D., Koeune, F., Bonaventure, O., Quisquater, J.-J.: Authenticated Wireless Roaming via Tunnels: Making Mobile Guests Feel at Home. In: Proc. of ASIACCS 2009, pp. 92–103 (2009)
18. Eduroam: http://www.eduroam.org
19. Linden, M., Viitanen, V.: Roaming Network Access Using Shibboleth. In: TERENA Networking Conference 2004, pp. 1–1 (2004)
20. OpenSAML libraries, https://spaces.internet2.edu/display/OpenSAML/Home

Privacy-Preserving Statistical Analysis on Ubiquitous Health Data

George Drosatos and Pavlos S. Efraimidis

Electrical and Computer Engineering, Democritus University
of Thrace, University Campus, 67100 Xanthi, Greece
{gdrosato,pefraimi}@ee.duth.gr

Abstract. In this work, we consider ubiquitous health data generated from wearable sensors in a Ubiquitous Health Monitoring System (UHMS) and examine how these data can be used within privacy-preserving distributed statistical analysis. To this end, we propose a secure multi-party computation based on a privacy-preserving cryptographic protocol that accepts as input current or archived values of users' wearable sensors. We describe a prototype implementation of the proposed solution with a community of independent personal agents and present preliminary results that confirm the viability of the approach.

Keywords: Ubiquitous health data privacy, Distributed statistical analysis, Personal data, Secure multi-party computation, Mutli-agent system.

1 Introduction

The use of statistical methods is an integral part of medical research. A medical statistic may comprise a wide variety of data types, the most common of which are based on vital records (birth, death, marriage), morbidity (incidence of disease in a population) and mortality (the number of people who die of a certain disease in relation with the total number of people). Other well-known statistical data that are used are the health care costs, the demographic distribution of a disease based on geographic, ethnic, and gender criteria, and data on the socioeconomic status and education of health care professionals.

At the same time, the advances in wearable sensor technology have dramatically increased the amount of health monitoring data that can be efficiently generated, stored and processed. This led to the emergence of Ubiquitous Health Monitoring Systems (UHMS's) [11,19,17] that use these health data. The data from wearable sensors like any health data are sensitive personal data. Thus, the operation of UHMS's systems must ensure the protection of the patients' privacy. Examples of data types that are used in health monitoring as they are reported in [4] are: heart rate, blood pressure, galvanic skin response, skin temperature, heat flux, subject motion, speed and the distance covered. One of the main features of a UHMS is to automatically generate alerts to notify the family or the patient's doctor about a possible health emergency. The need for UHMS

S. Furnell, C. Lambrinoudakis, and G. Pernul (Eds.): TrustBus 2011, LNCS 6863, pp. 24–36, 2011.

systems is expected to continuously rise in the foreseeable future. The population of the developed world is growing older, medical costs are rising, and there are not enough doctors to heal the elderly. UHMS systems are also important for special groups of people of any age who have the need of continuous health monitoring. The (aimed) benefits of a UHMS is both to reduce the number of visits to the hospitals and to support better health services that may lead to saving the lives of patients.

In this work, we examine how ubiquitous health data generated from wearable sensors in a Ubiquitous Health Monitoring System (UHMS) can be used within privacy-preserving distributed statistical analysis. To this end, we propose a secure multi-party computation based on a privacy-preserving cryptographic protocol that accepts as input current or archived values of users' wearable sensors. This distributed computation is performed by a community of personal agents; each patient has a personal agent which is continuously on-line and collects the medical data of its owner. In addition to the data that are obtained by wearable sensors, the agents may also contain other data such as demographic elements about the patient and further information about his health records, as well. Finally, we describe a prototype implementation of the proposed solution with a community of personal data management agents and present preliminary results that confirm the viability of the approach.

Some of the advantages of our approach in comparison to traditional statistical analysis techniques are:

– Performing statistical analysis on real time, up-to-date data.
– Utilizing valuable, sensitive personal data while ensuring privacy.
– Simplifying the process and reducing the time and cost for conducting a statistical analysis.
– Avoiding errors in data entry, which leads to more reliable results.

In the proposed solution, each patient must have a personal agent at his disposal and permanent access to the Internet. The personal agent collects and preserves the personal data of the patient. The computational requirements for the personal agent can be fulfilled with commodity hardware and hence its cost is not high. Thus, it is plausible to assume that patients with a UHMS can afford the extra cost for such an agent.

2   Related Work

The problem of distributed statistical analysis of this work is a secure multi-party computation (MPC) on extremely critical personal medical data. The general model of a MPC was firstly proposed by Yao [20] and later was followed by many others. In general, a MPC problem concerns the calculation of a function with inputs from many parties, where the input of each participant is not disclosed to anyone. The only information that should be disclosed is the output of the computation. The general solution for MPC presented in [20] is powerful but commonly leads to impractical implementations.

A secure two-party computation (S2C) for the calculation of statistics from two separate data sets is presented in [8]. Each data set is owned by a company and is not disclosed during the computation. Similar results are shown in [9], this time focusing on linear regression and classification and without using cryptographic techniques. Two indicative works from the related field of privacy-preserving data mining are [15,10]; A major difference of our work from the above is that in our approach every participant is in control of his health data and that the distributed computation is performed by the community of the personal agents.

Another approach for statistics on personal data is anonymization, i.e., the sanitization of a data collection by removing identifying information. The data anonymization approach and some of its limitations are discussed for example in [2,16]. Data anonymization applies to collections data in central databases and is not directly comparable to our decentralized approach. Finally, an example of an efficient privacy-preserving distributed computation is given in [7], where personal agents of doctors execute a distributed privacy-preserving protocol to identify the nearest doctor to an emergency. The focus of the present work is on privacy-preserving distributed statistical analysis using a massive number of participants.

3   The Proposed Solution

We propose a system for performing privacy-preserving statistical analysis. The system is build on top of a UHMS, and more precisely, on top of the privacy-enhanced UHMS presented in [6]. An overview of the architecture of the statistical analysis system is shown in Figure 1 with emphasis on the extra components that have to be added to a UHMS; the Network Community of Personal Agents and the Statistical Analysis Service (SAS). More analytically, all the data that are obtained by users' wearable sensors are sent and stored in their personal agents. The personal agent of each patient manages his personal data, provides controlled access to these data, and has the ability to participate in distributed computations. In addition to the medical data obtained by the wearable sensors, the personal agent may also contain other personal data such as demographic information, medical drugs and health record data of the patient.

The personal agents are organized into a virtual topology, which may be a simple ring topology or a more involved topology for time-critical computations. On the other hand, the SAS is a server that initiates the distributed computation on the users' medical data and collects the aggregate results. Each researcher who wishes to carry out a statistical research can submit his task to the SAS.

4   The Main Steps of the Calculation

The main steps of the proposed statistics calculation procedure are:

- Initially, the researcher who wishes to carry out a statistical analysis on the critical medical data submits his request to the SAS.

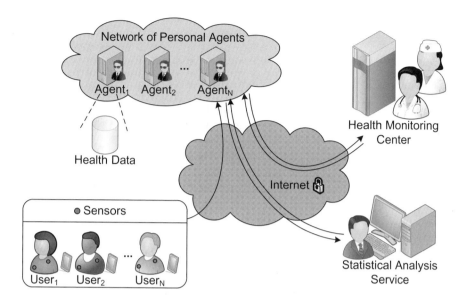

Fig. 1. The general architecture of our system

– The SAS accepts the request after verifying the credentials of the researcher.
– The SAS picks one of the personal agents which will serve as the root node for the specific computation and submits the request to it.
– The root-node coordinates a distributed computation that calculates the specified statistical function.
– At the end of the distributed computation, the SAS and the researcher will only learn aggregate results of the computation without any additional information of the actual personal data.

5 The Secure Distributed Protocol

In this section, we present the main idea of the cryptographic protocol that is used in the privacy-preserving statistical computations. The protocol is secure in the Honest-But-Curious (HBC) model (see Section 7), where the users' agents participating in the computation follow the protocol steps but may also try to extract additional information. During the calculation the actual users' personal data are not disclosed in any stage of the process but only the aggregate results are revealed at the end. An instance of a statistical computation consists of:

– **N patients** $P_1, P_2, \ldots, P_N$ and their personal data.
– **The statistical computation:** The agents of all patients perform a distributed privacy-preserving computation.
  • **Input:** The type of the statistical function/s and its parameters. In addition, selectivity constraints for the data set may also be specified.

- **Output:** The necessary values (e.g. w_x, u_x, z_{xy} and n) that are needed
  to calculate the statistical function/s.

Assume the following statistical computation instance: Computing the average
of the female patients' age in a city. Given the computation instance, the SAS
chooses a node from the network of the users' agents as the root-node for the
particular computation. Then, the SAS sends the type of the requested computation and its parameters to the root node. The parameters of the computation,
i.e., the female gender and the city name, are used to filter the data set. Each
personal agent, decides privately if it participates in the statistic research.

A simple topology for the personal agents is a virtual ring topology that
contains as nodes all agents (Figure 2.b). For time-critical computations, more
complex topologies like a virtual tree can be used (Figure 2.a). The tree topology
is used in [7]. At the end of the execution, the root-node collects the results of
the calculation as an encrypted message and sends it to the SAS. The message is
encrypted with the public key of the SAS, which should be known to all nodes.
In this way, the protocol ensures k-anonymity (see Definition 4), where $k = N$
and N is the number of all the nodes in the network.

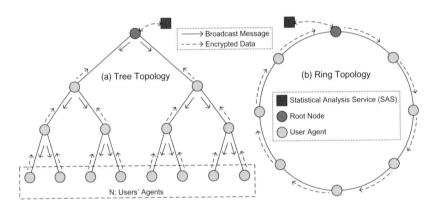

Fig. 2. Possibles network topologies

We use the Paillier public key cryptosystem [18] for the proposed cryptographic protocol. An important feature of the Paillier cryptosystem is its
homomorphic property.

Definition 1. Paillier Cryptosystem: *The Paillier cryptosystem is a prob-
abilistic asymmetric algorithm for public key cryptography that is based on the
Diffie-Hellman key agreement.*

Definition 2. Homomorphic Encryption: *The homomorphic encryption is
a form of encryption where one can perform a specific algebraic operation on the
plaintext by performing a (possibly different) algebraic operation on the
ciphertext.*

The additive homomorphic property of the Paillier cryptosystem is shown in the following equation:

$$\mathcal{E}(x_1) \cdot \mathcal{E}(x_2) = (g^{x_1} \cdot r_1^{n_p}) \cdot (g^{x_2} \cdot r_2^{n_p})$$
$$= g^{[x_1 + x_2 \bmod n_p]} \cdot (r_1 r_2)^{n_p} \bmod {n_p}^2$$
$$= \mathcal{E}([x_1 + x_2 \bmod n_p])$$

where

- x_1 and x_2 are two plain messages such that $x_1, x_2 \in \mathbb{Z}_{n_p}$,
- (n_p, g) is the Paillier public key,
- r_1 and r_2 are two random numbers such that $r_1, r_2 \in \mathbb{Z}_{n_p}^*$, and
- $\mathcal{E}(m) = g^m r^{n_p} \bmod {n_p}^2$ is the encryption of message m.

6   The Computations

In this section, we use our approach to calculate representative statistical functions with a distributed privacy-preserving computation. Wherever it is necessary, the expression of the statistical function is brought to a form that is appropriate for the distributed computation.

6.1   Arithmetic Mean

The arithmetic mean of a variable X (with sample space $\{x_1, \ldots, x_n\}$) is computed by the following equation:

$$\bar{x} = \frac{1}{n} \sum_{i=1}^{n} x_i$$

We use the additive homomorphic property of Paillier to calculate the value of the terms $u_x = \sum_{i=1}^{n} x_i$ and n. The calculation is privacy-preserving; no single x_i information is disclosed. Once the SAS learns the values of the terms u_x and n, it can compute the arithmetic mean. More analytically, using the homomorphic property of Paillier, the two terms u_x and n can be transformed into the following form:

$$E_{pk}(u_x) = \prod_{i=1}^{n} E_{pk}(x_i) \quad \text{and} \quad E_{pk}(n) = \prod_{i=1}^{n} E_{pk}(1)$$

where the E_{pk} indicates that the message is encrypted with the current public key of SAS for the specific statistical analysis. Each agent i that participates in the statistical analysis, calculates the $E_{pk}(x_i)$ and $E_{pk}(1)$ and multiplies the current two encrypted values that are calculated from the above two products. Agents that do not participate in the statistical computation (because for example they do not satisfy some selection criterion) multiply each of the above two products with a different encryption of zero $E_{pk}(0)$.

6.2   Frequency Distribution

The frequency distribution is a tabulation of the values that one or more variables take in a sample. Each entry in the table contains the frequency or count of the occurrences of values within a particular group or interval, and in this way the table summarizes the distribution of values in the sample. The graphical representation of frequency distribution is the well known histogram. Figure 3 indicates how the frequency distribution would become by using ciphertext as counters in each range, where each ciphertext is represented by the following equation:

$$E_{pk}(n_v) = \prod_{i=1}^{n} E_{pk}(m) \ , \text{ where } m = \begin{cases} 1, & x \in [x_{v-1}, x_v) \\ 0, & x \notin [x_{v-1}, x_v) \end{cases}$$

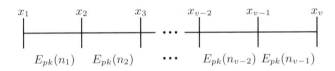

Fig. 3. Representation of a frequency distribution

6.3   Linear Regression

The linear regression of a dependent variable Y of the regressors X is given by the equation $y = a + bx$, where a and b are parameters. The determination of a and b gives an approximate line, which connects the values of Y with the corresponding values of X. This line can be constructed by using the method of least squares and the parameters a and b are given by the following equations:

$$b = \frac{n \sum_{i=1}^{n} x_i y_i - \sum_{i=1}^{n} x_i \sum_{i=1}^{n} y_i}{n \sum_{i=1}^{n} x_i^2 - \left(\sum_{i=1}^{n} x_i \right)^2} \ \text{ and } \ a = \frac{1}{n} \sum_{i=1}^{n} y_i - b \frac{1}{n} \sum_{i=1}^{n} x_i$$

The unknown terms that are required to calculate the parameters of line y with the help of the homomorphic property of Paillier are the $w_x = \sum_{i=1}^{n} x_i^2$, $u_x = \sum_{i=1}^{n} x_i$, $u_y = \sum_{i=1}^{n} y_i$, $z_{xy} = \sum_{i=1}^{n} x_i y_i$ and n, by taking the following form:

$$E_{pk}(w_x) = \prod_{i=1}^{n} E_{pk}(x_i^2), \ E_{pk}(u_x) = \prod_{i=1}^{n} E_{pk}(x_i),$$

$$E_{pk}(u_y) = \prod_{i=1}^{n} E_{pk}(y_i), \ E_{pk}(z_{xy}) = \prod_{i=1}^{n} E_{pk}(x_i y_i) \ \text{ and } \ E_{pk}(n) = \prod_{i=1}^{n} E_{pk}(1) \ .$$

6.4   Covariance

The covariance $cov(X, Y)$ of two random variables X and Y is a measure of the strength of the correlation between the two variables and is defined as:

$$cov(X, Y) = \frac{1}{n}\sum_{i=1}^{n} x_i y_i - \frac{1}{n}\sum_{i=1}^{n} x_i \cdot \frac{1}{n}\sum_{i=1}^{n} y_i = \frac{1}{n}\sum_{i=1}^{n} x_i y_i - \frac{1}{n^2}\sum_{i=1}^{n} x_i \sum_{i=1}^{n} y_i$$

The unknown terms that are required to calculate the covariance with the help of the homomorphic property of Paillier are the $u_x = \sum_{i=1}^{n} x_i$, $u_y = \sum_{i=1}^{n} y_i$, $z_{xy} = \sum_{i=1}^{n} x_i y_i$ and n, by taking the following form:

$$E_{pk}(u_x) = \prod_{i=1}^{n} E_{pk}(x_i), \;\; E_{pk}(u_y) = \prod_{i=1}^{n} E_{pk}(y_i)$$

$$E_{pk}(z_{xy}) = \prod_{i=1}^{n} E_{pk}(x_i y_i) \;\; \text{and} \;\; E_{pk}(n) = \prod_{i=1}^{n} E_{pk}(1)$$

6.5   Comments

From the analysis of the above statistical functions, we conclude that, except the frequency distribution, all other can be simultaneously calculated by computing once the required unknown terms. Moreover, it is clear that the proposed solution can be used to calculate also other statistical functions, such as the variance, the linear correlation coefficient and so on.

7   The Protocol's Security

In this section, we demonstrate that the proposed protocol of a distributed statistical analysis in a UHMS does not violate the privacy of participants. The security holds for the model of Honest-But-Curious (HBC) users.

Definition 3. Honest-But-Curious (HBC): *An honest-but-curious party (adversary) [1] follows the prescribed protocol properly, but may keep intermediate computation results, e.g. messages exchanged, and try to deduce additional information from them other than the protocol result.*

The security of the Paillier cryptosystem and its homomorphic property ensures that the personal medical data are not disclosed and cannot be associated with any particular patient. We will use the concept of k-anonymity.

Definition 4. k-anonymity: *An informal definition of k-anonymity in the context of this work is that no less than k individual users can be associated with a particular personal value. For a more general definition of k-anonymity that is also valid in databases see [5].*

The main security features of the protocol are:

- Each agent that receives a message from the previous node cannot obtain information about the contents of the message, because the ciphertexts are encrypted with the Paillier encryption.
- Each node alters the ciphertexts of the computation. Even the nodes that do not participate in the statistical function multiply the ciphertexts with an encrypted number "0", which is the neutral element of the additive homomorphic property of Paillier.
- At the end of the protocol, only the variables that are needed for a particular statistical function are revealed. As a result, no individual can be associated with the value that he had used in the computation. Consequently, the proposed protocol preserves k-anonymity for $k = N$, where N is the number of all agents in the network.

Another criterion for protecting privacy is the concept of differential privacy.

Definition 5. ϵ-Differential privacy [12]: *A randomized function $\mathcal{K}$ gives ϵ-differential privacy if for all data sets D_1 and D_2 differing on at most one element, and all $S \subseteq Range(\mathcal{K})$, the following holds:*

$$Pr[\mathcal{K}(D_1) \in S] \leq exp(\epsilon) \times Pr[\mathcal{K}(D_2) \in S]$$

The probability is taken is over the coin tosses of $\mathcal{K}$.

In our solution, the differential privacy is meaningful only if the SAS may find out the identities of participants in the distributed computation. Otherwise, the privacy is guaranteed by k-anonymity. If the SAS knows or may find out the identify of participants, then the concept of differential privacy applies and the common technique to assure differential privacy is to add appropriate additive random noise to the results [13]. In addition, for statistical computations on dynamic data such as the wearable sensors' data, the data which are used in the calculations contain by default some kind of random noise and this enhances the differential privacy.

8   Experimental Results

To evaluate our solution, we developed a prototype that carries out distributed statistical analysis on medical data. The application is implemented in Java and for the cryptographic primitives the Bouncycastle [3] library is used. The personal agents of the Polis platform developed in [14] are used as the personal data management agents of the patients. For this approach, the Polis agents were suitably modified so as to be able to manage both health records and health data that would actually be collected through a secure communication channel by the patients' wearable sensors. The community of the personal agents are organized as a Peer-to-Peer network. At this stage of development of the prototype, the backbone of the topology is a virtual ring topology. The ring offers a simple and reliable solution for the interconnection of the agents. For time-critical calculations or even real-time calculations of statistics a more involved topology like a virtual tree should be used.

The personal agents use production-ready cryptographic libraries and employ 1024 bits RSA X.509 certificates. The communication between agents is performed over secure sockets (SSL/TLS) with both client and server authentication. Below we describe an experiment of a distributed statistical analysis with 6 agents and the SAS. The requested statistic:

– *The arithmetic mean of the current body temperature of patients who are aged between 55 and 65 years old and their gender is female.*

For the needs of the experiment, each agent generated random values for the age and the gender, and for the current body temperature as well. In brief, the process has as follows. Initially, the SAS randomly chooses a node from the agents' network, in this case the agent 'Patient2', as the root-node and forwards the description of the statistical computation to it. The values of each agent which are related to the computation are shown in Table 1. The last two columns show the aggregate values that are encrypted after the corresponding agent applies its values to the results. Since the homomorphic property of Paillier applies to integers, the body temperature should be rounded to a number with at most two decimal digits and then multiplied by 100 to become an integer.

Table 1. Example of computation, where the agents in gray rows did not take part in computation

Agent	Curr. Temp.	Age	Gender	$E_{pk}(u_x) = \prod_{i=1}^{n} E_{pk}(x_i)$	$E_{pk}(n) = \prod_{i=1}^{n} E_{pk}(1)$
Patient2	36.68 ^{o}C	51	Female	$E(0)$	$E(0)$
Patient3	36.50 ^{o}C	56	Female	$E(3650)$	$E(1)$
Patient4	37.70 ^{o}C	60	Female	$E(7420)$	$E(2)$
Patient5	38.10 ^{o}C	65	Female	$E(11230)$	$E(3)$
Patient6	37.12 ^{o}C	59	Male	$E(11230)$	$E(3)$
Patient1	36.20 ^{o}C	63	Female	$E(14850)$	$E(4)$

At the end of the computation, the agent 'Patient2' as the root-node collects the results and sends them back to the SAS. Finally, the SAS decrypts the results and eventually finds that the average of the question which was submitted is 37.125 ^{o}C. A snapshot of the application during the execution of the experiment is shown in Figure 4.

We evaluated the efficiency of our solution with a series of experiments on a gradually increasing number of up to 300 agents. The corresponding running times are shown in Figure 5. For this experiment, a network of 30 computer workstations with Intel Core 2 Quad Q8300 CPU's at 2.5 GHz, 2 GB RAM and a 100 Mbps network, was used. Each computer was shared by at most 10 agents, to ensure that no single workstation will be overloaded; an overloaded workstation would become a bottleneck that could significantly delay the execution of the whole protocol.

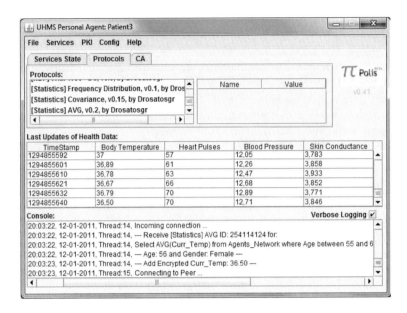

Fig. 4. A snapshot of the agent 'Patient3'

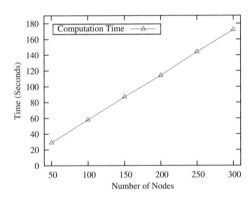

Fig. 5. Computation times of the protocol with respect to the number of agents

9   Conclusion

In this paper, we proposed the use of the ubiquitous health data that are obtained by the wearable sensors in a UHMS for carring out statistical researches. The proposed scheme utilizes the users' personal data while ensuring their privacy. The protection of privacy is achieved by using cryptographic techniques and performing a distributed computation within a network of personal agents. We described how representative statistical functions can be executed distributedly by using the proposed cryptographic protocol. Finally, we developed a prototype implementation and confirmed the viability and the efficiency of the proposed solution.

The present work can be extended to support more complex statistical functions like nonlinear regression and possibly to conduct privacy-preserving time series analysis on sensors' data. Another interesting direction would be to investigate the optimal adaptation of the differential privacy criterion (and the required random noise) in the context of our distributed computation.

References

1. Acquisti, A., Gritzalis, S., Lambrinoudakis, C., De Capitani di Vimercati, S.: Digital privacy. Auerbach Publications, Taylor & Francis Group (2008)
2. Aggarwal, C.C.: On k-anonymity and the curse of dimensionality. In: VLDB 2005, pp. 901–909 (2005)
3. Bouncycastle Java Library (January 2011), http://www.bouncycastle.org/
4. Camous, F., McCann, D., Roantree, M.: Capturing personal health data from wearable sensors. In: SAINT 2008, pp. 153–156. IEEE, Los Alamitos (2008)
5. Ciriani, V., Capitani di Vimercati, S., Foresti, S., Samarati, P.: κ-anonymity. In: Secure Data Management in Decentralized Systems. Advances in Information Security, vol. 33, pp. 323–353. Springer, Heidelberg (2007)
6. Drosatos, G., Efraimidis, P.S.: Privacy-enhanced management of ubiquitous health monitoring data. In: PETRA 2011. ACM, New York (2011)
7. Drosatos, G., Efraimidis, P.S.: A privacy-preserving protocol for finding the nearest doctor in an emergency. In: PETRA 2010, pp. 18:1–18:8. ACM, New York (2010)
8. Du, W., Atallah, M.: Privacy-preserving cooperative statistical analysis. In: ACSAC 2001, pp. 102–112. IEEE, Los Alamitos (2001)
9. Du, W., Chen, S., Han, Y.S.: Privacy-preserving multivariate statistical analysis: Linear regression and classification. In: SDM 2004, pp. 222–233 (2004)
10. Duan, Y., Youdao, N., Canny, J., Zhan, J.Z.: P4P: practical large-scale privacy-preserving distributed computation robust against malicious users. In: USENIX Security Symposium, pp. 207–222 (2010)
11. Durresi, A., Durresi, M., Barolli, L.: Secure ubiquitous health monitoring system. In: Takizawa, M., Barolli, L., Enokido, T. (eds.) NBiS 2008. LNCS, vol. 5186, pp. 273–282. Springer, Heidelberg (2008)
12. Dwork, C.: Differential privacy: a survey of results. In: Agrawal, M., Du, D.-Z., Duan, Z., Li, A. (eds.) TAMC 2008. LNCS, vol. 4978, pp. 1–19. Springer, Heidelberg (2008)
13. Dwork, C., McSherry, F., Nissim, K., Smith, A.: Calibrating noise to sensitivity in private data analysis. In: Halevi, S., Rabin, T. (eds.) TCC 2006. LNCS, vol. 3876, pp. 265–284. Springer, Heidelberg (2006)
14. Efraimidis, P.S., Drosatos, G., Nalbadis, F., Tasidou, A.: Towards privacy in personal data management. J. IMCS 17(4), 311–329 (2009)
15. Kantarcioglu, M., Kardes, O.: Privacy-preserving data mining in the malicious model. Int. J. IJICS 2(4), 353–375 (2008)

16. Muntés-Mulero, V., Nin, J.: Privacy and anonymization for very large datasets. In: CIKM 2009, pp. 2117–2118. ACM, New York (2009)
17. Otto, C., Milenkovic, A., Sanders, C., Jovanov, E.: System Architecture of a Wireless Body Area Sensor Network for Ubiquitous Health Monitoring. J. JMM 1, 307–326 (2006)
18. Paillier, P.: Public-key cryptosystems based on composite degree residuosity classes. In: Stern, J. (ed.) EUROCRYPT 1999. LNCS, vol. 1592, pp. 223–238. Springer, Heidelberg (1999)
19. Yamazaki, A., Koyama, A., Arai, J., Barolli, L.: Design and implementation of a ubiquitous health monitoring system. Int. J. Web Grid Serv. 5, 339–355 (2009)
20. Yao, A.C.C.: Protocols for secure computations (extended abstract). In: FOCS 1982, pp. 160–164. IEEE, Los Alamitos (1982)

A Safety-Preserving Mix Zone for VANETs

Florian Scheuer[1], Karl-Peter Fuchs[2], and Hannes Federrath[2]

[1] University of Regensburg
[2] University of Hamburg

Abstract. In vehicular ad hoc networks, vehicles may be tracked due to the frequent sending of beacons containing telemetic data. Even changing the vehicle's pseudonym cannot prevent attackers from linking beacons. Previously published solutions require vehicles to stop sending beacons when changing their pseudonyms, resulting in the loss of safety. We propose a novel concept based on the approach of mix zones, providing a compromise between privacy and safety. Therefore we introduce a communication proxy inside the mix zones. Simulations show that this approach is technically feasible, even with common hardware.

1 Introduction

Vehicular ad hoc networks (VANETs) are an upcoming technology to interconnect vehicles for data exchange by wireless ad hoc communication. The goal is to increase safety and convenience on the road and enable new applications such as warnings about dangerous situations or road conditions, advanced driver assistance systems (*ADAS*), real-time traffic information, or simply using the internet inside a vehicle.

The sending of false information, attacking of devices, and tracking of vehicles has to be prevented. This paper focuses on the privacy aspects that have to be considered when enabling the so-called beaconing.

Most proposals for VANET communications work on the assumption that each vehicle has a unique identifier (*UID*) that is sometimes covered by a pseudonym that is changed frequently ([16,15]). All messages sent during the validity period of a pseudonym contain it and can therefore be linked to each other. However, considering a system without pseudonyms suffers from different other problems like for instance missing accountability or high communication overhead due to broadcasting.

Beacons (sometimes also called *heartbeat messages*) are the most frequently sent messages in VANETs. They consist of telemetric data of the sender (like position, speed, acceleration, direction) and the sender's pseudonym and are broadcasted in intervals of 100 to 300 ms ([6,17]). Those beacons are used by the *ADAS* of any receiver.

Since beacons are sent frequently and are linkable with the contained pseudonym, an attacker is able to track a certain vehicle during its whole journey. Of course, this is not desirable and has to be prevented. However simply changing the pseudonym is not sufficient to prevent tracking as shown in figure 1.

S. Furnell, C. Lambrinoudakis, and G. Pernul (Eds.): TrustBus 2011, LNCS 6863, pp. 37–48, 2011.

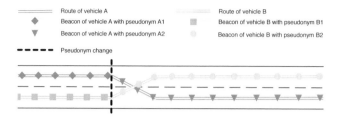

Fig. 1. Using beacons to track vehicles [21]

Two vehicles are driving next to each other sending beacons. Even if they change their pseudonyms simultaneously and even if they change their positions, an attacker can easily distinguish between them simply from the position information contained in the beacons. Even if a vehicle brakes rather strongly immediately after sending a beacon, its deviation from the expected position of the next beacon can only be around 20 cm (supposing a strong break application right after sending the previous beacon, see [21]). Taking the size of a vehicle into consideration, it becomes clear that this deviation is not enough to prevent an attacker from tracking it.

In the next section, we will examin the concept of *mix zones*, a common technique for an unobservable pseudonym change. After considering requirements and attacker models in section 3, we present our contribution in section 4. Our proposal enhances the idea of *mix zones* by enabling a compromise between privacy (unlinkability) and safety. In section 5, we evaluate our concept with regard to the requirements and conclude in section 6. Our contribution is to demonstrate a way to steer an adjustable middle course between safety features and the level of privacy.

2   Mix Zones

Solutions proposed for this tracking issue base on the *mix zone* of Beresford and Stajano [1] which transfers David Chaum's concept of communication MIXes [4] to the mixing of mobile nodes in an ad hoc network. Vehicles entering a certain area (called *mix zone*) stop sending messages and change their pseudonyms. They resume their communication when leaving the zone. So the vehicles transiting the *mix zone* at the same time form an anonymity group and (in theory) cannot be distinguished without further knowledge. This is shown in figure 2 where two vehicles enter a *mix zone*, change their pseudonyms and their lanes. An attacker has to guess which of these two vehicles is the one he wants to track.

This concept has been adapted and evaluated by several authors (for instance [21,2]). The main problem of *mix zones*, that ceasing all communication results in the loss of all VANET safety features, is adressed by Freudiger et al. in [6] and Ma et al. in [13]. Both publications propose to encrypt beacons in *mix zones* instead of stopping all communication. However this concept cannot prevent a

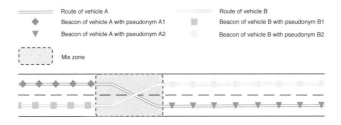

Fig. 2. A pseudonym change inside a *mix zone* [21]

sophisticated attacker from tracking vehicles because it is easy for an attacker to enter the *mix zone* as well and take part in the encrypted message exchange. In addition, other proposals generally encrypt beacons (e. g. [16]) and therefore a *mix zone* with encpted messages would not provide any benefit.

Another approach does not establish *mix zones* on certain geographical positions. Huang et al. and Sympigethaya et al. discuss in several publications ([7,8,9,11,19,20]) the opportunity to let the participants decide when it is reasonable or necessary to cease all communication and change pseudonyms (in so-called *silent periods*). However their approach suffers from the same problems as the *mix zones*: without message exchange, no safety features or *ADAS* are available.

Wasef and Shen present in [22] a scheme for changing pseudonyms that combines the proposals of encrypting messages and user-initiated periods (here called *random encryption periods*). A vehicle that needs to change its pseudonym contacts nearby vehicles and arranges a period of time in which all messages are encrypted and pseudonyms are changed. Once again, an attacker may easily participate in the encryption of messages and therefore can observe the pseudonym change.

Buttyan et al. propose a different solution for the potentially dangerous time frame where no beacons are broadcasted: in their proposal called *SLOW* [3] each vehicle may stop sending messages when its speed is below a threshold of 30 kph. Obviously, crashes at low speed are much less fatal and the lack of *ADAS* may be tolerated. However, this only works in cities where cars are forced to break at crossroads. Vehicles travelling for a long time on motorways may be tracked easily since no pseudonym changes are attempted.

3   Attacker Model and Requirements

Attacker Model. We do not consider outsiders (i. e. attackers not taking part in the VANET) because it is rather easy to become an inside attacker by simply owning a VANET-enabled car. Our attacker has a global view of all exchanged messages however he cannot break encryption. He is not able to locate vehicles by triangulation or other physical layer-based attacks. These attacks are difficult to perform with fast-moving vehicles and the only protection against them would be radio silence. In addition, the attacker is able to appear in the role of a regular VANET participant. This strong attacker does not seem realistic but an attacker might get full coverage in a certain region and the infrastructure operator may also be able to have a global view.

The operators of mix zone infrastructures are not necessarily trustworthy but have to obey the protocol. Disobedience may result in dangerous traffic situations and will therefore be discovered by vehicles. As in Chaum's concept of communication mixes, we assume that operators of different mix zones do not collude.

Safety Requirements. Beacons are used to implement *ADAS* and other important safety features. Those cannot work satisfactory without communication between nearby vehicles. We want to provide vehicles participating in the VANET with beacons from their relevant neighbors all the time.

Security Requirements. Vehicles in the VANET have to be protected against false messages, the manipulation or suppression of forwarded data, all sensitive data has to be encrypted and all entities should be protected from DoS attacks. There are several publications tackling those issues like accountability, message integrity, spoofing protection, etc, for instance [16,12,15,14,18,17,10]. Since we regard our proposal as an extension to previously published works, we do not focus on these requirements in detail but refer to the before-mentioned references.

As in previous work we consider the use of a trusted hardware module (*THM*) that securely contains all cryptographic keys. However *ADAS* need to use data contained in beacons so this information leaves the *THM* and may be used by the attacker.

Privacy Requirements. The frequent broadcasting of beacons endangers the privacy of persons with VANET-enabled vehicles since they can be tracked relatively easily as described in section 1. We have to implement mechanisms to prevent attackers from following their victims along their whole journey. We need a way to change a vehicle's pseudonym securely so that linking of pseudonyms is impossible. However, we are aware that we cannot prevent any attacks that are possible without the VANET (like simply driving behind another car and following it all its way) by technical means.

Performance Requirements. Since VANETs use an air interface with limited bandwidth, the communication overhead has to be kept low. Secondary, any entity of the VANET has to be able to process all accumulating data in due time.

4   Beaconing in Mix Zones via Proxy

4.1   Architecture and Principle

We assume that each vehicle i possesses a set of asymmetric key pairs (consisting of a public key c_i and a private key d_i) and a corresponding certificate $cert_i$

issued by a certification authority CA. These key pairs are used for communication inside mix zones (if beacons are usually sent symmetrically encryped as described in [16]) or to sign all beacons (if beacons should be asymmetrically secured as for instance in [18]) and may be stored in a tamper proof hardware device (cf. [16,18]), though we do not focus on the security of these key pairs. Each vehicle sends beacons $B_{i,t}$ every 200 ms. Those beacons contain an identifier that is the current pseudonym $P_{i,t}$ of the sending vehicle and its current position $pos_{i,t}$, speed $v_{i,t}$, acceleration $a_{i,t}$ and direction $dir_{i,t}$. These beacons are not retransmitted (single-hop messages) which means that only nearby vehicles obtain the included information and use it for their $ADAS$. Figure 3a illustrates the structure of a regular beacon as published in [16] or [18].

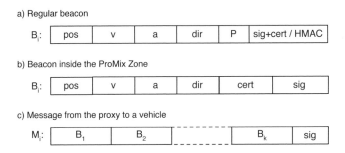

Fig. 3. Structure of messages

As a solution to the problems discussed in section 1, we propose the implementation of mix zones at crossroads and highway intersections in which vehicles change their pseudonym. We do not present a distribution strategy for pseudonyms in this paper. For further information on this topic see [5,21]. In contrast to the mix zone proposals described before, we introduce a mix zone called *ProMix Zone (Mix zone with communication via proxy, PMZ)* that allows sending beacons via a proxy to provide a certain level of privacy.

Each of the *ProMix Zones* is operated by a different provider and contains a set of infrastructure units refered to as *proxy* that are interconnected, contain a computational unit and cover the whole *PMZ* with wireless tranceivers. The computational component (that is part of the *proxy*) owns an asymmetric key pair c_p and d_p as well as a certificate $cert_p$ issued by the CA. This certificate is broadcasted at the borders of the *PMZ* so that each vehicle entering it already received the *proxy*'s public key. The rest of the protocol is divided in three steps:

Step 1: A vehicle i inside the *PMZ* substitutes the pseudonym $P_{i,t}$ with the certificate $cert_i$ of the key pair that will also be used to secure communication inside the zone and signs this beacon with d_i as shown in figure 3b. The beacon $B_{i,t}$ is then encrypted with c_p so that only the *proxy* is able to take note of its contents. The *proxy* decrypts all received beacons $B_{i,t}$, $i \in [1 \dots n]$ of the vehicles currently in the *PMZ* and pools them. After 200 ms, the *proxy* possesses n beacons – one of each vehicle inside the *PMZ*.

Step 2: At this point in time, the *proxy* has full knowledge about all vehicles currently inside the *PMZ* and the complete traffic situation. It now decides from this situation which vehicle i, $i = 1 \ldots n$ needs to receive the beacons of which other vehicles j, $j = 1 \ldots k$, $k < n$. The way a *proxy* may decide, which beacons are relevant for a certain vehicle is discussed in section 4.2.

Step 3: After creating the subset of relevant beacons for each vehicle i, the *proxy* removes the certificate $cert_{j,t}$ and the signature from the beacons and creates a new message $M_{i,t}$ containing these beacons. Then, this message is signed with d_p, encrypted for the receiver with its public key c_i and sent. Its composition is shown in figure 3c.

Each vehicle i receives a message $M_{i,t}$ that can be decrypted with its private key d_i and contains the set of relevant beacons $B_{j,t}$. Since all relevant beacons are received, the vehicle's *ADAS* is fully functional even inside the *PMZ*.

When leaving the *PMZ*, each vehicle changes its pseudonym (this could also be done during the crossing of the *PMZ*) and returns to sending regular beacons.

4.2   Selection of Relevant Beacons

The selection of beacons B_j that are relevant for a vehicle i is the most interesting aspect of our *ProMix Zone*. If too few beacons are sent, the *ADAS* cannot operate safely and the situation is as in any other mix zone proposal. If the number of beacons is n (the number of vehicles inside the *PMZ*), no privacy gain can be achieved since all vehicles nearby can observe the pseudonym change (similar to the *cmix* proposal).

The actual set of beacons with size k that has to be considered as required, depends on the actual implementations of the *ADAS* available in the VANET. However some vehicles can be considered as irrelevant independently from any implementation:

- Vehicles that do not cross ways and do not follow each other. For instance vehicles coming in the opposite direction on a divided highway or a vehicle crossing another one on a bridge or underpass.
- Vehicles coming in the opposite direction that have passed each other.
- Vehicles that are far from each other or have many other vehicles between them.

Other vehicles are definitely relevant:

- Vehicles crossing each other.
- Vehicles coming in the opposite direction still going towards each other.
- Vehicles following each other without any other vehicles between them.
- Vehicles that show an abnormal behaviour like wrong way drivers.

Figure 4 shows a possible situation in a *PMZ* from the point of view of the black vehicle. It depends on the implementation of the *ADAS* which vehicles are considered relevant, irrelevant or maybe relevant. The decision in this figure is simply based on the rules mentioned before. However the specific decision rule has to be based on the $ADAS$ and the required data as well as empiric data of traffic situations.

Obviously reducing the number of vehicles that receive the beacons of a certain vehicle makes it more difficult for an attacker to be among the relevant receivers and therefore improves the privacy of the mix zone.

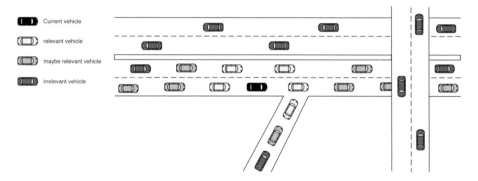

Fig. 4. Relevance of vehicles

5   Evaluation

5.1   Safety and Security Aspects

PMZ allows vehicles to exchange beacons while changing their pseudonyms. Accordingly all safety features of the $ADAS$ are available and the safety requirements are met.

As mentioned in section 3, we do not evaluate the security features of VANETs in detail since we intend to extend previously published VANET security architectures or frameworks. However all relevant messages are encrypted with asymmetric cryptography and signatures are used to provide accountability.

5.2   Privacy

The PMZ provides the same protection against attackers outside the zone as common mix zones. Linking of pseudonyms is only possible if the traffic density is too low or additional knowledge is used to perform intersection attacks.

Complete protection against attackers entering the mix zone can only be provided with radio silence. However our proposal reduces the number of vehicles that are able to track another vehicle inside the zone and therefore link its pseudonyms. The privacy protection is based mainly on the actual number of vehicles k, that receive the beacons of the observed vehicle. Reducing k might cause problems with $ADAS$ however attacks on the privacy become more difficult. With a small k, attackers can only observe vehicles via their beacons, if they drive close to them. Since following right behind a tracked vehicle is always possible and can not be prevented by technical means our solution comes close to the maximum level of privacy achievable in practice.

The operator of the *proxy* knows all telemetric data of the vehicles inside the *PMZ* and therefore can observe pseudonym changes. Since in order to track the route of a vehicle, all *PMZ*s the victim crosses would have to collude, which is in contradiction to the attacker model presented in section 3.

5.3   Performance

In order to evaluate the performance of *PMZ*, we have implemented a simulation environment, which allows conclusions on the complexity of the cryptographic processes required. The upper bound of the delay introduced by our system depends on the accuracy requirements of the beacons (B_i): The telemetric data contained in the beacons can only be considered useful, if it still reflects the prevalent traffic situation at the point of arrival. Given a strong deceleration (a) of $-9\frac{m}{s^2}$ and the assumption, that a divergence of a vehicle's position (Δs) of $1m$ is acceptable (considering the size of a vehicle), we obtain a maximum delay of about $600ms$ according to $\Delta s = a * \frac{t^2}{2}$. Accordingly, the three steps of the *PMZ* (*receive, select* and *send*) must not exceed this bound. Since we consider the participants to send beacons every $200ms$, the *proxy* must be capable of performing all actions of *step 1* for each participant within that timeframe.

While we estimate a length of $153byte$ for regular beacons ($pos = 64bit, v = 10bit, a = 10bit, dir = 9bit, p = 100bit, sig = 1024bit$), the beacons in our simulation consume $524byte$ due to the additional overhead of a certificate. We use a X.509 certificate ($3072bit$) containing a $1024bit$ RSA key and a $1024bit$ RSA signature. Although the new beacon size is about 3.5 times the size of the normal one, the total size is still low enough for efficient sending via air interface[1].

Our simulation environment is implemented in Java 1.6.0_20 64 and uses the *Bouncy Castle* Cryptography Provider 1.45[2]. All tests where run on an Intel Core 2 Duo T9300 CPU (2x 2.50GHz) with 4 GB DDR2 SDRAM. We use RSA for asymmetric cryptography (key size: $1024bit$) and AES for symmetric cryptography (key size: $256bit$). Simulation results are summarized in Fig. 5.

Figure 5a shows how the number of participants n affects *step 1* (decryption of beacons, validating signatures). Obviously, the time consumption grows linear with the number of clients. According to the upper bound of $200ms$ for this step, our test system was able to handle about 120 participants simultanously.

Figure 5b illustrates to what extent the number of participants n affects *step 3* (encrypting and signing replies). Unsurprisingly, the time consumption for this step grows linear with the number of clients, too, since again two costly asymmetric cryptographic operations per participant dominate the runtime. If we consider $20ms$ for *step 2* (chosing the relevant beacons for each user), $380ms$ are left for *step 3*. Accordingly, about 235 participants could be handled by our

---

[1] Using elliptic curve cryptography (*ECC*) for encryption and signing, the length could be reduced to $212bytes$, considering $192bit$ key size.

[2] http://www.bouncycastle.org/

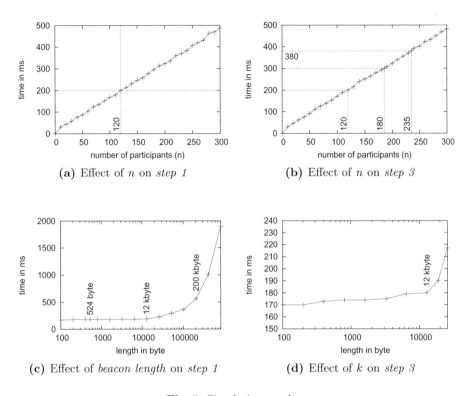

(a) Effect of n on *step 1*

(b) Effect of n on *step 3*

(c) Effect of *beacon length* on *step 1*

(d) Effect of k on *step 3*

Fig. 5. Simulation results

test system simultanously. The simulation results for *step 1* limits the number of participants to 120, however, this result is of theoretic use only. For 120 participants, *step 3* takes only about $200ms$. Accordingly $200ms$ are left for *step 2* and additional delays (e.g. network latency). *Step 1* turns out to be the bottleneck, due to its limitation to $200ms$. If we try to reduce this obviously oversized buffer for additional delays in order to utilize the full *proxy* calculation capacity, about 180 participants could be handled. This would result in a maximum allowed sending rate of $290ms$ per participant. Although the total performance seems to scale linear with the maximum allowed sending rate, no periods longer than $290ms$ should be used due to the accuracy requirements of the beacons.

Figure 5c illustrates how the length of the beacons affects *step 1*. The execution time is almost constant for any length less than $12kbyte$, since the expenses for the symmetric cryptograhpic operations needed to decrypt the additional data is lower than the measurement uncertainty in comparison to the computationally expensive asymmetric cryptograhpic operations. Between 12 and $200kbyte$, a slow increase of the execution time is legible, as the expenses for encrypting the additional data symetrically becomes more and more relevant. Above $200kbyte$, the execution time scales linear with the beacon length, since the expenses for symmetric cryptograhpy outweigh the constant expenses for asymmetric cryptograhpy. In any case, our expected beacon length of $524byte$ is far from the relevant bound of $12kbyte$.

Figure 5d shows the effect of k (the average number of beacons sent to each participant) on *step 3*. Again, we see an almost constant runtime until the beacon length exceeds $12kbyte$. According to the expected size of regular beacons (without the, in this context, unnecessary signature) of $193bit$, about 500 beacons[3] could be sent to each participant without measurable effects on runtime. Regarding the limit of 120 participants due to *step 1*, which is the upper bound for k, the average number of beacons sent to each participant has no measurable effect in the relevant range.

The simulation results show that the performance is linearly dependent on the number of vehicles n inside the *PMZ* and, of course, the transmission rate of the beacons. The length of the beacons and the average number of beacons relevant per participant k has a constant effect and can therefore be considered almost irrelevant in practice.

The messages do not gain much in size and number and therefore the bandwidth overhead should be acceptable. However, the size of the messages could be further reduced by employing *ECC*.

Considering these simulation results on common hardware for client PCs, we do not expect performance issues on dedicated harware for cryptographic operations. In addition, all operations scale linearly with the number of vehicles n and are independent. Accordingly scaling and parallelization are possible.

6   Conclusion

In this paper we reviewed different approaches for unobservable pseudonym changes and introduced a way to find a compromise between the secure change of pseudonyms and the possibility to continuously use safety applications in vehicular ad hoc networks. Our proposal should fit into the previously published frameworks for VANET security because we rely on common techniques like asymmetric cryptography with a PKI and few roadside units.

The evaluation shows that the concept fullfills the requirements presented in section 3 and is technically feasible on common hardware.

References

1. Beresford, A.R., Stajano, F.: Location privacy in pervasive computing. IEEE Pervasive Computing 2 (2003)
2. Buttyán, L., Holczer, T., Vajda, I.: On the effectiveness of changing pseudonyms to provide location privacy in vanets. In: Stajano, F., et al. (eds.) ESAS 2007. LNCS, vol. 4572, pp. 129–141. Springer, Heidelberg (2007)

---

[3] $(12000byte * 8)/193bit = 497$ Beacons.

3. Buttyan, L., Holczer, T., Weimerskirch, A., Whyte, W.: SLOW: A practical pseudonym changing scheme for location privacy in VANETs. In: Proceedings of the IEEE Vehicular Networking Conference (VNC), Tokyo, Japan. IEEE, Los Alamitos (2009)

4. Chaum, D.L.: Untraceable electronic mail, return addresses, and digital pseudonyms. Communications of the ACM 24(2) (1981)

5. Fonseca, E., Festag, A., Baldessari, R., Aguiar, R.: Support of anonymity in vanets – putting pseudonymity into practice. In: Proceedings WCNC, Hong Kong (March 2007)

6. Freudiger, J., Raya, M., Félegyházi, M., Papadimitratos, P., Hubaux, J.-P.: Mix-Zones for Location Privacy in Vehicular Networks. In: ACM Workshop on Wireless Networking for Intelligent Transportation Systems (WiN-ITS, Vancouver (2007)

7. Huang, L., Matsuura, K., Yamane, H., Sezaki, K.: Enhancing wireless location privacy using silent period. In: Proceedings of the 2005 IEEE Wireless Communications and Networking Conference (WCNC), New Orleans, LA, USA, pp. 1187–1192 (March 2005)

8. Huang, L., Yamane, H., Matsuura, K., Sezaki, K.: Towards modeling wireless location privacy. In: Danezis, G., Martin, D. (eds.) PET 2005. LNCS, vol. 3856, pp. 59–77. Springer, Heidelberg (2006)

9. Huang, L., Yamane, H., Matsuura, K., Sezaki, K.: Silent cascade: Enhancing location privacy without communication qoS degradation. In: Clark, J.A., Paige, R.F., Polack, F., Brooke, P.J. (eds.) SPC 2006. LNCS, vol. 3934, pp. 165–180. Springer, Heidelberg (2006)

10. Kamat, P., Baliga, A., Trappe, W.: An identity-based security framework for VANETs. In: VANET 2006: Proceedings of the 3rd International Workshop on Vehicular Ad Hoc Networks, pp. 94–95. ACM, New York (2006)

11. Li, M., Sampigethaya, K., Huang, L., Poovendran, R.: Swing & swap: user-centric approaches towards maximizing location privacy. In: Juels, A., Winslett, M. (eds.) Proceedings of the 2006 ACM Workshop on Privacy in the Electronic Society, WPES 2006, Alexandria, VA, USA, pp. 19–28. ACM, New York (2006)

12. Lin, X., Lu, R., Zhang, C., Zhu, H., Ho, P.-H., Shen, X.: Security in vehicular ad hoc networks. IEEE Communications Magazine 46(4), 88–95 (2008)

13. Ma, Z., Kargl, F., Weber, M.: Pseudonym-on-demand: a new pseudonym refill strategy for vehicular communications. In: Proceedings of the 68th IEEE Vehicular Technology Conference, VTC Fall 2008, September 21-24, pp. 1–5. IEEE, Los Alamitos (2008)

14. Papadimitratos, P., Buttyan, L., Holczer, T., Schoch, E., Ma, Z., Kargl, F., Kung, A., Hubaux, J.-P.: Secure vehicular communication systems: design and architecture. IEEE Wireless Communications Magazine, 100–109 (November 2008)

15. Papadimitratos, P., Buttyan, L., Hubaux, J.-P., Kargl, F., Kung, A., Raya, M.: Architecture for secure and private vehicular communications. In: Proceedings of the 7th International Conference on ITS Telecommunications (June 2007)

16. Plößl, K., Federrath, H.: A privacy aware and efficient security infrastructure for vehicular ad hoc networks. In: Proceedings of the 5th International Workshop on Security in Information Systems – WOSIS (2007)

17. Raya, M., Hubaux, J.-P.: Securing vehicular ad hoc networks. Journal of Computer Security 15(1), 39–68 (2007)

18. Raya, M., Papadimitratos, P., Hubaux, J.-P.: Securing vehicular communications. IEEE Wireless Communications 13(5), 8–15 (2006)

19. Sampigethaya, K., Huang, L., Li, M., Poovendran, R., Matsuura, K., Sezaki, K.: CARAVAN: Providing location privacy for VANET. In: Embedded Security in Cars (ESCAR) (2005)
20. Sampigethaya, K., Li, M., Huang, L., Poovendran, R.: Amoeba: Robust location privacy scheme for vanet. IEEE Journal on Selected Areas in Communications 25(8), 1569–1589 (2007)
21. Scheuer, F., Plößl, K., Federrath, H.: Preventing profile generation in vehicular networks. In: WIMOB 2008: Proceedings of the 2008 IEEE International Conference on Wireless & Mobile Computing, Networking & Communication, pp. 520–525. IEEE Computer Society, Washington, DC, USA (2008)
22. Wasef, A., Shen, X.: REP: Location privacy for VANETs using random encryption periods. Mobile Networks and Applications 15(1), 172–185 (2010)

A Secure Smartphone Applications Roll-out Scheme

Alexios Mylonas, Bill Tsoumas, Stelios Dritsas, and Dimitris Gritzalis

Information Security and Critical Infrastructure Protection Research Laboratory
Dept. of Informatics, Athens University of Economics & Business (AUEB)
76 Patission Ave., GR-10434, Athens, Greece
{amylonas,bts,sdritsas,dgrit}@aueb.gr

Abstract. The adoption of smartphones, devices transforming from simple communication devices to smart and multipurpose devices, is constantly increasing. Amongst the main reasons for their vast pervasiveness are their small size, their enhanced functionality, as well as their ability to host many useful and attractive applications. Furthermore, recent studies estimate that application installation in smartphones acquired from official application repositories, such as the Apple Store, will continue to increase. In this context, the official application repositories might become attractive to attackers trying to distribute malware via these repositories. The paper examines the security inefficiencies related to application distribution via application repositories. Our contribution focuses on surveying the application management procedures enforced during application distribution in the popular smartphone platforms (i.e. Android, Black-Berry, Apple iOS, Symbian, Windows Phone), as well as on proposing a scheme for an application management system suited for secure application distribution via application repositories.

Keywords: Smartphone, Security, Mobile Applications, Software Roll-out.

1 Introduction

Smartphones appear to be devices that fall really close to enhance Weiser's vision of ubiquitous computing [1]. Their small size, together with their mobility and connectivity capabilities, as well as their multi-purpose use, are some of the reasons for their vast pervasiveness over the last few years [2].

Malicious software, or malware [3], [4], [5] has also appeared [6] in smartphones, but its occurrence and severity currently appear to be limited. Nonetheless, recent reports show that the risk introduced by malware on smartphones is severe and contingent [7], [8]. In addition, by considering that smartphones extend the infrastructure perimeter of an organization, the impact and risk of the threats introduced by mobile devices, and especially from malware attacks, is expected to be amplified [9].

Apart from the increasing smartphone sales [2], the annual downloads of smartphone applications that are distributed from application repositories are expected to be increased by 117% in 2011 [10]. Moreover, several popular web applications (e.g. YouTube) and social networks (e.g. Facebook) are being accessed on mobile devices through native applications, instead of their web browser interface. In this context, smartphones contain a vast amount of users' personal data and, thus, introduce a serious privacy threat vector [11], [12], [13]. These data are augmented with smartphone sensor data (e.g. GPS) and data created by everyday use (personal or business),

S. Furnell, C. Lambrinoudakis, and G. Pernul (Eds.): TrustBus 2011, LNCS 6863, pp. 49–61, 2011.

making the device a great source of data related to the smartphone owner. This data source is attractive to attackers trying to harvest data to increase their revenues (e.g. with blackmail, phishing, surveillance, espionage attacks, etc.). In addition, everyday use of smartphones by non-technical and non-security savvy people increases further the likelihood of using smartphones as a security and privacy attack vector.

Currently, every smartphone platform applies different and non-standardized application submission procedures, while their effectiveness is controversial [14]. The security scheme [15] of smartphone platforms should, under these circumstances, be extended to provide a managed application repository, where specific security controls are enabled towards the protection from malware spreading in the repository.

This paper examines security inefficiencies related to application distribution via application repositories. Our contribution focuses on surveying the application management procedures enforced by current smartphone official repositories, as well as on proposing a scheme for an application management system suited for application submission in the official application repositories.

The rest of the paper is organized as follows: Section 2 provides background information, regarding current smartphone operating systems; in Section 3 existing application management approaches are presented. The suggested scheme for an application repository system is presented in Section 4, followed by discussion in Section 5. The paper concludes in Section 6.

2 Smartphone Platforms

In this section the security schemes of the most popular smartphone platforms, namely Android, BlackBerry, iOS, Symbian, and Windows Phone are summarized. Security mechanisms employed for physical device protection (e.g. data encryption, anti-theft solutions, etc.) are not analyzed herein.

2.1 Android Platform

Android OS is a Linux-based open source operating system maintained by Google. Core elements of the Android security scheme [16] are the application permissions that control access to protected resources. By default, every application runs in a sandboxed environment and requests permission authorization to be granted by the user at installation time. No further permission checks are made during application execution.

A developer distributes her application either in the official application repository maintained by Google, the Android Market, or in other sources (e.g. Amazon Appstore for Android). Android does not enforce any restriction in the installation of applications originating outside its repository. Nonetheless, Google developed technologies to remove applications [17] from devices and the Android Market in case they pose a threat to the Android platform. Moreover, applications in the Android Market are provided to end-users without being previously tested for malicious behavior. Hence, a developer must only provide her Google account credentials and pay a small fee for application distribution in the Android application repository. It is evident that in this context, potential malicious developers can use the Android Market as a malware distribution point.

The Android security scheme requires every application to be digitally signed by its developer. Nonetheless, the developer's certificate does not mandatorily need to be signed by a trusted certificate authority. Thus, applications are digitally signed with self-signed certificates, providing only poor source origin and integrity protection. This preserves the anonymity of a potential attacker, since the certificate is not verified by a Trusted Third Party (TTP).

2.2 BlackBerry Platform

The BlackBerry OS is an operating system maintained by Research In Motion Inc. (RIM). The BlackBerry security scheme [18] enforces restrictions to third party application access to protected APIs by mandating application signing with a cryptographic key provided by RIM [19]. A developer must pay a (small) fee to obtain a valid RIM key pair. However, since this process does not include any application testing, it only provides poor source origin and code integrity, without offering any assurance about third party application validity and/or security level.

Similar to the Android platform, a developer distributes her applications either in the official application repository, the BlackBerry App World, or outside the official repository. Application distribution in the official repository requires registration for a vendor account. However, before application publication in the repository, the application is not examined for malicious behaviour by RIM. Moreover, the employment of a remote application removal mechanism is not documented by the platform's security scheme, but RIM can potentially restrict execution by revoking the key pair of a particular developer.

2.3 Symbian Platform

Symbian OS is an operating system maintained by Nokia. The cornerstone in Symbian's security scheme [20] is the use of capabilities for defining restrictions to sensitive platform APIs. Basic functionality (e.g. network access) is granted during application installation by the user, whereas access to more sensitive APIs is only granted by device manufacturers and after the application's certification by Symbian Signed [21]. Application signing is mandated for application installation. The signing process ensures that the application is not using API, apart from the ones corresponding to the application's signing level. If the application uses only basic API, the developer can self sign it [22]. The smartphone user will be prompted with security warnings at installation time, since the signing key is not trusted. To eliminate the warnings and access sensitive capabilities the developer submits her application to Symbian Signed.

Applications are not required to reside in the official application repository, the OVI store, to be installed in Symbian devices. For application submission in the official repository a developer must [23]: (a). register as an OVI publisher, (b). pay a one-time registration fee and (c). submit an application that complies with the Symbian Signed Test Criteria [21]. It must be noted that the criteria include application scanning for malicious code presence.

2.4 iOS Platform

iOS is an operating system maintained by Apple and executed in Apple smartphones and tablets (i.e. iPhones, iPADs). iOS security scheme only permits the installation of applications that have been signed by Apple [24] and are available in the official application repository, the App Store. Before being signed, an application is tested for its functionality consistency and malicious behaviour. However, the testing process and criteria applied by Apple are not publicly available. For application submission in the App Store, the developer incurs an annual enrollment cost.

Once an application is installed on a device it runs on a sandboxed environment, but the user neither controls, nor is prompted when the application accesses some OS' sensitive resources. All the device resources that are available to applications in iOS version 3 are presented in [25].

2.5   Windows Phone Platform

Windows Phone is an operating system maintained by Microsoft. The security scheme of Windows Phone [26] is based on the least privilege concept and application sandboxing in conceptual chambers, where access to protected resources is granted via capabilities. Third party applications are executed in a least privileged chamber, where access to resources is controlled by capabilities that are granted by the user at installation time and cannot be elevated during execution time.

The Windows Phone security scheme permits third party application installation only from the official application repository, the App Hub. Before application submission in the App Hub the application is tested and the developer is authenticated during registration, in an attempt to maintain a managed application repository. During registration a developer pays an annual registration fee. According to [27], developer authentication is applied to hinder unauthorized developers from using a company's brand name and to assure the users that applications are authentic and their sources are known. Each submitted application is tested for compliance with Windows Phone Application Certification Requirements [28]. The requirements apart from testing the application's functionality and performance involve security tests for malware detection. Moreover, Microsoft employs a remote application removal mechanism to remove malicious applications that manage to enter the application repository and Windows Phone devices.

3   Current Application Management Approaches

From the above-mentioned smartphone security schemes, it is obvious that a reliable security scheme must include an *Application Management System (AMS)* providing a managed application repository. The AMS must impede malicious applications from entering the repository and be able to authenticate their developers. Therefore, the AMS must include secure and robust procedures for developer registration and application submission. In this context an AMS must at least include mechanisms that provide: (a). Application Integrity, (b). Application Testing, (c). Remote Application Removal, (d). Application Testing Documentation, and (e). Developer Strong Authentication. These mechanisms are described and analyzed in the following paragraphs.

Application Integrity ensures that an application's binary is not altered, e.g. by malicious code injection in pirated versions of the application. As mentioned previously, in all smartphone platforms - apart from the Android platform - the security scheme mandates application digital signing with a certificate controlled by the platform. On the contrary, Android allows users to sign applications with custom self-signed certificates not validated by a TTP. As a result, a malicious developer may download and repack an application with a new certificate and submit it to the Android Market or in an alternative application repository. Apart from monetary loss to the original application's developer, a rogue developer can infect the application with malware, compromising the security of Android devices [14].

Application Testing employs static and/or dynamic binary analysis to ensure application functionality reliability, official API usage and rational resource consumption. It typically contains tests for copyright infringements and, in some platforms, security testing [21], [28]. In a managed application repository, we argue that the security testing process should be mandatory. This will ensure that malware cannot easily be spread through the application repository. Only Symbian, iOS and Windows Phone platforms mandate application testing before submission in their repositories, whereas it is unclear if Apple's iOS employs security testing procedures.

Remote Application Removal also referred as "application remote kill switch" ensures that a malicious application will stop being executed in smartphone devices, if it has not been detected during application testing. The security scheme must ensure that (a) the mechanism will not be used for application censorship and (b) that it is conformant with legislation protecting access to a user's device. Among the surveyed smartphone platforms, only Symbian and BlackBerry do not use a documented remote application removal mechanism.

Application Testing Documentation on the one hand mandates developers into submitting applications that satisfy strict requirements and, on the other hand, informs smartphone users about these testing criteria before application acceptance. From the surveyed platforms only Symbian and Windows Phone document application tests.

Developer Strong Authentication prevents unauthorised developers from using a company's brand name and assures the application repository users that the applications are authentic and their sources are known. All smartphone platforms examined in this paper do not enforce strong authentication during developer registration. The platforms require a fee paid via a credit card during registration, but this does not imply reliable validation, since attackers may use credit cards acquired from the underground market. Windows Phone is the only platform trying to verify the developer identity [27] by outsourcing identity verification to GeoTrust. However, an attacker can use an ID acquired in the underground market (identity theft) or use a fake ID service, e.g. the service provided in [29] during her registration [27], [30], [31].

Table 1. Current Application Management Approaches

Management Functionality	Android OS	BlackBerry OS	Symbian OS	iOS	Windows Phone
Application Integrity	✗	✓	✓	✓	✓
Application Testing	✗	✗	✓	✓	✓
Remote Application Removal	✓	✗	✗	✓	✓
Application Testing Documentation	✗	✗	✓	✗	✓
Developer Strong Authentication	✗	✗	✗	✗	✗

The adoption of the management functionalities by the surveyed security schemes is summarized in Table 1 above.

4 Application Repository System Scheme

In this section an Application Repository System Scheme (ARSS) providing the entities and AMS procedures required for a managed application repository is proposed. The proposed ARSS consists of four main entities, namely: Developer, User, Application and Application Repository. A detailed analysis of the entities, as well as, their role in our scheme is described in the following sections. The proposed scheme satisfies the requirements presented in the previous section, regarding an efficient and robust application management system. Our scheme is also cross-platform, since its definition is not dependent on any smartphone platform. Finally, its underlying security mechanisms are fully documented and extensible.

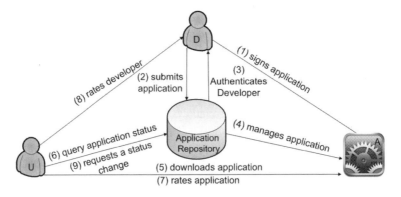

Fig. 1. Entities in the Application Repository System Scheme (the "pyramid")

An overview of the scheme is given in Fig.1. Initially, a developer signs the application and submits it in the application repository. The application repository AMS (referred to as AMS) authenticates the developer and tests the application. If the application is accepted for submission, then its lifecycle in the repository starts. During this lifetime, users are able to download the application, query for an application status, request a status change and optionally rate the application and/or the developer.

4.1 The Developer Entity

In the proposed scheme, the developer - upon application implementation - hashes the application binary. In the sequel, the hash is signed and inserted in the application file, ensuring the application's binary integrity. For the signing process the developer creates a unique signing key contained in a digital certificate. This certificate (referred hereinafter as *application certificate*) contains a subset of the developer's identity data, e.g. her logo, her employer brand and application data, e.g. application title, version, web links etc. The decision to allow developers to create *application certificates* provides flexibility to the developers and the application repository owner. The former avoids certificate creation costs from a TTP and delays stemming from this creation procedure. The latter avoids computation costs stemming from the creation, management and delivery of each *application certificate*.

In the sequel, the developer includes identity information in the application binary by signing the *application certificate* with a certificate verified by a Public Key Infrastructure (PKI) TTP (referred hereinafter as *developer certificate*). As a result, the certificate chain shown in Fig. 2 is created. In this paper, we propose the use of qualified certificates [32] as *developer* certificates, which apart from providing strong developer authentication, they also provide legal equivalence of a hand-written signature. In this context, the AMS could mandate developers to digitally sign a Computer Misuse Act (CMA) compliant [33] or an equivalent statement. Each developer could state in this statement that she is providing an application which is not impairing the repository management system functionality or the end user device. Nonetheless, the use of qualified certificates and the legal binding of the developers is not mandatory in this scheme. However, the implementation of the proposed scheme must use developer certificates providing strong developer authentication.

TTP Certificate   Developer Certificate   Application Certificate

Fig. 2. Certificate Chain in the ARSS

Subsequently, the developer concatenates the signed hash and inserts the developer and application certificates in the application. Then, if the developer submits an application for the first time, she enrols to the application repository. The developer provides authentication data and pays a registration fee during enrolment.

4.2   Application Repository Entity

The application repository entity is responsible for developer authentication and application management in the ARSS - i.e. controlling application (a). submission, (b). testing, and (c). remote removal - during the application's lifecycle in the repository. In addition, the AMS uses mechanisms to deter attackers from inserting malicious applications in the repository and misusing its operations and resources.

Strong developer authentication is required during application submission to: (a). avoid application spoofing\phishing attacks, (b). bind the developer with legal responsibilities (e.g. conformance with CMA – like legislation), and (c). give penalties to miscreant developers. In this paper, qualified certificates are proposed for user authentication and hence user management (e.g. user identity checking, secure storage of personal data, etc.) is outsourced to a PKI TTP.

The developer uses her *developer certificate* during developer enrolment. The validity of the certificate is verified and part of its contents are parsed and stored in the application repository. The repository examines only the developer's certificate validity in subsequent application submissions. If the certificate is invalid, then the application submission is rejected and the developer is informed via email for the rejection reasons. The enrolment in the application repository ends with the reception of an enrolment fee, via a credit card linked to a valid bank account. The credit card number is securely stored, in case monetary penalties are given to miscreant developers. The registration fee, as well as, the penalty monetary amounts are system parameters and must be carefully selected so as: (a). to deter attackers from enrolling and misusing the repository's resources, and (b). not to deter freelancer developers from enrolling to the application repository.

In the sequel, the application hash is verified, ensuring the application's integrity. Similarly, if the integrity check fails the developer is informed via an email. Upon hash verification the application undergoes application testing where the conformance to testing criteria, such as [21], [28] is verified. These criteria must control many application execution aspects and may involve manual inspection or automated testing via static or dynamic binary analysis.

Although this paper does not focus on the application testing procedure, we argue that an application upon submission in the repository, must be tested against a variety of criteria such as: (a). successful execution start and termination, (b). protected API use, (c). unofficial API avoidance, (d). malicious code presence, (e). device resource consumption, (f). application's graphical interface consistency, (g). brand misuse - copyright abuse, etc. Nonetheless, the testing criteria and procedures that the AMS implements must be documented. This informs expert users about the tests and ensures that application censorship is avoided in the repository.

If the application conforms to the testing criteria, test metadata are appended in the application. The AMS may mandate a specific structure and content in the application metadata to facilitate the application testing procedure. Subsequently, the AMS hashes and signs the application. For application signing the AMS uses a certificate that is verified by a PKI TTP. Signing and hashing the application by the ARSS provides, apart from application integrity, protection against malicious ARSS spreading malware through rogue application repositories.

The AMS removes applications from the repository in case they are later proved to be malware. Upon application removal, the AMS has two options: (1). removing a class of applications implemented by the same developer, or (2). removing an individual application from the application repository. In the first case, the AMS inserts the developer's certificate in a blacklist. Similarly, in the second case, the AMS places the application's certificate in a blacklist. In both cases, the AMS gives the miscreant developer monetary penalties. Optionally, the AMS may take legislation action against the developer, especially when the developer has signed a CMA-conformant, or an equivalent, statement with a qualified certificate. In addition, an ARSS user is able to request an application status change, if she can prove that it contains malware. In this scenario the AMS re-checks the application and if malware is found, the application is removed. The user must pay a fee for her request, where the fee is a system parameter, to avoid application removal service misuse by attackers. If the application is found to be malicious then the user is refunded and given a reward (e.g. application discount). This would motivate users to report malicious applications.

4.3 The Application Entity

A conceptual application structure in the ARSS is depicted in Fig. 3. As discussed before, the developer hashes, signs, and inserts the developer hash in the application file, providing binary integrity. In this paper the use of a hashing algorithm belonging to the SHA-2 family [34] is recommended, since it is widely implemented and resistant to collisions [35]. Furthermore, the application contains a section for metadata, containing data required for application execution, or providing information aiding the repository's application management system, e.g. requested permissions, imported libraries, developer and application certificates, etc.

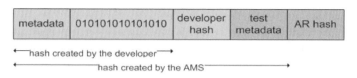

Fig. 3. Application structure in the ARSS

The application contains test metadata that depend on the application testing mechanism that the ARSS employs. At minimum, they must include a vector indicating the execution or not of a test, the test date, etc. These metadata must not be space demanding. Towards this direction, the test metadata can be stored in an online database maintained by the ARSS, and only the AR hash may be included in the application file along with a link to the online database entry. This decision depends on implementation details and our scheme is not imposing restrictions about it. Finally, the application structure contains the AMS-signed hash that provides protection against malicious ARSS spreading malware through rogue application repositories.

4.4   The User Entity

The user enrols to the ARSS by providing identity information - where the identity verification is a system parameter - and a valid credit card. The user selects and downloads an application from the application repository. Consequently, the validity of the application's ARSS certificate is examined. During this validity check, we assume that the device has an up-to-date list of known ARSS certificates. If the application is signed with a valid certificate, then the user trusts that the application is managed by an application repository, i.e.: (a). the application's developer has been authenticated, (b). the application repository has used reasonable care and skill to test the application, (c). the application has not been found to contain malware, and (d). the user will be informed in case the application is later proved to contain malicious code.

Subsequently, the user optionally inspects the developer information contained in the application file, as a second level of defence against spoofing attacks, and installs the application. Upon application installation, we assume that the smartphone's security scheme either checks the developer metadata, or the application is installed, since it has been inspected by the application repository. Furthermore, we assume that the security scheme allows any user to manually inspect both the developer and AR metadata stored in the application. The user must be able to decide whether some application permissions will be denied during execution. In this context, the user's control of the application execution in the device is preserved, while he is aware of the security tests that the application successfully passed.

Software in the user's device periodically queries the repository for blacklisted applications. Hence, in this scheme it is assumed that the device connects regularly to the Internet and that this software - which is included in the application's security scheme - queries for application status change upon application launch. Before querying the AMS, the software may occasionally prompt for Internet access authorization, giving the user control on the query frequency. The query frequency is a system parameter and ensures that the device will be updated in predefined intervals and that the AMS will not be overwhelmed with queries.

The application binary is not deleted from the device when an application certificate is blacklisted. Only the user has the authorization to remove the application. This option is given to avoid unfair application censorship in the application repository and to conform the mechanism with legislation protecting access to a user's device.

Furthermore, in the current scheme, the device's security scheme must block the application execution when its certificates are blacklisted. Nonetheless, the user should have authorization to run the application. In this case before its execution the security scheme must: (a). prompt the user with security warnings, (b). revoke all application's permissions, and (c) enable the user to manually inspect and select, which blocked application permissions will be granted again. The ARSS user optionally rates an application / developer w.r.t. application functionality and user friendliness.

5 Discussion

The proposed scheme includes mechanisms that satisfy the security requirements which were not provided by the surveyed smartphone security schemes, namely: (a). application integrity, (b). application testing, (c). remote application removal, (d). application testing documentation, and (e). developer strong authentication. The scheme is cross-platform, since its definition is not dependent on any smartphone platform implementation details. Moreover, its security mechanisms must be fully documented and extensible. The scheme deters malicious developers from submitting malware in the repository, as well as users from misusing the repository's resources, by giving penalties to miscreant activities. It may optionally deter malicious developers from entering the application repository, by using qualified certificates and imposing the digital signing of a CMA, or an equivalent, statement during developer registration.

The proposed scheme does not focus on the application testing criteria. It considers application testing as a black box containing the state of the art of application testing such as [21], [28]. Nonetheless, the application testing mechanisms and criteria in the scheme's implementation must be documented and carefully selected to avoid performance bottlenecks in this component. Furthermore, the proposed scheme is based on PKI certificates verified by TTP providing strong authentication. The scheme employs authentication only during developer registration, to avoid delays in user registration that could deter user access to the ARSS. The developer incurs a certificate creation cost, for the acquisition of a developer certificate, which is equal to the developer registration cost in current official application repositories. Hence, the enrolment cost must be carefully selected in the scheme implementation so as to not deter developers from enrolling to the repository.

6 Conclusions

This paper examined the necessity of an Application Management System (AMS) embedded in the security scheme of smartphone platforms, providing a managed application repository that hinders malicious application submission in the repository, and is able to authenticate their developers. The proposed approach contributes towards this direction by: (a) surveying the application management procedures enforced in current smartphone official repositories, and (b) proposing a scheme for AMS suited for application submission in application repositories.

The proposed scheme is extensible, cross platform and fully documented. It also includes mechanisms that provide: (a). application integrity, (b). application testing, (c). remote application removal, (d). application testing documentation, and (e). developer strong authentication, which are not provided in whole by current smartphone security schemes. To the best of our knowledge, this is the first time that an AMS is proposed to be included in smartphone security schemes.

Future work will focus on the implementation of the scheme in test and real environment, in order to evaluate its effectiveness and address performance issues. In addition, we plan to survey and amend the state of the art application testing procedures of the scheme. Also, we will explore legal issues protecting application repositories from malware submission and alternative developer authentication schemes that provide strong developer authentication at low cost. Finally, we plan to examine security economics of the proposed scheme to determine optimum values for the scheme's monetary parameters (e.g. registration cost, misuse penalties, rewards, etc).

Acknowledgments. This work has been partially funded by the European Union (European Social Fund) and Greek national funds through the Operational Program *Education and Lifelong Learning* of the National Strategic Reference Framework - Research Funding Program: HERACLEITUS II - Investing in Knowledge Society. The work was, also, supported by the SFINX (09SYN-72-419) project, which is partly funded by the Hellenic General Secretariat for Research & Technology, under the Synergasia Programme.

References

1. Weiser, M.: The computer for the 21st century. Scientific American 265(3), 94–104 (1991)
2. Gartner: Gartner Newsroom (accessed April 15, 2011),
   http://www.gartner.com/it/page.jsp?id=1543014
3. Adleman, L.: An abstract theory of computer viruses. In: Goldwasser, S. (ed.) CRYPTO 1988. LNCS, vol. 403, pp. 354–374. Springer, Heidelberg (1990)
4. Cohen, F.: Computational aspects of computer viruses. Computers & Security 8(4), 325–344 (1989)
5. Kephart, J., White, S.: Directed graph epidemiological models of computer viruses. In: Lunt, T., et al. (eds.) Proc. of IEEE Symposium on Research in Security and Privacy (SP), pp. 343–359. IEEE Press, USA (1991)
6. Hypponen, M.: Malware goes mobile. Scientific American 295(5), 70–77 (2006)
7. McAfee Labs, 2011 Threats Predictions, Technical Report (December 2010)

8. Cisco: Cisco 2010 Annual Security Report (accessed April 15, 2011),
   `http://www.cisco.com/en/US/prod/vpndevc/annual_security_report.html`

9. Forrester: Forrester Research (accessed April 15, 2011),
   `http://www.forrester.com/rb/Research/security_of_b2b_enabling_unbounded_enterprise/q/id/56670/t/2`

10. Gartner: Gartner Newsroom (accessed April 15, 2011),
    `http://www.gartner.com/it/page.jsp?id=1529214`

11. PAMPAS, Pioneering Advanced Mobile Privacy and Security (accessed April 15, 2011),
    `http://www.pampas.eu.org/`

12. Hogben G., Dekker M.: Smartphone security: Information security risks, opportunities and recommendations for users, Technical report (December 2010)

13. GSM World, Mobile Privacy (accessed April 15, 2011),
    `http://www.gsmworld.com/our-work/public-policy/mobile_privacy.htm`

14. Security on MSNBC, Malware infects more than 50 android apps (accessed April 15, 2011), `http://www.msnbc.msn.com/id/41867328/ns/`

15. Goguen, J., Mesajue, J.: Security Policies and Security Models. In: Neumann, P. (ed.) Proc. of the 1982 IEEE Symposium on Security and Privacy (SP), pp. 11–20. IEEE Press, USA (1982)

16. Google, Security and Permissions (accessed April 15, 2011),
    `http://developer.android.com/guide/topics/security/Security.html`

17. Google, Android Developers (accessed April 15, 2011),
    `http://android-developers.blogspot.com/2010/06/exercising-our-remote-application.html`

18. RIM, Security overview (accessed April 15, 2011),
    `http://docs.blackberry.com/en/developers/deliverables/21091/Security_overview_1304155_11.jsp`

19. RIM, Code Signing Keys (accessed April 15, 2011),
    `http://us.blackberry.com/developers/javaappdev/codekeys.jsp`

20. Nokia, Symbian Platform Security Model (accessed April 15, 2011),
    `http://wiki.forum.nokia.com/index.php/Symbian_Platform_Security_Model`

21. Nokia, Symbian Signed Test Criteria V4 Wiki version (accessed April 15, 2011),
    `http://wiki.forum.nokia.com/index.php/Symbian_Signed_Test_Criteria_V4_Wiki_version`

22. Nokia, Developer_certificate (accessed April 15, 2011),
    `http://wiki.forum.nokia.com/index.php/Developer_certificate`

23. Nokia, OVI Publisher Guide, Technical Report (December 2010)

24. Apple, iOS Dev Center (accessed April 15, 2011),
    `http://developer.apple.com/devcenter/ios/index.action`

25. Seriot, N.: iPhone Privacy. Black Hat Technical Security Conference, Technical report (February 2010)

26. Microsoft, Windows ® Phone 7 security model, Technical report (December 2010)

27. Microsoft, App Hub (accessed April 15, 2011),
    `http://create.msdn.com/en-US/home/about/developer_registration_walkthrough_confirmation`

28. Microsoft, Windows Phone 7 Application Certification Requirements, Technical report, ver. 1.4 (October 2010)
29. Fluxcard, Fluxcard Fake ID (accessed April 15, 2011),
    `http://www.fluxcard.com/`
30. GeoTrust, GeoTrust Repository (accessed April 15, 2011),
    `http://www.geotrust.com/resources/repository/legal/`
31. GeoTrust, GeoTrust Technical Support (accessed April 15, 2011),
    `https://knowledge.geotrust.com/support/`
    `knowledge-base/index?page=chatConsole`
32. European Parliament and of the Council of the European Union. Community Framework for Electronic Signatures, Directive 1999/93/EC (December 1999)
33. Legislation.gov.uk, Computer Misuse Act 1990 (accessed April 15, 2011),
    `http://www.legislation.gov.uk/ukpga/1990/18/contents`
34. NIST, Secure Hash Standard (SHS), Technical Report FIPS PUB 180-3 (October 2008)
35. Dang, Q.: Recommendation for Applications Using Approved Hash Algorithms. NIST Special Publication 800-107 (February 2009)

Privacy Preserving Tree Augmented Naïve Bayesian Multi–party Implementation on Horizontally Partitioned Databases

Maria Eleni Skarkala, Manolis Maragoudakis, Stefanos Gritzalis, and Lilian Mitrou

Department of Information and Communication Systems Engineering, University of the
Aegean, Karlovassi, Samos 83200, Greece
{mes,mmarag,sgritz,l.mitrou}@aegean.gr

Abstract. The evolution of new technologies and the spread of the Internet
have led to the exchange and elaboration of massive amounts of
data. Simultaneously, intelligent systems that parse and analyze patterns within
data are gaining popularity. Many of these data contain sensitive information, a
fact that leads to serious concerns on how such data should be managed and
used from data mining techniques. Extracting knowledge from statistical
databases is an essential step towards deploying intelligent systems that assist in
making decisions, but also must preserve the privacy of parties involved. In this
paper, we present a novel privacy preserving data mining algorithm from
statistical databases that are horizontally partitioned. The novelty lies to the
multi-candidate election schema and its capabilities of being a basic foundation
for a privacy preserving Tree Augmented Naïve Bayesian (TAN) classifier, in
order to obviate disclosure of personal information.

Keywords: Privacy, Distributed data mining, Horizontally partitioned
databases, Tree Augmented Naïve Bayes, Homomorphic encryption.

1 Introduction

Technological progress has led to ever-increasing storage, retrieval and processing of
data collections stored in large–scale databases. Statistical databases with financial,
medical or social data have usually been exploited for analysis and discovery of
useful patterns. Database owners wish to share the data contained therein, on the
premise there is no leakage of sensitive information. A crucial issue arises when this
information can be misused for various reasons in favor of some expectant aggressors
[8]. Data is usually distributed across several parties, thus the usage of secure
protocols is required for sharing information. In order to efface possible disclosure of
sensitive data, resulting in privacy violation while data mining processes are applied,
various techniques have been proposed. A privacy preserving data mining algorithm
should support the following features; prevent disclosure of sensitive information,
resist to potential security holes that many traditional data mining algorithms pose,
not degrade access and use of non-sensitive information, be useful for large volume of
data and not have exponential computational complexity. An algorithm to be effective

S. Furnell, C. Lambrinoudakis, and G. Pernul (Eds.): TrustBus 2011, LNCS 6863, pp. 62–73, 2011.
© Springer-Verlag Berlin Heidelberg 2011

must simultaneously manage large number of participants owning large databases, but ensuring at the same time that personal data are not revealed to other parties, or to a trusted third party (Miner). Involved databases can be either horizontally [10, 12, 24, 28] or vertically [20, 23] partitioned, with each party holding its own sensitive data. In the former case each party holds a different set of records but a unified set of attributes, while in the latter case, different sets of attributes for the same recordset are distributed to participants [1]. The parties involved are considered to be mutually mistrustful and in some cases are curious to learn information about other participant's data. If a party does not deviate from a protocol during its execution and sends its data, then it is considered semi-honest, but in case it sends specific inputs in order to discover other participant's data, it is considered malicious. In real world applications, the former case behaviors are more often. The problem of privacy preservation has been addressed in different ways such as randomization, perturbation and k-anonymity. Several techniques that have been proposed using data encryption are based in the idea of Yao [25]. Secure multi party computation [11], an extension of Yao's idea, is also widely used to prevent leakage of any information other than the final results. The contribution of cryptography is essential as the original data are not transformed in any way, like randomization or transformation methods do, a fact that can lead to inaccurate outcomes [28].

In this paper, we present a novel protocol which utilizes a robust Bayesian algorithm that unlike the widely used Naïve Bayesian classifier is not based on the unrealistic assumption about the independence of attribute variables given the class. More specifically, we propose the privacy preserving version of the Tree Augmented Naïve Bayesian classifier used by our protocol which aims to extract global information from statistical databases horizontally partitioned. In comparison with work [28] which uses only binary attributes' type, our approach uses databases containing numerical (included binary) but also nominal data. The protocol presented in this work was developed in a client-server (C2S) environment and the participants can only be connected with the Miner, making communication among them unfeasible. Privacy is preserved using cryptographic techniques exploiting homomorphic primitive first proposed by Yang [24], through which the Miner who collects the data of at least three semi-trusted parties is unable to identify the original records. Because of some "curiosity", the protocol requires the existence of at least three participants in order to maintain privacy, as to the subsequent analysis of the results sensitive information in the model of two parties may be leaking. The contribution of the present work lies within the exploitation of a variation of the multi-candidate selection model, used for mining frequencies of attribute-class vectors in a secure and efficient manner, and inspired from the work of [14]. We stress that the protocol presented is a sketch of a generic privacy preserving data mining scheme in the fully distributed setting, where there are k-out-of-l selections [4].

The rest of the paper is structured as follows. Next section addresses previous work on the topic. Section 3 introduces the security and design requirements and analyzes the proposed protocol, while section 4 presents the results from experiments carried out and the total evaluation of the protocol. This paper closes with some conclusions drawn from this study.

2 Related Work

A categorization of privacy preserving data mining algorithms is presented in [22]. The algorithms were categorized in five segments; apportionment of data, modification of data, data mining algorithm for which the privacy technique has been designed for, type of data that need to be protected from disclosure and technique adopted for the preservation of privacy. The authors in [1] explored various methods such as randomization, k-anonymity and transformations for hiding personal information. Randomization and cryptography as privacy preservation techniques have been studied widely by researchers. The first method was used in association rules [20] and decision trees [3] for vertically and horizontally partitioned data respectively. The technique proposed in [3] was based on the reconstruction of data. The privacy provided is measured by the facility of finding the factual data of a modified attribute. This measure is suffering from inconsistencies with regards to the distribution of the actual and the transformed data. Instead, the work [2] uses the entropy of information as a measure of privacy and thus solves the problem in [3].

The second method was applied in models which most of them are based in the idea of Yao [25], extended by Goldreich [11] who studied the secure multi-party computation problem (SMC). This approach is widely used in distributed environments, where parties wish to estimate through a function, with their data as input, the final mining results, but in a way that privacy is ensured. Cryptographic techniques have been applied for horizontally [10] partitioned databases to build decision trees [13, 17], Naive Bayesian classifiers [12, 24, 26, 21] and Association Discovery Rules [10], or for vertically partitioned data to construct association rules [7, 23] and Naïve Bayesian classifiers [21]. One technique based on cryptography proposed in [10], where the first participant transmits a number of frequencies and a random value to her neighbor, encrypted. Another method proposed by Clifton [6] on distributed environments, is the local execution of data mining methods. Then the results are sent to a trusted third party who combines the results of each participant to obtain the final results. This technique, however, can lead to inaccurate outcomes [12]. Naive Bayes classification was employed in many researches [12, 24, 26] because of its simplicity and straightforward approach. Simplified Bayesian Networks have also been used for data mining processes by either applying the Tree Augmented Naïve Bayes (TAN) [28] or K2 [23] algorithm as structure search methods. The authors in [28] use an algebraic technique to perturb original data. Our approach uses cryptographic techniques to build a simplified Bayesian Network using TAN as search algorithm. Such networks are considered more efficient in relation to Naïve Bayes classifiers as they take into account the dependency among databases' attributes.

A tool used in the literature is the homomorphic primitive first used in the work of Yang et.al. [24]. Our protocol employs the Paillier cryptosystem [16] in which this primitive is applied, which can assure both privacy and accurate results. As a conclusion, while randomization methods are efficient, on the other hand they are not completely secure, and the results can be inaccurate. Unlike, cryptographic methods are secure and the results are more accurate, but are lagging in terms of efficiency.

3 System Description

Privacy preservation emerges nowadays, as collections of data are daily exchanged. Data mining techniques that used to derive statistics from distributed databases must ensure that personal data will not be disclosed. This work aims to develop a mining algorithm which extracts accurate results, while privacy is preserved using efficient encryption that satisfies the essential security requirements. A Miner contributes in the creation of a classification model by collecting from at least three parties the overall frequencies of each value per attribute in relation to each class value. The attributes' type can be either numerical (binary data are included) or categorical. These frequencies are encrypted using asymmetric cryptography [16] which exploits the homomorphic primitive, ensuring that sensitive data remain secret and only aggregated results can be exported. The communication among parties is infeasible as the only data flow is between each party and the Miner, in order to prevent any collusion attacks. As mentioned, much of the work is based on the study of [14] and thus, many of the motivating features used as well as theoretical requirements to be met spring up from theirs quotations.

3.1 Tree – Augmented Naïve Bayesian Classifier

The objective and the novelty of this work is the development of a protocol through which global information is extracted using the Tree Augmented Naive Bayesian algorithm [5]. The traditional Naive Bayes algorithm computes the conditional probability of each attribute A_i given the class C during training. When classifying, the Bayes theorem is applied thereafter, to compute the probability of C given a particular instance vector $<A_1 ..... A_n>$, where n is the total number of attributes. This classifier assumes that all attributes are independent given the value of C, an over restrictive and often unrealistic assumption. In order to improve the performance of such classifiers is necessary to alleviate the issue of the independence assumption. Bayesian Networks exploit possible dependencies among attributes in order to compute more efficiently the Bayesian probabilities. However, unrestricted Bayesian networks are not very successful classifiers [15] since they do not have any prior knowledge on the class variable when they are learned from data, resulting in network structures that do not favor classification. An interesting variation of Bayesian networks is the Tree – Augmented Naïve Bayesian classifier (TAN). TANs usually behave more robust as regards to classification since they combine the initial structure of the Naïve Bayes algorithm. This classifier allows the existence of additional edges between attributes that represent the relations among them. The full TAN structure is depicted in Figure 1.

In a TAN network the class variable has no parents and each attribute has as parents the class variable and at most one other attribute. In an augmented structure, an edge from attribute A_i to A_j implies that the influence of A_i on the assessment of the class variable also depends on the value of A_j. The procedure for learning these edges, which is based on a method proposed by Chow and Liu [5], reduces the problem of constructing a maximum likelihood tree to finding a maximal weighted spanning tree in a graph. The problem of finding such a tree is to select a subset of arcs such that the sum of weights attached to the selected arcs is maximized.

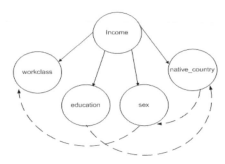

Fig. 1. TAN structure created from simplified dataset "Adult" [19]

The procedure consists of four main steps. At first, for each attribute pair the mutual information is computed using Equation 1, measuring how much information the attribute y provides about x. In the second step an undirected graph is built in which the vertices are the variables in x (the weight of an edge connecting two attributes). In the third step a maximum weighted spanning tree is created while in the final step the undirected tree is transformed to a directed one by choosing a root variable and setting the direction of all edges to be outward from it.

$$I_p(X;Y) = \Sigma_{x,y} P(x, y) \log p(x, y)/p(x)p(y) \tag{1}$$

TAN results are significantly improved over those produced by the classical Naive Bayes classifier and the Bayesian networks as the assumption of independence is removed, but at the same time the robustness and computational complexity are maintained, showing better accuracy [9].

3.2 Paillier Cryptosystem

Paillier algorithm [16] is used for encryption and exploits the additive homomorphic primitive [24] achieving privacy and un-linkability between data and participants' identities. The Miner and each participant create, at their own side, a key pair of 1024 bits size. The public key of each user is the product N of two random prime numbers (N=p*q), and a random number g which belongs to $Z_{n^2}^*$. The private key is the result of two equations, *lambda* and *mu* (Equation 2 & 3).

$$Lambda = lcm(p-1, q-1) = (p-1)*(q-1)/gcd(p-1, q-1) \tag{2}$$

$$mu = (L(g^{lambda} \bmod N^2)^{-1} \bmod N) \text{ where } L(u) = (u-1)/N \tag{3}$$

Generally, if a party j wishes to send frequency i, encrypts the message with the Miner's public key. Paillier encryption is performed as shown in Equation 4, where M is a random value produced at the Miner's side and send to each participant encrypted.

$$E[m_{i,j}] = g^{M^{\wedge i}} x^N \pmod{N^2} \tag{4}$$

When at least three participants have sent their data to the Miner, homomorphic primitive is used to calculate the total frequencies by decrypting all the messages received at once. The decrypted message can be written as presented in Equation 5.

$$T = a_0 M^0 + a_1 M^1 + \ldots\ldots + a_{l-1} M^{l-1} (\mathrm{mod} N) \tag{5}$$

3.3 Security Requirements and Possible Threats

In distributed environments every party is considered to be either semi-honest or malicious. Semi-honest adversaries follow the protocol specifications, they do not collude but are curious to learn more information during the execution of the protocol. Malicious adversaries can be either internal or external. Internals deviate from the protocol and send specific inputs in order to infer other parties' private data. An external one tries to impersonate a legal party and then behave as an internal. In order to confront such behaviors in our scheme, external adversaries cannot participate as every party has to send her digital signature which is assigned by a Certification Authority. The Miner and each participant are *mutually authenticated*, thus unauthorized users are excluded and the authorized ones are connected with the literal server indisputably. Internals are restricted to send blank inputs, or missing values, so are not able to gain any further information other than the final results. Three clients must participate in order to prevent any probing attacks and revelation of other participants' data. Semi-honest adversaries cannot learn more information from the final results as they cannot communicate and collude with each other. Data are transmitted only among the Miner and each client. The case in which parties collaborate outside the protocol is not considered in the present work. *Privacy* can be preserved if the requirements of *confidentiality*, *anonymity* and *un-linkability* are fulfilled. Using asymmetric encryption all data exchanged among one party and the Miner are encrypted and only the participant for whom the message is intended for can decrypt it, so eavesdropping attacks or data leaking is infeasible. Anonymity and un-linkability can be achieved as through homomorphic primitive the Miner cannot identify which participant submits specific inputs to the system. The Miner could also be considered as an internal adversary, if he tries to decrypt partial transmitted messages resulting to privacy violation. This is infeasible as the Miner can decrypt only the overall distributions. Paillier cryptosystem at its initial mode is vulnerable to chosen plaintext attacks. The usage of a random variable (in our scheme M value) is important to confront such attacks. *Integrity* mechanisms are implemented in case any active attacker tries to modify the transmitted messages, and cause variations to the final results or even disclosure of sensitive data.

3.4 Protocol Analysis

The proposed protocol combines both privacy preservation, through Paillier cryptosystem that follows the homomorphic model, and data mining capabilities in a fully distributed environment. Our approach is based on the classical homomorphic election model, and particularly on an extension for supporting multi-candidate elections, where each participant has k-out-of-l selections [4]. Both the Miner and each participant possess a key pair for creating digital signatures, in order to be mutually authenticated, which is used only in the first phase of the protocol and is generated by a Certificate Authority. We assume that the Miner is able to obtain all the public keys of each participant, and each participant can retrieve the Miner's public key. All transmitted messages are encrypted with the keys created during the key generation phase of Paillier cryptosystem, and each one includes a SHA-1 digest to confirm that no modification has been accomplished. Figure 2 presents the main procedures that are being carried out by the protocol using the notations given in Table 1. The Miner regroups all data sent by the participants (clients) of the protocol. His purpose is focused on building a TAN classifier in order to extract the final results by finding the correlations among the attributes and the network structure that represents them. These results will be sent later to each one of the three clients who participated in the creation of the mining model.

Initially, the Miner generates the encryption key pair (S_{pu} and S_{pr}) through Paillier key generation phase and an RSA key pair (S_{Dpu} and S_{Dpr}) of 1024 bit and uses MD5 hash function to create the digital signature. We assume that a client is able to obtain the public key S_{Dpu}. Then a random number M is generated which will be sent, in later phase encrypted to every client that is aware of the Miner's password. This variable is used during the encryption of the sensitive data. When a client request connection with the Miner she sends her public key C_{pu} and her digital signature encrypting the C_{pu} key with her private key C_{Dpr}. The Miner decrypts the digital signature with the client's public key C_{Dpu} obtained by the Certificate Authority and creates a digest of the message send (C_{pu}). If the Miner verifies the client's identity, stores the public key C_{pu} of the client. In return the Miner sends his public key S_{pu} and his digital signature encrypted with his private key S_{Dpr}. The client decrypts the Miner's signature with his public key S_{Dpu} and creates a digest of the S_{pu} key, and is now able to verify that she is connected to the legal server. Afterwards she stores the public key S_{pu}. The purpose of this phase is to prevent any unauthorized access to the system. After the completion of this phase, temporary identities are given to each client. In order to proceed to the mining process, the client must be aware of the Miner's password. If she provides the correct one she can possess the random variable M. Once the mutual authentication process is completed the Miner can gather the clients' personal data. A client can participate in the exportation of statistics giving her personal data. However, requires the sensitive data contained in the database can be disclosed, in the notion of verbatim records, neither to the Miner nor to other participants, nor to a malicious one not involved in the protocol. Every client that consents to the creation of the classification model sends each value of the class and each value of every attribute subsequently. These messages are encrypted with the Miner's public key S_{pu}. This procedure is necessary for the Miner to initialize the TAN classifier, after the collection of at least three clients' data. After the completion of the model initialization, the Miner inquires about the frequencies that correspond to the first attribute. Each client sends the count of every value for this specific attribute in relation to every class value. This count is encrypted using the random variable M and the message send contains also the name of the attribute value and the name of the class value that the count is related with.

When the Miner has collected the data from the three clients he proceeds to their decryption, applying homomorphic primitive. Later on, the Miner asks the frequencies for the next attribute and this process is continuing for all attributes. Then the Miner creates the classification model, as described in section 3.1., and the final results are sent to all participating clients.

Table 1. Notations used in protocol

S_{pu}	Server's public key for encryption/decryption
S_{pr}	Server's private key for encryption/decryption
C_{pu}	Client's public key for encryption/decryption
C_{pr}	Client's private key for encryption/decryption
$H(m)$	SHA-1 hash of message m
$Enc\{m\}k$	Encryption of message m with key k
$Decr\{m\}k$	Decryption of message m with key k
S_{Dpr}	Server's private key for digital signature
S_{Dpu}	Server's public key for digital signature
C_{Dpu}	Client's public key for digital signature
C_{Dpr}	Client's private key for digital signature

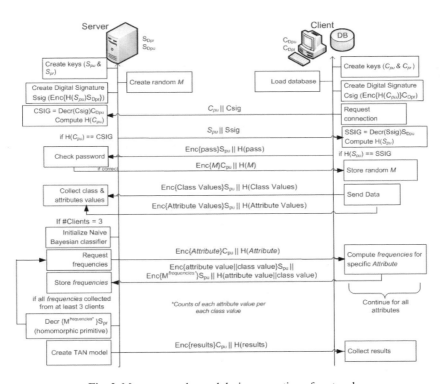

Fig. 2. Messages exchanged during execution of protocol

4   Evaluation

In this section, the main procedures of our protocol are evaluated as we aim to demonstrate that they portray a low level of computation time but at the same time privacy is preserved. We measure the time needed for the key generation phase, the mean authentication time and login time. In order to measure the performance of our scheme we use three scenarios in which three clients participate and the number of records and attributes varies, and compare the secure modes with the corresponding insecure modes of our proposal. For the secure versions we measure the mean encryption and decryption time of messages exchanged. In section 4.2 we present an evaluation of the TAN classifier using Recall and Precision variables as metrics. The experiments were conducted to a computer system with Intel Core 2 Duo T5750 processor at 2.00 GHz, with 3GB DDR2 RAM. The operating system of the machine is MS Windows 7.

4.1   Experiments

For the measurement of mean authentication time, mean login time and mean key generation time we collected measurements from 50 runs. The mean times are presented in milliseconds (ms). Key generation phase includes the encryption key pair generation and the creation of the RSA digital signature. We assume that each client knows the Miner's S_{Dpu} key and the Miner is aware of all public keys C_{Dpu} of the clients. A client requires 513 ms and 133 ms to create the encryption key pair and the digital signature, respectively. The Miner requires 465 ms for the encryption keypair, 45 ms to create the digital signature, and 68 ms to generate the random variable M. In total, 289 ms are required for the key establishment phase. As authentication time we mean the time that is needed for the Miner and each client to mutually be authenticated. From the measurements we calculate that 29 ms are needed for the mutual authentication and 289 ms for the login phase. In this phase the client sends the Miner's password encrypted with the S_{pu} key and the Miner in return respond with the correctness of the password received by sending the random variable M. The mean login time is significant larger than the mean authentication time as decryption and encryption operations are involved.

In order to evaluate our protocol we examined three scenarios to compute the time that is required for the completion of some main procedures. For each scenario we compare the secure mode and an insecure one. The insecure mode is similar to the secure one described in section 3.4 without the authentication phase and the encryption and decryption procedures. Every message is send in cleartext and the client is authenticated only by providing the correct password to the Miner. We use three different scenarios, each one including different number of attributes and different number of records, and three clients are involved to each setting. The horizontally partitioned database used for these experiments comes from a real dataset [19], which is tailored for each case. For the first scenario each client's database consist of 50 records and 5 attributes, in the second scenario it consists of 100 records and 5 attributes and in the third scenario 100 records and 10 attributes are involved. These sets were selected in order to compare if the performance of the protocol depends on the number of attributes and records. From the outcomes, which are presented in Table 2 in comparison with each insecure scenario, as it was expected the mean times are smaller for the insecure versions as encryption and decryption operations are not involved. The classifier initialization time is low and is increased only if the number of attributes is growing. The higher time is when the Miner collects the frequencies for each attribute from all the clients, and is affected when the number of instances is raising. Regarding to the creation of the TAN model, the time is increased when the number of instances is growing. The time to send the final results to all clients is raising both in cases the number of instances and attributes is increased, but the exact opposite happens to the insecure scenarios. We can conclude that the overall time to complete all the steps is determined by the mining process time which is mostly increased when the number of the attributes is growing.

Because of the different number of characters that have been encrypted and decrypted during the execution of the protocol, we collected from the above scenarios the mean times of all messages being exchanged and evaluate them. The average time to encrypt a message is equal to 60 ms. Similar results obtained for the decryption time, as 70 ms is the average time that resulted. We conclude that the mean times are low, so the Paillier cryptosystem is not only effective but also efficient.

Table 2. Experiments' results

Basic Procedures	1st scenario	1st Insecure	2nd scenario	2nd Insecure	3rd scenario	3rd Insecure
Classifier initialization	13	14	16	16	30	22
Mining Process	31777	563	35502	559	94793	3069
BN creation	39	19	117	29	68	171
Final results	2407	5,4	4258	2,2	4476	1,2

4.2 Classifier Evaluation

The evaluation of the TAN classifier is also an important affair. In order to examine the classifier created by the Miner we calculate two variables, Recall and Precision. Variable Recall is the percentage of records categorized with the correct class in relation to the number of all records with this class. Variable Precision is the percentage of records that have truly a certain class over all the records that were categorized with this class.

Table 3. Classifier evaluation results

Records	Naïve Bayes Classifier						TAN classifier					
	1000		2000		5000		1000		2000		5000	
Correct	49		49		50		54		55		56	
Incorrect	51		51		50		46		45		44	
ClassValue	<=50	>50	<=50	>50	<=50	>50	<=50	>50	<=50	>50	<=50	>50
Recall	0,42	0,54	0,48	0,52	0,50	0,8	0,42	0,63	0,52	0,6	0,54	0,6
Precision	0,43	0,53	0,77	0,23	0,47	0,2	0,48	0,57	0,73	0,38	0,73	0,39

Three different sets of data were used as training sets each one holding 1000 records, 2000 records and 5000 records with 14 attributes. As test set, 10% of the training records were kept off the training phase. Our aim is to figure if the created model classifies correctly and more accurate, in relation to the Naïve Bayes classifier, the given records. The results are presented in Table 3. The evaluation has presented fairly good results, from which we can presume that as the training set is getting larger, the Miner classifies more instances correctly, and the TAN model shows better accuracy in relation to the Naïve Bayes model.

5 Conclusion

Classification is considered as a key factor for the detection of hidden information within voluminous data being exchanged. The data stored in databases often contain sensitive information, so possible disclosure during mining processes can compromise fundamental rights of individuals such as privacy or the right to be free from discrimination. This problem can be solved using privacy preserving TAN classifier, which was the purpose of the present work. A protocol developed in a C2S environment where data are horizontally partitioned to participants. Communication among them is infeasible and the only data flow is between a Miner and each participant. Data exchanged during the execution of the protocol, which are the incidences of each attribute value in relation to each class value, are encrypted. The Miner is not in position to know which one of the participants has sent specific frequencies, and so each party remains anonymous. This is achieved by exploiting the homomorphic primitive, and by decrypting the data from at least three parties who consented to participate to the mining process. The data are also been examined for modifications during transmission. From experiments conducted we conclude that the proposed protocol is effective but also efficient. From the security perspective, the cryptographic approach is considered the most appropriate in terms of accuracy of the final results, because the data are not altered in any mode and therefore accurate results are extracted. It was demonstrated that the proposed protocol is safe from possible disclosure of sensitive information. This work focused primarily on ensuring the informational privacy of persons related with.

References

1. Aggarwal, C.C., Yu, P.S.: A General Survey of Privacy-Preserving Data Mining Models and Algorithms. In: Aggarwal, C.C., Yu, P.S. (eds.) Privacy-Preserving Data Mining, pp. 11–52. Springer, US (2008)
2. Agrawal, D., Aggarwal, C.: On the Design and Quantification of Privacy Preserving Data Mining Algorithms. In: 12th ACM SIGMOD-SIGACT-SIGART Symposium on Principles of Database Systems, pp. 247–255. ACM, New York (2001)
3. Agrawal, R., Srikant, R.: Privacy-preserving data mining. In: 2000 ACM SIGMOD Conference on Management of Data, vol. 29(2), pp. 439–450 (2000)
4. Baudron, O., Fouque, P.-A., Pointcheval, D., Stern, J., Poupard, G.: Practical multi-candidate election system. In: PODC 2001: Proceedings of the Twentieth Annual ACM Symposium on Principles of Distributed Computing, pp. 274–283. ACM, New York (2001)
5. Chow, C.K., Liu, C.N.: Approximating discrete probability distributions with dependence trees. IEEE Transactions on Information Theory 14, 462–467 (1968)
6. Clifton, C.: Privacy Preserving Distributed Data Mining. In: 13th European Conference on Machine Learning, pp. 19–23 (2001)
7. Clifton, C., Kantarcioglu, M., Vaidya, J., Lin, X., Zhu, M.Y.: Tools for Privacy Preserving Distributed Data Mining. ACM SIGKDD Explorations 4(2), 28–34 (2002)

8. Clifton, C., Marks, D.: Security and Privacy Implications of Data Mining. In: Proceedings of the 1996 ACM SIGMOD Workshop on Data Mining and Knowledge Discovery, Montreal, Canada, pp. 15–19 (1996)
9. Friedman, N., Geiger, D., Goldszmidt, M.: Bayesian network classifiers. Machine Learning 29(2-3), 131–163 (1997)
10. Kantarcioglu, M., Clifton, C.: Privacy preserving distributed mining of association rules on horizontally partitioned data. IEEE Transactions on Knowledge and Data Engineering 16(9), 1026–1037 (2004)
11. Goldreich, O.: Secure multi-party computation. Working Draft (1998)
12. Kantarcioglu, M., Vaidya, J.: Privacy Preserving Naive Bayes Classifier for Horizontally Partitioned Data. In: IEEE ICDM Workshop on Privacy Preserving Data Mining, pp. 3–9 (2003)
13. Lindell, Y., Pinkas, B.: Privacy Preserving Data mining. Journal of Cryptology 15(3), 177–206 (2002)
14. Magkos, E., Maragoudakis, M., Chrissikopoulos, V., Gritzalis, S.: Accurate and Large-Scale Privacy-Preserving Data Mining using the Election Paradigm. Data and Knowledge Engineering 68(11), 1224–1236 (2009)
15. Mitchell, T.: Machine Learning. McGrawHill, New York (1997)
16. Paillier, P.: Public-key cryptosystems based on composite degree residuosity classes. In: Stern, J. (ed.) EUROCRYPT 1999. LNCS, vol. 1592, pp. 223–238. Springer, Heidelberg (1999)
17. Pinkas, B.: Cryptographic techniques for privacy-preserving data mining. ACM SIGKDD Explorations Newsletter 4(2), 12–19 (2002)
18. Sweeney, L.: k-Anonymity: a model for protecting privacy. International Journal on Uncertainty, Fuzziness and Knowledge-based Systems 10(5), 557–570 (2002)
19. UC Irvine Machine Learning Repository, http://archive.ics.uci.edu/ml/index.html
20. Vaidya, J., Clifton, C.: Privacy preserving association rule mining in vertically partitioned data. In: 8th ACM SIGKDD International Conference on Knowledge Discovery and Data Mining, pp. 639–644 (2002)
21. Vaidya, J., Kantarcioglu, M., Clifton, C.: Privacy-preserving Naive Bayes classification. The VLDB Journal 17(4), 879–898 (2008)
22. Verykios, V., Bertino, E., Fovino, I., Parasiliti Provenza, L., Saygin, Y., Theodoridis, Y.: State-of-the-art in privacy preserving data mining. ACM SIGMOD Record 33(1), 50–57 (2004)
23. Wright, R., Yang, Z.: Privacy-Preserving Bayesian Network Structure Computation on Distributed Heterogeneous Data. In: Proceedings of the 10th ACM SIGKDD International Conference on Knowledge Discovery and Data Mining (KDD 2004), Seattle, WA, USA, pp. 713–718 (2004)
24. Yang, Z., Zhong, S., Wright, R.: Privacy-preserving classification of customer data without loss of accuracy. In: SIAM International Conference on Data Mining, SDM 2005 (2005)
25. Yao, A.C.: How to generate and exchange secrets. In: 27th Annual Symposium on Foundations of Computer Science, pp. 162–167 (1986)
26. Yi, X., Zhang, Y.: Privacy-preserving naive Bayes classification on distributed data via semi-trusted mixers. Information Systems 34(3), 371–380 (2009)
27. Zhan, J., Matwin, S., Chang, L.: Privacy-Preserving Naive Bayesian Classification over Horizontally Partitioned Data. Data Mining: Foundation and Practice (118), 529–538 (2008)
28. Zhang, N., Wang, S., Zhao, W.: On a new scheme on privacy-preserving data classification. In: Proceedings of the Eleventh ACM SIGKDD International Conference on Knowledge Discovery in Data Mining, pp. 374–383. ACM, NewYork (2005)

Secure Cloud Storage: Available Infrastructures and Architectures Review and Evaluation

Nikos Virvilis, Stelios Dritsas, and Dimitris Gritzalis

Information Security and Critical Infrastructure Protection Research Laboratory
Dept. of Informatics, Athens University of Economics & Business (AUEB)
76 Patission Ave., Athens, GR-10434 Greece
{nvir,sdritsas,dgrit}@aueb.gr

Abstract. Cloud Computing is an emerging technology paradigm, enabling and facilitating the dynamic and versatile provision of computational resources and services. Even though the advantages offered by cloud computing are several, there still exists thoughts as per the thus offered security and privacy services. Transferring and storing data to a cloud computing infrastructure, provided by Storage-as-a-Service (STaS) tenants, changes an organization's security posture, as it is challenging to control or audit the cloud provider's infrastructure in terms of the way the underlying risks are controlled and mitigated. Therefore, it is necessary that the organizations understand the new threats and risks introduced by the cloud technology. On the other hand we need to adopt, develop, and deploy mechanisms that can effectively and efficiently preserve the confidentiality and integrity of the data. In this paper we examine available cloud computing architectures, focusing on their security capabilities regarding the storage of the data. We then define a set of comparative criteria, so as to evaluate these architectures. Finally, we evaluate current commercial secure storage services, in order to demonstrate their strengths and weaknesses as well as their supported features and usability.

Keywords: Cloud Computing, Security, Storage Services, Evaluation, Review.

1 Introduction

Storage as a Service (STaS) enables end-users and organizations store their data remotely, using data centers deployed and managed by third party storage providers. This model of remote data storage has been enhanced by the aggressive data volume growth, the provision of large data storage capabilities, and the decrease of the related costs. On the other hand, the thus emerging security threats and risks have been increased. In particular, the transition and storage of critical data to a third-party storage provider gives rise to a number of security and privacy issues.

In this paper we provide an analysis of available and state-of-the-art cloud storage approaches, focusing on the integrity and confidentiality protection mechanisms. We also compare the most popular commercial cloud storage providers, focusing on their underlying security features. Although the paper is focused on cloud storage services, we also present generic schemes addressing data security issues in untrusted stores.

S. Furnell, C. Lambrinoudakis, and G. Pernul (Eds.): TrustBus 2011, LNCS 6863, pp. 74–85, 2011.

The rest of the paper is organized as follows. In Section 2 we define the need for secure storage in the cloud and we summarize the related security requirements. In Section 3 we present a state-of-the-art review on integrity verification protocols, followed with a state-of-the-art review on confidentiality preserving protocols in Section 4. The evaluation of the proposed schemes is presented in Section 5, whilst the commercial cloud storage solutions and their evaluation are described in Section 6. We conclude our analysis in Section 7.

2   Problem Definition

Secure data storage in untrusted stores has gained the attention of the research community, introducing a series of security concerns [29]. In the past, this was a problem affecting mainly corporate users and organizations in general, as individuals had rarely access to a remote storage server. Cloud storage enables both individuals and organizations to easily store their data on the cloud, enjoying the benefits offered by such technology. Use of these services alters the risk profile, because some security responsibility is transferred to the cloud provider, while the security perimeter is extended to include the provider's computing resources and personnel.

Transferring and storing data to a cloud computing infrastructure changes an organization's information technology security posture. When moved to a public or community cloud, controls and measures previously provided within a physical location no longer apply. The data is stored and processed on the cloud provider's hardware at the provider's data center. In this environment, encryption and digital signature schemes replace physical location, as a means of protecting data confidentiality and integrity. Moreover, as encryption replaces physical protection, organizations need to be able to verify that either the cloud provider's encryption capabilities fulfill their data protection requirements, or additional encryption capabilities can be provided.

Given the above changes and issues, it is necessary for the organizations to understand the new threats and risks and adopt, develop, and deploy mechanisms that can effectively and efficiently preserve the confidentiality and integrity of data, while providing appropriate usability and transparency levels, so even non-technical users would be able to use them.

In this context we examine and evaluate available approaches regarding secure data storage. Hence, our work contributes by: a) presenting a state-of-the-art review of the current integrity and confidentiality mechanisms for cloud/remote storage, b) defining and introducing evaluation and comparison criteria, c) comparing and evaluating current schemes, and d) reviewing the most popular cloud storage providers and comparing their underlying security mechanisms and supported features.

3   Integrity Protection

Depending on the sensitivity of the outsourced data a user might only be interested in protecting data integrity - but not confidentiality. This could be, for example, the outsourcing of a digital library. In such scenarios, the verifier (end-user) is interested in verifying data integrity with high probability and low communication and computational overhead. For addressing this challenge the research community follows mainly two approaches [5]:

a) *Proof or Retrievability Schemes (POR)*, i.e. a challenge-response protocol enabling a cloud-storage provider to demonstrate to its client that a file *F* is retrievable, without any loss or corruption [5].

b) *Provable Data Possession Schemes (PDP)*, i.e. a challenge response protocol which is weaker than a POR, as it does not offer guarantees that the client can actually retrieve the file.

The main benefit of the above approaches is that the integrity or retrievability of the data can be verified without actually re-downloading them, thus reducing significantly communication complexity and overhead.

Since detecting data corruption is not that helpful if the user does not maintain any other copy of the whole data set, PDP and POR schemes are mainly useful in environments where the data is distributed across multiple systems [5]. In that sense, if a user detects corruption within a given server, then she can recover the file from redundant data on other servers.

In the remainder of this Section we present an overview of the existing schemes and approaches, which are focusing on protecting the integrity of the data stored on the cloud.

Ateniese, et al. [1] have proposed a model for provable data possession (PDP), by enabling a client to verify the integrity of her outsourced data located at a third party. This is achieved by sampling random sets of data blocks from the server. The client maintains a constant amount of metadata to verify the proof. The challenge/response protocol provided by PDP transmits a small amount of data (minimizing network overhead), in addition to low overhead on the server side. Even though this approach only supports verification of static data, it provides public verifiability by the use of RSA-based homomorphic tags [28]. In order to enhance their technique, the authors presented a revised PDP scheme [2], which was entirely based on symmetric key cryptography. The scheme supports append, modify, and delete operations on the outsourced data. Moreover, only an *a priori* number of integrity verifications are provided, whilst block insertions and public verifiability are not supported.

In [3], a POR scheme was introduced, by which the server proves to the client that an outsourced file *F* is retrievable with high probability. The proposed approach uses special blocks (called sentinels), inserted between normal data, and asks the server to retrieve randomly these blocks so as to prove that the file is retrievable. The sentinel method supports only static data and allows only a fixed number of integrity verifications. There is inevitably data expansion due to the introduction of the sentinels. As the sentinels have to be indistinguishable from other data blocks, all blocks must be encrypted, which significantly affects the overall performance.

A similar technique is presented in [4], which achieves lower storage requirements and a higher level of assurance, with minimal computational overhead. As with the previous techniques, it only addresses static data. In their subsequent work, Bowers et al. [5] extended the POR model to support distributed systems. Their main point was that PORs or PDPs can help a user detect data corruption, but as there is no way to recover the corrupted data the usefulness of these schemes is actually limited. Storing the data in distributed systems enables data recovery from redundancy on intact servers.

In [9], Shacham, et al. proposed the use of homomorphic authenticators for file blocks, which are integrity values that can be efficiently aggregated to reduce bandwidth in a POR protocol. Their scheme addresses only static data. It also supports public verifiability and unlimited number of queries. Wang et al. introduced a model that supports dynamic data operations and distributed server support [6]. Similar to the method proposed in [2], just a few operations are supported (update, delete, append) and public verifiability is missing.

Erway, et al. [7] presented the first fully dynamic PDP model enabling a client to insert, modify, or delete stored blocks or files. Their model supports only private verification of dynamic data, while the efficiency of file updates remains a question. In [8], Wang et al. propose an improved version of their previous scheme, offering dynamic data operation and public verifiability.

In [17], the proposed storage system enables users not only to detect integrity, write-serializability and freshness violations, but also to prove the occurrence of such violations to a third party. Furthermore, the protocol offers read and write access to outsourced data. It also offers high scalability and performance. According to the authors, the proposed POR or PDP schemes can be compromised; the provider could keep the data intact and correctly respond to the verification requests of the client. However, there are no guarantees that she will not refuse to transmit the data (or transmit junk data), when the client tries to retrieve them.

4 Confidentiality Protection

Outsourcing data to a cloud provider (trusted or not) may require confidentiality protection, when the data are sensitive. In the following paragraphs we provide the reader with an overview of existing approaches for ensuring data confidentiality in cloud environments.

In [10], researchers propose the use of data fragmentation as a means for protecting data confidentiality. According to the authors, encryption introduces significant key management issues and may not be adequate for a long period of time and large amount of data, due to new cryptanalytic techniques and the increase in computational power. However, their model introduces significant storage overhead and poor performance.

In [11], a cryptographic cloud storage scheme is presented. It addresses confidentiality and integrity, and supports searchable encryption. Data is indexed and then encrypted using symmetric cryptography with a unique key for each data file. The index file is then encrypted using searchable encryption. Finally, the encrypted data and index are encoded in such way that the end-user (client) can later verify their integrity. Searchable encryption enables the client to perform actions on encrypted data, without having to reveal the encryption keys to the cloud provider. However, the performance overhead imposed by searchable encryption makes the approach impractical.

In [12], researchers propose a generic scheme for access control of outsourced data. The scheme uses a different symmetric key for encrypting each data block. It supports update, deletion, insertion, and appending operations. Each data block is encrypted using a unique symmetric encryption key. It uses a key derivation method based on key hierarchy, in an effort to limit the imposed overhead that is due to key management.

In [13], a file encryption scheme for cryptographic distributed file system is proposed. It is based on optimized Merkle hash trees. In an effort to enhance the performance of the hash tree, authors proposed a universal hash-based MAC scheme, providing confidentiality and integrity of the outsourced data. Data is split into chucks, called blocks, which are symmetrically encrypted. The scheme requires additional trusted storage space.

In [18], researchers propose a Cloud Provider Agnostic protocol, which uses hybrid encryption and message authentication codes (MAC) to protect the confidentiality and integrity of the data. All processing is performed on the client side, thus the model can be used transparently with any cloud storage provider, requiring no modifications from the provider's side. Distribution between multiple providers is supported and no storage overhead is imposed. However, only single user access is supported at the moment.

Several schemes have also been introduced for addressing secure data storage on untrusted environments over insecure protocols, like NFS. In [14], a protocol for secure data storage is proposed. It does not require modifications on the server side, but it is not optimized for storage over the Internet, where network latency is considerably higher than LAN storage. Also, it does not support write serializability (thus two users can read a file at the same time), placing updates subsequently with the second user ignorantly overwriting the first user's update. In its basic form it does not hide the file structure or the filenames of the encrypted data, thus information to a malicious user could be disclosed.

A similar scheme addressing confidentiality is presented in [15]. In this scheme the key generation procedure, which depends on power modular computation and key rolling, introduces significant overhead.

In [16], authors suggest a secure file system that offers fork consistency by having clients check histories of snapshots of file versions. It neither provides read access control, nor scales well to a large number of users [17].

Finally, in [19] researchers propose a secure sharing scheme offering advanced sharing capabilities, similar to the *nix* sharing model (read, write, execute permissions) and supporting user groups. The model does not require modifications on the server side, thus can be used transparently with any cloud provider. It also requires users manage only their private public-private key pair. The use of all other keys is transparent to the user.

5   Cloud Storage Approaches Comparison and Evaluation

We define a set of evaluation criteria that allows us to evaluate and compare the proposed solutions. The criteria are based on the main characteristics of the solutions (security, performance, etc.). Although the list of the proposed criteria is not exhaustive, it helps us analyze and check the pros and cons of each solution, as well as pinpoint and identify new research areas.

- *Type of integrity mechanism,* by which the type of the underlying integrity safeguarding protocol (PDP or POR), is examined.
- *Public Verifiability.* Existence of the appropriate means and techniques in order to prove the possession and validity of the data to third parties. In such schemes a Trusted Third Party (TTP) can be used to verify the integrity of data, thus removing the burden of the user/client.

- *Number of Verifications*, through which we examine if there is an upper bound in the number of integrity verification cycles supported by POR/PDP protocols.
- *Access Control.* The existence of a built-in access control mechanism in the protocol is evaluated, regardless of the native access control that the provider may support.
- *Encryption:* Identification of the encryption techniques used by the protocol for safeguarding data confidentiality.
- *Overhead* is used to flag if a significant overhead (storage, computational, network) is introduced by the protocol.
- *Transparency.* Identifies if the adoption of the scheme requires significant changes or the adoption of a specific protocol by the cloud provider.
- *Distributed Support,* whereas the ability to distribute data to multiple servers for redundancy, is supported.
- *Protocol Performance.* The performance of the protocol, in terms of throughput, is evaluated.
- *Scalability.* How the protocol scales with large data volume or users.
- *Dynamic Data Support.* Integrity verification support for dynamic data. This feature enables users to update the outsourced data and still be able to verify their integrity without need to reprocess the data set.

Tables 1 and 2 depict the comparison of the above schemes. The majority of the schemes share some common characteristics, especially in terms of the underlying encryption technique, which is based on symmetric algorithms so as to minimize computational overhead. In addition, most of schemes satisfactorily deal with scalability issues in order to be able to handle the potential increase in their users' base. On the other hand, the mechanisms partially elaborate with the dynamic data support and with the distributed support. Also, the mechanisms do not offer transparency capabilities, so as to better support usability issues and moreover the transition to other STaS providers, enhancing, in this way, the lock-in effect for their users.

In this context, even though the examined mechanisms offer some basic security services, they do not handle the security issues in a holistic approach. At this point it is useful to introduce cloud storage schemes, capable of offering robust security techniques by preserving usability and transparency properties, as well as by providing performance capabilities.

6 Commercial Solutions

There is a large number of existing commercial solutions for data storage on the cloud. In this Section we present a brief description of current services, focusing on their underlying security mechanisms.

SugarSync [21] is an online backup, file sync and sharing service, offering 5GB free data storage (up to 250 GB for paying customers). Sugarsync application is available for Windows and Mac OS, as well as for smartphone platforms. Linux is currently not supported. Automatic backup, file versioning, synchronization amongst many computers, and file sharing are some of the provided services. SugarSync uses TLS/SSL for all data transfers and files are stored encrypted using AES with 128 bit key in two different geo-redundant data centers. It is not clear enough where the file encryption takes place and how the encryption keys are generated and stored.

Wuala [22] is a storage provider focused on secure storage, offering 1 GB of free storage. Currently it supports Windows, Mac OS X, and Linux OS's. It supports file sync and file versioning. Compared to the rest commercial solutions, only a part of its underlying mechanisms used to secure the data is known [27]. Wuala client encrypts all data on the client system using AES (with 128 bit key) before they get transmitted to the cloud. Then, the encrypted data are split into redundant data fragments using Reed Solomon codes. When a user signs up for a Wuala account, a primary key is automatically generated. This is the key used to encrypt all data. The key itself is encrypted using the username and password of the user and is stored on Wuala Server(s). When a user requests access to her files, the encrypted key is downloaded from the Wuala servers, it gets decrypted locally, and it is used to decrypt/encrypt new files. There is no support for multi factor authentication.

Table 1. Integrity and confidentiality-oriented comparison

	Integrity oriented Criteria			Confidentiality oriented Criteria	
	Type	Public Verifiability	Limited Number of verifications	Access Control Support	Encryption
[1]	PDP	YES	NO	N/A	N/A
[2]	PDP	NO	YES	N/A	N/A
[3]	POR	NO	YES	N/A	Symmetric or Asymmetric
[4]	POR	NO	YES	N/A	N/A
[5]	POR	NO	NO	N/A	N/A
[6]	PDP	NO	YES	N/A	N/A
[7]	PDP	NO	NO	N/A	N/A
[8]	POR	YES	NO	N/A	N/A
[9]	POR	YES	NO	N/A	N/A
[17]	Other	TTP	NO	YES	Symmetric
[10]	N/A	N/A	N/A	NO	N/A
[11]	N/A	N/A	N/A	YES	Symmetric
[12]	N/A	N/A	N/A	YES^2	Symmetric
[13]	N/A	N/A	N/A	NO	Symmetric
[14]	N/A	N/A	N/A	NO	Symmetric
[15]	N/A	N/A	N/A	YES	Symmetric
[16]	N/A	N/A	N/A	NO	Symmetric
[18]	N/A	N/A	N/A	NO	Symmetric
[19]	N/A	N/A	N/A	YES	Symmetric

Table 2. Generic criteria oriented evaluation

	Overhead	Transparency	Distributed Support	Performance	Scalability	Dynamic Data Support
				Generic Criteria		
[1]	Low	NO	NO	Normal	Normal	NO
[2]	Low	NO	NO	Normal	Normal	Partial
[3]	-	NO	NO	Normal	Normal	NO
[4]	-	NO	NO	Normal	Normal	NO
[5]	-	NO	YES	Normal	Normal	NO
[6]	-	NO	YES	Normal	Normal	Partial
[7]	Network	NO	YES	Normal	Normal	YES
[8]	Network	NO	NO	Normal	Normal	YES
[9]	Network	NO	NO	Normal	Normal	NO
[17]	-	NO	NO	Normal	Normal	NO
[10]	Storage	NO	YES	Poor	Poor	YES
[11]	-	NO	NO	Poor	Normal	YES
[12]	-	NO	NO	Normal	Normal	YES
[13]	Storage	YES	NO	Normal	Normal	YES
[14]	Network	YES	NO	Normal	Poor	YES
[15]	Computational	NO	NO	Normal	Poor	YES
[16]	-	NO	NO	Normal	Poor	YES
[18]	-	YES	YES	Normal	Poor	YES
[19]	-	NO	NO	Normal	Normal	YES

Spideroak [23] is a cloud storage service offering automatic backup, file sync, file versioning, and file sharing. Currently, Windows, Linux, Mac OS X OS, iPhone OS, and Android are supported. It offers 2 GB of free storage (100 GB for paying customers). All data is stored in encrypted form on the cloud. The encryption key is derived from the user's password using *pdkdf2* algorithm (16384 rounds) and a 32 bit salt, and it is stored on the cloud. Even with physical access to the cloud servers an attacker can only see sequentially numbered containers of encrypted data. Original file names and folder names are protected. Spideroak uses its own data center and offers an option for geographic redundancy at additional cost.

Ubuntu One [24] is another cloud storage provider. It offers a free account of 2 GB of data (a paying account of 20 GB is also available). It currently supports file syncing, music streaming on iPhone and Android phones, as well as file sharing and contact backup (either from phone or computer). Currently, only Ubuntu and Windows OS are supported. All data transmitted between the client and the cloud server is encrypted using SSL/TLS. The files are stored in plaintext on the Ubuntu one servers.

Carbonite [25] is a secure cloud storage service that supports Windows, Mac OS X, iPhone, Android, and Blackberry phones. It offers 15 days of free trial. After that a standard yearly fee is applied, regardless of the data volume. It supports automatic backup, file sync, and file versioning. It does not support file synchronization between multiple computers. Data is encrypted using Blowfish with 128 bit key on the client side and it is transmitted over TLS/SSL. It enables users to manage their encryption key themselves, thus even if the access credentials are stolen, the attacker will also have to steal the encryption key, to gain access to data, thus providing two factor authentication. Carbonite is using its own datacenters.

Mozy is a flat rate cloud storage service. Currently, only Windows and Mac OS are supported. Mozy supports automatic backup and file versioning. Users are able to request a DVD restore of their files, apart from downloading them. Data are encrypted locally and transferred over TLS/SSL. Users are given the option to manage their personal encryption key, thus having a two factor authentication. Supported encryption options are AES-265 or Blowfish-448 and encryption is carried out on the client side.

Windows Azure Storage is not an "out of the box" storage service *per se*, but rather a Platform as a Services (PaaS) environment. It enables developers to build applications that support secure data storage using Cryptographic Service Providers (CSP). CSP are implementations of cryptographic standards, algorithms, and functions that are implemented by Microsoft to develop a secure storage solution. Thus, developers do not have to rewrite their own implementation of an encryption algorithm or to use other third party cryptographic libraries.

Amazon S3 is a cloud storage service, with no supported encryption. Amazon encourages users to encrypt their data before storing them to the cloud. However, users are able to choose the encryption mechanisms (i.e. an encrypted file system).

6.1 Commercial Solutions Comparison and Evaluation

Keeping in mind the above mentioned commercial solutions for cloud storage, we propose a list of criteria for comparing and evaluating them. The criteria are focused on the provided security mechanisms, as well as on their underlying features. These criteria are:

- *Syncing Between Multiple Computers:* the support of syncing between multiple computers is reviewed.
- *Data Encryption during Transmission*: check if the provider offers secure data transmission (e.g. TLS/SSL).
- *Data Encryption at Store*: refers to the data encryption algorithm used to encrypt the data. We differentiate between schemes that encrypt the data on the client side and schemes that encrypt data on the server side.
- *Multi-factor Authentication:* refers to the ability of the service to enable users to manage their own encryption key and/or to support multifactor authentication.
- *Own Datacenter:* checks if the provider stores the data on its own datacenter, or uses a third party datacenter.
- *Free Space*: the free storage space offered by the provider is examined.

Table 3. Commercial solutions comparison

Cloud Solutions	Own Data Center	Sync	Secure transmission	Data encryption	Multifactor authentication	Free space
Amazon S3	Yes	-	-	No	No	-
Azure	Yes	-	-	No	No	-
Carbonite	Yes	No	Yes	Blowfish-128 Symmetric at client side	Yes	-
Mozy	Yes	Yes*	Yes	AES-256 or Blowfish-448 Symmetric at client side	Yes	2GB
Spideroak	Yes	Yes	Yes	AES-256 Symmetric at client side	No	2GB
Sygarsync	Yes	Yes	Yes	AES-128	No	5GB
Ubuntu One	No	Yes	Yes	No	No	2GB
Wuala	Yes	Yes	Yes	AES-128 Symmetric at client side	No	1GB

*At additional cost, per machine.

Table 3 depicts the evaluation and comparison results regarding the commercial solutions for cloud data storage. Based on the table and the underlying characteristics of each commercial solution we can conclude that the majority of the STaS providers offer many useful services along with some basic security mechanisms. However, we argue that the most important issue to deal with is the support of multifactor authentication, through which the providers must support the encryption of the data at the clients (users)-side. This way, the potential user encrypts the data with a personal key before transmit them to the cloud and therefore has more control over her data. This service is an essential attribute, which can motivate a user to choose her STaS provider.

7 Conclusion

Cloud Computing is a rapidly evolving technology paradigm, enabling and facilitating the dynamic and versatile provision of computational resources and services. Cloud environments and infrastructures and, especially secure storage services are rapidly gaining popularity, making this new computational model extremely successful. On the other hand, one should also highlight the resulting threats and risks. As security and privacy issues are very important, they should be addressed before cloud computing establishes an important market share. In this paper we presented a state-of-the-art review on current cloud storage schemes, with focus on the provided confidentiality and integrity services and mechanisms. More specifically, we have defined and elaborated a set of comparison and evaluation criteria. These criteria are used for analyzing, comparing and evaluating current cloud storage approaches and solutions in an effort to pinpoint their advantages and possible drawbacks. Furthermore, the set of criteria also encompasses performance and usability properties in order to provide us with a thorough evaluation of the STaS approaches. In a similar way, we have compared and evaluated the most popular commercial cloud storage providers based on their underlying security features and properties.

The analysis and evaluation of the STaS mechanisms and techniques have enabled us to identify weaknesses and drawbacks in the current schemes and to pinpoint specific issues that should be reviewed and enhanced so as to preserve the confidentiality and integrity of the data stored into the cloud. We consider that the majority of the proposed research approaches and solutions are mature enough, but, on the other hand, they do not handle the security issues in a holistic approach in order to provide security as well as user transparency (usability) services. Based on our analysis and evaluation it is obvious that that the introduction of cloud storage schemes, capable of offering robust security techniques by preserving usability and transparency properties, as well as by providing performance capabilities, is necessary.

In this context, and by taking into consideration the above-mentioned issues, our future research work will focus on the study, development and deployment of an enhanced and holistic STaS model. The proposed model will deal with usability and performance issues and will be able to deliver full control of the desired security and privacy services and attributes to its users.

References

1. Ateniese, G., Burns, R., Curtmola, R., Herring, J., Kissner, L., Peterson, Z., Song, D.: Provable Data Possession at Untrusted Stores. In: Proc. of the 14th ACM Conference on Computer and Communications Security, USA, pp. 598–609 (2007)
2. Ateniese, G., di Pietro, R., Mancini, V., Tsudik, G.: Scalable and efficient provable data possession. In: Proc. of the 4th International Conference on Security and Privacy in Communication Networks, Turkey (2008)
3. Juels, A., Kaliski, B.: Pors: Proofs of Retrievability for Large Files. In: Proc. of the 14th ACM Conference on Computer and Communications Security, USA, pp. 584–597 (2007)
4. Bowers, K., Juels, A., Oprea, A.: Proofs of Retrievability: Theory and implementation. In: Proc. of the 2009 ACM Workshop on Cloud Computing Security, USA, pp. 43–54 (2009)
5. Bowers, K., Juels, A., Oprea, A.: HAIL: A High-Availability and Integrity Layer for Cloud Storage. Cryptology ePrint Archive, Report 2008/489 (2008)
6. Wang, Q., Wang, K., Ren, W., Lou: Ensuring Data Storage Security in Cloud Computing. In: 17th IEEE International Workshop on Quality of Service (IWQoS 2009), USA (2009)
7. Erway, A., Kupcu, C., Papamanthou, R., Tamassia : Dynamic Provable Data Possession. In: Proc. of the 16th ACM Conference on Computer and Communications Security, USA, pp. 213–222 (2009)
8. Wang, Q., Wang, C., Li, J., Ren, K., Lou, W.: Enabling Public Verifiability and Data Dynamics for Storage Security in Cloud Computing. In: Backes, M., Ning, P. (eds.) ESORICS 2009. LNCS, vol. 5789, pp. 355–370. Springer, Heidelberg (2009)

9. Shacham, H., Waters, B.: Compact proofs of retrievability. In: Pieprzyk, J. (ed.) ASIACRYPT 2008. LNCS, vol. 5350, pp. 90–107. Springer, Heidelberg (2008)

10. Stoner, M., Greenan, K., Miller, E., Voruganti, K.: POTSHARDS: Secure Long-Term Storage without Encryption. In: Proc. of the USENIX Annual Technical Conference, USA, pp. 143–156 (2007)

11. Kamara, S., Lauter, K.: Cryptographic Cloud Storage. In: Proc. of the Financial Cryptography: Workshop on Real-Life Cryptographic Protocols and Standardization, Spain (2010)

12. Wang, W., Li, Z., Owens, R., Bhargava, B.: Secure and Efficient Access to Outsourced Data. In: Proc. of the 2009 ACM Workshop on Cloud Computing Security, USA, pp. 55–66 (2009)

13. Aaram, Y., Chunhui, S., Yongdae, K.: On Protecting Integrity and Confidentiality of Cryptographic File System for Outsourced Storage. In: Proc. of the 2009 ACM Workshop on Cloud Computing Security, USA, pp. 67–76 (2009)

14. Goh, U.-J., Shacham, H., Modadugu, N., Boneh, D.: SiRiUS: Securing Remote Untrusted Storage. In: Proc. Network and Distributed Systems Security Symposium, USA, pp. 131–145 (2003)

15. Kallahalla, M., Riedel, E., Swaminathan, R., Wang, Q., Fu, K.: Plutus: Scalable secure file sharing on untrusted storage. In: Proc. of the 2nd Conference on File and Storage Technologies (FAST 2003), USA, pp. 29–42 (March 2003)

16. Li, J., Krohn, M., Mazieres, D., Shasha, D.: Secure Untrusted Data Repository. In: Proc. of the 6th Symposium on Operating Systems Design and Implementation (OSDI), USA, pp. 121–136 (2004)

17. Popa, A., Lorch, J., Molnar, D., Wang, H., Zhuang, L.: Enabling Security in Cloud Storage SLA with CloudProof. Microsoft Research, TechReport MSR-TR-2010-46 (May 2010)

18. Virvilis, N., Dritsas, S., Gritzalis, D.: A cloud provider-agnostic secure storage protocol. In: Proc. of the 5th International Conference on Critical Information Infrastructure Security (CRITIS-2010), Greece (September 2010)

19. Singh, A., Lin, L.: Sharoes: A Data Sharing Platform for Outsourced Enterprise Storage Environments. In: Proc. of Data Engineering 2008, pp. 993–1002. PRC (April 2008)

20. Dropbox (accessed February 2, 2011), https://www.dropbox.com/

21. Sygarsync (accessed February 2, 2011), https://www.sugarsync.com/

22. Wuala (accessed February 2, 2011), http://www.wuala.com/

23. Spideroak (accessed February 2, 2011), https://spideroak.com/

24. Ubuntu One (accessed February 2, 2011), https://one.ubuntu.com/

25. Carbonite (accessed February 2, 2011), http://www.carbonite.com/

26. Mozy (accessed February 2, 2011), http://mozy.ie

27. Grolimund, D., Meisser, L., Schmid, S., Wattenhofer, R.: Cryptree: A folder tree structure for cryptographic file systems. In: Proc. of the 25th IEEE Symposium on Reliable Distributed Systems (SRDS 2006), pp. 189–198 (2006)

28. Johnson, R., Molnar, D., Song, D., Wagner, D.: Homomorphic signature schemes. In: Preneel, B. (ed.) CT-RSA 2002. LNCS, vol. 2271, pp. 244–262. Springer, Heidelberg (2002)

29. Armbrust, M., Fox, A., Griffith, R., Joseph, A., Katz, R., Konwinski, A., Lee, G., Patterson, D., Rabkin, A., Stoica, I., Zaharia, M.: A view of cloud computing. Communications of the ACM 53(4) (April 2010)

TRAP: Open Decentralized Distributed Spam Filtering

Nahid Shahmehri, David Byers, and Rahul Hiran

Department of Computer and Information Science
Linköping University, SE-58183 Linköping, Sweden
{nahid.shahmehri,david.byers,rahul.hiran}@liu.se

Abstract. Spam is a significant problem in the day-to-day operations of large networks and information systems, as well as a common conduit for malicious software. The problem of detecting and eliminating spam remains of great interest, both commercially and in a research context. In this paper we present TRAP, a reputation-based open, decentralized and distributed system to aid in detecting unwanted e-mail. In TRAP, all participants are equal, all participants can see how the system works, and there is no reliance on any member or subset of members. This paper outlines the TRAP system itself and shows, through simulation, that the fundamental component of TRAP, a distributed low-overhead trust management system, is efficient and robust under the normal conditions present on the Internet.

Keywords: reputation; trust; spam; electronic mail.

1 Introduction

E-mail is one of the most widely used Internet applications. However, today most e-mail is unwanted – spam. The Messaging Anti-Abuse Working Group estimates that in the second quarter of 2010, nearly 90% of all e-mail was spam [18]. The Internet abounds with solutions to the spam problem, none of which actually *stop* spam, but many of which reduce the number of unwanted messages that reach their recipients. However, this is something of an arms race: as spam protection gets better, spammers get smarter, so we need to keep developing new techniques to deal with spam. Spam is more than just a nuisance. It consumes resources and time, and is a vehicle for malicious software. In this paper we present TRAP, a distributed reputation-based system that can help e-mail recipients determine if messages are spam or not. Ultimately, we envision TRAP being used with conventional detection tools to form a complete spam detection and filtering solution. TRAP could also be used to throttle spam at the source: ISPs could use data in the TRAP system to identify (potential) spam sources within their networks, and e.g. limit their ability to send e-mail.

TRAP differs from currently deployed reputation-based filtering systems in that it is completely decentralized and completely open. Decentralized means that all participants in the system are equal: there is no central point of control or data collection point, and no hierarchy among participants. This can make the system very

S. Furnell, C. Lambrinoudakis, and G. Pernul (Eds.): TrustBus 2011, LNCS 6863, pp. 86–97, 2011.

robust, since there is no single point to compromise or attack. Open means that the inner workings of the system are completely exposed: users can find out exactly how messages are processed and why TRAP yields the results it does. This allows participants to understand why the system behaves the way it does, which is vital when troubleshooting e-mail systems. However, adversaries have the same insight, which may help in attempting to subvert the system.

This paper presents the design of the TRAP system and an evaluation of the behavior of the reputation system. The reputation system in TRAP is distributed with a very low overhead. Through simulations we show that despite the simplistic protocol, the reputation system is stable under normal (and many abnormal) Internet conditions.

2   The TRAP System

TRAP is intended to operate in tandem with mail servers that can use external software for spam detection (e.g. sendmail's milter [20] or Postfix's content filtering [22]). TRAP consists of mail sending nodes (senders), mail receiving nodes (receivers), trust holders (holders), trust requesting nodes (requesters) and experience reporting nodes (reporters). Figure 1 shows an overview of how these interact.

Senders are Internet hosts that send e-mail to TRAP participants (i.e. MTAs). Senders do not have to participate in TRAP; they are simply the subject of trust calculations. Receivers are hosts that receive mail and use TRAP, to detect spam. Receivers participate in TRAP by being or using requesters and reporters.

A holder is a TRAP participant that stores the trust values of one or more senders. Any node in TRAP is eligible to be a holder, and each sender is handled by multiple holders. Requesters are hosts that request trust values from holders. Reporters are hosts that report experiences to the holders in the TRAP system. Requesters and reporters either are mail receivers, or are used by mail receivers.

When a receiver receives an e-mail from a sender, it either uses or acts as a requester to get the trust value for the sender. The requester contacts the holder(s) for the sender to collect reputation values. These are processed by the requester to create a single trust value, which is then reported to the receiver. The receiver performs spam detection using the trust value, and finally reports its experience to the holders(s) for the sender by using or acting as reporter.

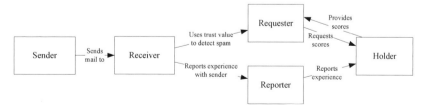

Fig. 1. Overview of the components of TRAP

The spam detection step is not specified by TRAP; any normal detection methods may be employed, but they can use the trust value from TRAP to increase their precision. For example, a threshold-based scheme (e.g. SpamAssassin [26]) could adjust the detection threshold based on the trust value of the sender, or a system could apply stricter filtering or more detailed checks to mail from untrusted senders.

2.1 Requirements

TRAP was designed to meet specific criteria: it must not rely on a central authority or central services; its operations must be open, so users know what it does and can diagnose failures; at the same time, it must be secure, so spammers cannot subvert the system; and it must be scalable and interoperate with existing systems. These overall criteria yielded the following requirements:

- TRAP should support large numbers of users, but be useful even when used by a small portion of the Internet.
- Communications overhead should be kept to a minimum.
- Holders must be assigned so it is impractical for a sender to choose a specific holder and to set up a holder that handles a specific sender.
- Holders must present consistent trust values for a given sender. Otherwise it becomes impossible to interpret the trust values (this is the focus of this paper).
- A sender should never be its own holder, and no node should report its own score.
- The system must be resilient to classical attacks on distributed hash tables.

2.2 The TRAP Overlay Network

TRAP uses the Pastry [25] peer-to-peer system for message routing and data lookup. Pastry provides a self-organizing distributed hash table with provable look-up times for queries; important properties for scalability. Each node has a 128 bit identifier (assignment of identifiers is discussed below). Note that only requesters, reporters and holders must be part of the Pastry network; senders do not need to participate.

2.3 The TRAP Protocol

The TRAP protocol messages contain a message type and zero or more attributes. Sender and receiver addresses and payload length are available from Pastry. Attributes consist of type, flags, length and value. One flag is currently used: *copy* (the attribute must be copied from request to response). There are four message types: reputation request, reputation response, experience report, and error.

Reputation request is sent from receiver to holder to get the reputation of a sender. The only required attribute is *target* (the hashed node ID for which the score is to be returned). Reputation response is sent in reply to a reputation request. The attribute *reputation* contains the reputation of the requested *target*. Experience report is sent from reporter to holder to update the reputation value. Required attributes are *timestamp* (the timestamp at which the experience occurred), *message-id* (a 128 bit integer that identifies the experience; message IDs must be monotonically increasing for each sender/reporter pair), and *target* (hashed node ID that the experience relates to). Holders do not respond to experience report messages. Error is sent when it is not possible to generate a response. The attribute *error-code* indicates the type of error. Nodes can match responses to requests in any way they want. We recommend the use of a custom attribute with the *copy* flag set.

2.4 Node Identifiers

In the TRAP system we assign node IDs by computing a cryptographic hash of the node's IP address; TRAP currently uses the low 128 bits of the SHA-256 function over the node's IP address: $ID^0(addr) = H(addr)$. This ensures that a node can choose its own ID only by searching the entire IP address space and gaining control of the part that contains the sought-after IP address, which is infeasible.

2.5 Trust Holders

Each sender is associated with several holders to ensure trust values are not lost and to make subverting the system more difficult. This, however, increases communications.

TRAP implicitly assigns holders to every IP address. To find the holder of a given node, its node ID is hashed and the result treated as a DHT key; the holder is the Pastry node that handles that key. Additional holders are assigned by repeatedly applying the hash function:

$$Holder^0(addr) = H(ID^0(addr))$$
$$Holder^i(addr) = H(Holder^{i-1}(addr))$$

2.6 Calculation of Reputation Values

TRAP uses a dynamic trust metric that is resilient to oscillatory behavior. It consists of a short-term trust factor, a long-term trust factor and a penalty factor that can be applied to either the short-term or the long-term trust factor [6], and has values from 0 to 1. The short-term factor reflects new experiences; it is defined as a reinforcement learning update rule for non-stationary problems, and can be tuned using a positive and a negative sensitivity factor: the positive factor determines how fast trust increases in response to positive experience and the negative factor determines how fast trust decreases in response to negative experiences [6]. The long-term factor reflects the long-term behavior of the subject, and is an average over all previous experiences, weighted by the number of available experiences. When a subject misuses its trust, the difference between trust invested and actual experience accumulates and is converted to a penalty factor that is applied to the short- or long-term trust factor, either permanently reducing trust or making it increasingly difficult to regain trust. The trust in a subject is calculated as the minimum of the short-term and long-term factors (either of which may be multiplied by the penalty factor). Full details of the trust metric are given in Duma et al. [6]. We have previously used this trust metric in an experimental peer-to-peer intrusion detection system [5].In TRAP unrated nodes start with a trust value of 0.4, which the evaluation shows is a value that only appears during the transition between extremes, and therefore can only be interpreted as unknown trust.

Using this method, the order in which experience reports are processed will affect the reputation value. Therefore, it is important that all holders process the experience report messages for a given sender in the same order. Conventional methods for ensuring that transactions are processed in the same order at all holders, such as distributed agreement, have unacceptably high communications overhead (several roundtrips per node). Therefore, TRAP uses a method that attempts to process experience reports in order at all holders, but makes no guarantees. This method requires no messages other than experience report itself.

In TRAP, every experience report message carries a timestamp and message ID. The experience report messages resulting from any given experience all have the same message ID and timestamp. We can define a total order for experience reports relating to any given sender based on timestamp, message ID and sender node ID:

$$R_i < R_j \quad \text{if timestamp}_i < \text{timestamp}_j$$
$$R_i < R_j \quad \text{if timestamp}_i = \text{timestamp}_j \text{ and sender}_i < \text{sender}_j$$
$$R_i < R_j \quad \text{if timestamp}_i = \text{timestamp}_j \text{ and}$$
$$\text{sender}_i = \text{sender}_j \text{ and message-id}_i < \text{message-id}_j$$

When a holder receives an experience report, it delays processing it until it is old enough that it is likely to have reached all holders. For this to work all TRAP nodes must have synchronized clocks; we specify that all nodes must use NTP [19] against a reliable reference to ensures that the clocks are not *too* far apart.

3 Security of TRAP

Since there is considerable economic incentive behind spam, TRAP must be resilient against attacks intended to disrupt its operations or manipulate the reputation of a given node. Here we briefly discuss how TRAP handles several typical attacks.

False addresses. If a sender were able to use false addresses, TRAP would be ineffective. However, in practice, senders are limited to the addresses they are assigned – it is infeasible to spoof the source address of an SMTP connection reliably. Since any given sender is limited to a small number of IPv4 addresses, attacks based on false addresses are impractical. With IPv6 TRAP would need to use network prefixes (e.g. the first 48 or 64 bits of the address) to construct the node ID in order to achieve the same effect.

Malicious or malfunctioning holders. The simplest attack on TRAP is for a holder to falsify trust values. Nodes can also oscillate between good and bad behavior, to build up and then abuse trust [29]. TRAP mitigates these attacks in two ways: the trust metric is resilient to oscillation [6], and because trust values converge to the extremes, false values are easily distinguished from real ones.

Collusion attacks. In this attack, one or more malicious nodes send false experience reports to the holder of a target node (either to improve or reduce its reputation) [11]. TRAP must tolerate collusion since membership is completely open. Prevention of collusion attacks is one of the most important topics of future work on TRAP.

TRAP also needs to contend with generic attacks on peer-to-peer systems such as the Sybil and eclipse attacks [4] [28]. For the most part these are mitigated in the Pastry layer, but the implicit node ID assignment in TRAP helps by ensuring that an entity receives only as many node IDs as they control network addresses (or in the case of IPv6, network prefixes).

4 Evaluation of the Reputation System

In TRAP holders must report reasonably consistent reputation values: otherwise requesters cannot interpret the values. Due to the best-effort nature of experience reports, some inconsistency between holders is inevitable, but if the normal degree of consistency is known, requesters can process the values, and even identify potentially malicious or malfunctioning nodes. We have conducted simulations to measure the consistency between holders in TRAP. Specifically, we examine:

- To what degree do trust values diverge over time if the maximum and minimum trust values are not constrained? This gives an idea of the stability of the system, exposing problems that might be hidden if values are constrained to a fixed range.
- To what degree do trust values diverge over time if the maximum and minimum trust values are constrained (as they must be in a reputation system)?
- How does message loss and TRAP processing delay affect convergence?
- How does the choice of parameters for the trust metric affect operation?

4.1 Method

Running a simulation of TRAP consists of creating an overlay network, generating mail messages and experience reports, randomly dropping messages, and calculating and observing trust values at the holders.

The simulation is created using the discrete event simulator in FreePastry [8], an open-source Pastry implementation. We place nodes randomly in Euclidian space and the delay between a pair of nodes is based on far apart they are. This topology does not accurately simulate the Internet, but is adequate for our purposes.

Mail messages are generated by single sender and sent to random recipients. E-mail sender behavior is modeled as a stochastic process with a Poisson distribution (i.e., messages are sent with a known average rate, independently of each other, in this case 20 messages per second) [14].

Unless otherwise specified, experience reports were dropped with a probability of 8%; this has been established as a typical drop rate on the Internet [12].

Trust values were periodically written to file so we could see how they developed over time. We applied the penalty factor to the long term trust value; since the sender exhibits oscillatory behavior, all trust values eventually converge to zero. We used a positive sensitivity value of 0.0010 and a negative sensitivity value of 0.0020.

4.2 Results

Divergence with unconstrained trust values. We simulated six separate TRAP networks and measured the maximum difference in trust values between any two holders over the course of the entire simulation. We found that divergence tends to increase over time, but remained very small in relation to the magnitude of the trust value. This indicates that we can expect holders to report very similar scores when the values are constrained.

Convergence with constrained values. Figures 2 and 3 show how trust values for a single sender develop over time for low and high rates of spam respectively when constrained between one and zero. The top charts show that the values rapidly move between 0 and 1, and the bottom that holders deviate significantly only during the transition between these extremes. We also found that the maximum deviation decreased with increasing spam rate, from 0.35 for 10% spam to 0.1 above 40% spam. This means that the meaning of trust values is easy to determine: near the extremes, the values are reliable and indicate whether a sender is a spam source or not; whereas other values indicate a transitional phase during which trust values cannot be reliably used. This also means that inaccurate values from holders can be detected quite easily. Note that the trust value for any given sender may move between the extremes any number of times due to changes in sender behavior.

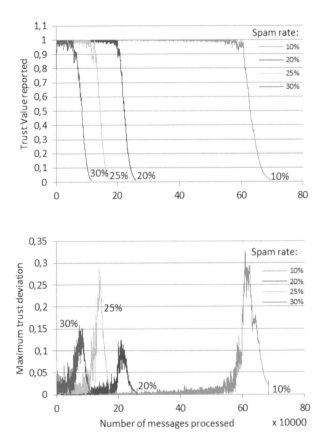

Fig. 2. The convergence and maximum difference of trust values for lower spam rates

Effect of drop rate on convergence speed. Since TRAP does not use a reliable transport, dropped messages can result in deviation between holders. We ran simulations to determine what effect message drop has on convergence speed and deviation between holders. We found that the maximum difference between holders increased only slightly with increased drop rate for a given spam rate, but that drop rates affected convergence speeds considerably, as shown in figures 4 and 5. However, the typical drop 8% rate on the Internet can be handled efficiently by TRAP.

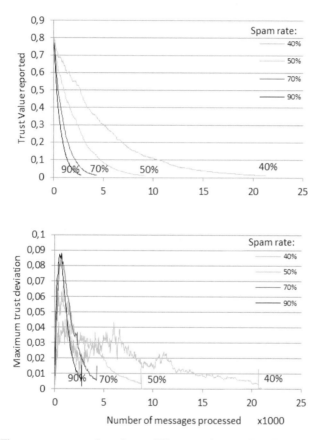

Fig. 3. The convergence and maximum difference of trust values for higher spam rates

Choice of parameters. As expected, when the processing delay *d* (for trust reports at the holders) is lower than the latency in the network, trust values diverge rapidly. With *d* higher than the average latency, trust values converged. With *d* set so 95% of packets had a latency of *d* or lower, convergence was rapid and maximum difference in trust values small. We assume that the clock skew between nodes is small compared to *d*.

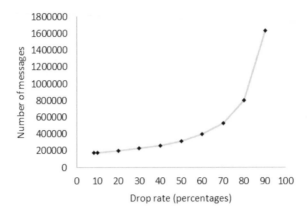

Fig. 4. Number of messages processed before the trust values converge for varying message drop rates (25% spam rate)

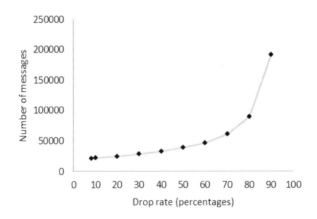

Fig. 5. Number of messages processed before the trust values converge for varying message drop rates (40% spam rate)

5 Related Work

Typically spam detection involves extracting features from a message and determining if the message is spam based on the features that are detected. Determination can be made by assigning weights to each filter (messages above a threshold weight are considered spam), or calculating the probability that a message is spam (e.g. by using a Bayesian network trained using a corpus of e-mail) [26] [9]. These methods can be applied at a single mail receiver; no collaboration is required. A number of collaborative systems exist, where users and/or mail servers collaborate to improve detection quality. An early effort was Vipul's Razor [23], where users could nominate messages as spam; messages with enough nominations were recorded as spam in a catalog server that users could query. Variants of this type of filtering are now used in several solutions, such as Cloudmark [27], the Distributed Checksum Clearinghouse (DCC) [1] and Pyzor [24] and appear in many proposed systems [3][13][30][10][15][21]. Unlike these systems, which detect spam messages, TRAP attempts to identify spam sources. Furthermore, many of the Razor-like systems rely on a central server for their operation. Content filtering and sender detection are typically both used in a complete spam filtering solution.

Trust and reputation frameworks have also been used to aid spam filtering. Two main variants exist: user reputations and sender trust. With user reputations, the (apparent) identity of the sender is used in spam filtering; with sender trust, trust is associated with the sending server. MailRank [2] assigns trust values to email addresses. Unlike TRAP, MailRank relies on a central server. TRAP is an example of a system that employs sender trust. McGibney and Botovich [17] proposed a system in which each mail server stores a trust value for each other mail server it is aware of. Mail servers exchange trust values with each other, and the trust in a sender is a combination of direct experience and reputation. This system has no central control, but unlike TRAP, experiences are only reported to the local neighborhood. The Internet is estimated to have 2-4 million mail servers [16]; it is not clear whether trust values in McGibney and Botovich's system would percolate through a network of that scale fast enough for the system to react to changes in sender behavior.

Foukia, Zhou and Neyman propose a collaborative system for defense against spam [7], in which federations of systems share trust and traffic volume information, so that all participants can calculate a global trust value and traffic rate for mail senders. It is unclear to what degree this system would or how rapidly it reacts to changes in sender behavior. TRAP differs from systems like this in that no special action is required to join or leave TRAP, and that it is designed to require a bare minimum of communication.

There are many more systems that could be described. In general, TRAP differs from all of them in at least one of the properties *open*, *distributed* or *decentralized*. One of the properties it shares with essentially all other approaches is that it has to be used in combination with other mechanisms for detecting and filtering spam.

6 Conclusions and Future Work

In this paper we have presented TRAP, a distributed reputation-based system for evaluating whether mail senders are sources of spam or not. Unlike previous reputation systems for spam filtering, TRAP is completely decentralized and completely open: there is no reliance on a central service of any kind, and the internals of the system are open for anyone to examine. This creates new challenges as it makes it easier for spammers to subvert the system, but in return the system can be made very robust and easy to join.

TRAP uses the Pastry protocol to implement the underlying peer-to-peer network, which gives proven performance for communication; and a dynamic trust metric that is resilient to oscillatory behavior; this makes it harder for spam sources to subvert the system. The results presented here show that the fundamental component of TRAP, the trust management system, is efficient and robust. We have presented initial findings concerning tuning the parameters of TRAP. However, a considerable amount of work still remains: the precise mechanics of joining and leaving the system are not defined; several security challenges remain; and the precise tuning of the various parameters in TRAP requires additional experimentation with the network.

TRAP is intended to be used as part of a spam solution; in itself it will be insufficient to determine what is spam or not, but we think that it can improve the accuracy of a complete system.

References

1. Distributed checksum clearinghouses, http://www.rhyolite.com/dcc
2. Chirita, P., Diederich, J., Nejdl, W.: MailRank: Using Ranking for Spam Detection. In: 14th ACM International Conference on Information and Knowledge Management, pp. 373–380. ACM, Bremen (2005)
3. Damiani, E., Vimercati, S.D.C.D., Paraboschi, S., Samarati, P.: P2P-Based Collaborative Spam Detection and Filtering. Peer-to-Peer Computing, pp. 176–183 (2004)
4. Douceur, J.R.: In: Druschel, P., Kaashoek, M.F., Rowstron, A.I.T. (eds.) The Sybil Attack: Revised Papers from the First International Workshop on Peer-to-Peer Systems, pp. 251–260. Springer, London (2002)
5. Duma, C., Karresand, M., Shahmehri, N., Caronni, G.: A Trust-Aware, P2P-Based Overlay for Intrusion Detection. In: 17th International Workshop on Database and Expert Systems Applications, pp. 692–697. Krakow, Poland (2006)
6. Duma, C., Shahmehri, N., Caronni, G.: Dynamic Trust Metrics for Peer-to-Peer Systems. In: Sixteenth International Workshop on Database and Expert Systems Applications, Copenhagen, Denmark, pp. 776–781 (2005)
7. Foukia, N., Zhou, L., Neuman, C.: Multilateral Decisions for Collaborative Defense Against Unsolicited Bulk E-mail: Trust Management. In: Stølen, K., Winsborough, W., Martinelli, F., et al. (eds.) iTrust 2006. LNCS, vol. 3986, pp. 77–92. Springer, Heidelberg (2006)
8. FreePastry, http://www.freepastry.org
9. Gong, Y., Chen, Q.: Research of Spam Filtering Based on Bayesian Algorithm. In: International Conference on Computer Application and System Modeling (ICCASM), Taiyuan, China, PP. V4-678–V4-680 (2010)
10. Gray, A., Haahr, M.: Personalised, Collaborative Spam Filtering. In: First Conference on Email and Anti-Spam, CA, USA (2004)
11. Hoffman, K., Zage, D., Nita-Rotaru, C.: A Survey of Attack and Defense Techniques for Reputation Systems. ACM Computing Surveys, 1:1–1:31 (2009)
12. Internet Traffic Report, http://www.internettrafficreport.com
13. Kong, J.S., Rezaei, B.A., Sarshar, N., Roychowdhury, V.P., Boykin, P.O.: Collaborative Spam Filtering using E-Mail Networks. Computer 39, 67–73 (2006)
14. Lee, Y., Kim, J.: Characterization of Large-Scale SMTP Traffic: The Coexistence of the Poisson Process and Self-Similarity. In: 2008 IEEE International Symposium on Modeling, Analysis and Simulation of Computer and Telecommunication Systems, MASCOTS (2008)
15. Li, K., Zhong, Z., Ramaswamy, L.: Privacy-Aware Collaborative Spam Filtering. IEEE Transactions on Parallel and Distributed Systems 20, 725–739 (2009)

16. Measuring the popularity of SMTP server implementations on the Internet,
    `http://www.stillhq.com/research/smtpsurveys_feb2010.html`
17. McGibney, J., Botvich, D.: A Trust Based System for Enhanced Spam Filtering. Journal
    of Software 3, 55–64 (2008)
18. MAAWG: Messaging Anti-Abuse Working Group, `http://www.maawg.org`
19. Mills, D.: Network Time Protocol Version 4 Reference and Implementation Guide.
    Technical report (2006)
20. Milter.org, `https://www.milter.org`
21. Mo, G., Zhao, W., Cao, H., Dong, J.: Multi-Agent Interaction Based Collaborative P2P
    System for Fighting Spam. In: 2006 IEEE/WIC/ACM International Conference on
    Intelligent Agent Technology, Washington, DC, USA, pp. 428–431 (2007)
22. Postfix, `http://www.postfix.org`
23. Vipul's Razor, `http://razor.sourceforge.net`
24. Pyzor, `http://sourceforge.net/apps/trac/pyzor`
25. Rowstron, A.I.T., Druschel, P.: Pastry: Scalable, Decentralized Object Location, and
    Routing for Large-Scale Peer-to-Peer Systems. In: IFIP/ACM International Conference on
    Distributed Systems Platforms, pp. 329–350. Springer, Heidelberg (2001)
26. The Apache SpamAssassin Project, `http://spamassassin.apache.org`
27. A Reputation-Based Approach for Efficient Filtration of Spam,
    `http://www.cloudmark.com`
28. Wallach, D.S.: A survey of peer-to-peer security issues. In: Okada, M., Babu, C. S.,
    Scedrov, A., Tokuda, H. (eds.) ISSS 2002. LNCS, vol. 2609, pp. 42–57. Springer,
    Heidelberg (2003)
29. Xiong, L., Liu, L.: Peertrust: Supporting Reputation-Based Trust For Peer-To-Peer
    Electronic Communities. IEEE Transactions on Knowledge and Data Engineering 16,
    843–857 (2004)
30. Zhou, F., Zhuang, L., Zhao, B.Y., Huang, L., Joseph, A.D., Kubiatowicz, J.: Approximate
    Object Location and Spam Filtering on Peer-to-Peer Systems. In: Endler, M., Schmidt,
    D.C. (eds.) Middleware 2003. LNCS, vol. 2672, pp. 1–20. Springer, Heidelberg (2003)

Best Effort and Practice Activation Codes

Gerhard de Koning Gans[1] and Eric R. Verheul[1,2]

[1] Institute for Computing and Information Sciences
Radboud University Nijmegen
P.O. Box 9010, 6500 GL Nijmegen, The Netherlands
{gkoningg,eric.verheul}@cs.ru.nl
[2] PricewaterhouseCoopers Advisory
P.O. Box 22735, 1100 DE Amsterdam, The Netherlands
eric.verheul@nl.pwc.com

Abstract. Activation Codes are used in many different digital services and known by many different names including voucher, e-coupon and discount code. In this paper we focus on a specific class of ACs that are short, human-readable, fixed-length and represent value. Even though this class of codes is extensively used there are no general guidelines for the design of Activation Code schemes. We discuss different methods that are used in practice and propose BEPAC, a new Activation Code scheme that provides both authenticity and confidentiality. The small message space of activation codes introduces some problems that are illustrated by an adaptive chosen-plaintext attack (CPA-2) on a general 3-round Feistel network of size 2^{2n}. This attack recovers the complete permutation from at most 2^{n+2} plaintext-ciphertext pairs. For this reason, BEPAC is designed in such a way that authenticity and confidentiality are independent properties, i.e. loss of confidentiality does not imply loss of authenticity.

Keywords: activation code, e-coupon, voucher, Feistel network, small domain encryption, financial cryptography.

1 Introduction

This paper introduces Activation Codes (ACs) as a generic term for codes that are used in many different digital services. They are known by many different names including voucher, e-coupon and discount code. The common properties of these codes are that they need to be short, human-readable, have a fixed length and can be traded for economic benefit. There are schemes [4,5,8] that include all kinds of property information in the code itself or include digital signatures [14,12]. This makes the codes unsuitable for manual entry and thus for printing on products, labels or receipts. The focus of this paper is on ACs that can be printed and manually entered such as the AC that is printed on a receipt in Figure 1. In this case the customer can enter the AC 'TY5FJAHB' on a website to receive some product. We propose a scheme called BEPAC to generate and verify this class of ACs. BEPAC is an acronym for Best Effort and Practice

S. Furnell, C. Lambrinoudakis, and G. Pernul (Eds.): TrustBus 2011, LNCS 6863, pp. 98–112, 2011.

Activation Codes. Here *'best practice'* covers the use of a keyed hash function to satisfy authenticity and *'best effort'* covers the use of a Feistel network to satisfy confidentiality.

Security plays an important role in the design of an AC system because of the economic value it represents. A system breach could result in big financial losses. Nevertheless, to the best of our knowledge, there are no guidelines on the design of secure AC systems that consider the previously mentioned properties. Despite the lack of general guidelines for good practice, ACs are extensively used. This underlines the need for a proper AC scheme that relies on elementary, well-studied, cryptographic primitives to provide authenticity and confidentiality. First, we discuss some examples that illustrate the need for a scheme that provides both confidentiality and authenticity. Then, we give a general definition of an AC scheme and use it as a reference throughout this paper.

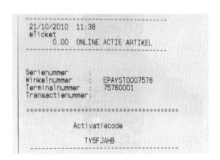

Fig. 1. Activation Code

Our Contribution. This paper addresses some known methods that are used to generate ACs and proposes BEPAC, an AC scheme that combines best effort with best practice. BEPAC is based on well-studied cryptographic primitives to guarantee unique and authentic codes that provide a satisfactory level of confidentiality. Confidentiality is obtained by a Feistel construction. The Feistel construction has weak theoretical bounds when it is used on a small domain, therefore we do not rely on it for authenticity. We use the work of Black and Rogaway [3] on small domain encryption and make some small changes to achieve confidentiality. A practical attack on a general 3-round Feistel network is presented to demonstrate the weak bounds of the Feistel construction. For authenticity, we solely rely on a keyed-hash message authentication code (HMAC) of the serial number, where the size of this HMAC determines the probability of successfully guessing a valid AC. This separated design allows a separate analysis of both confidentiality and authenticity. An advantage of this approach is that authenticity is not automatically compromised when confidentiality is broken. Finally, a BEPAC solution fits on a smart card and therefore allows AC generation and clearance to be performed in a controlled environment.

Related Work. Black and Rogaway [3] propose the Generalized Feistel Cipher (GFC) as a solution to small domain encryption. This elegant solution can be used to construct a permutation on any finite domain. In the BEPAC scheme we use their method in a slightly adapted way and solely to provide confidentiality. Black and Rogaway provide an adapted proof of Luby [15] to prove secrecy of a 3-round Feistel network. However, in their example configuration, the single DES round function does not give the 3×56-bit security since single DES can be broken by exhaustive key search [25]. Moreover, in this setting it can be broken round by round which actually means that we have 58-bit security. Bellare et al. [2] propose 128-bit AES as a pseudo-random function which drastically increases the effort needed to break one round of the Feistel network by brute-force. However, the adaptive chosen-plaintext attack (CPA-2) on a 3-round Feistel network presented in this paper shows that the key length of the pseudo-random function used in each round does not have any influence on the attack complexity. Research on Feistel networks [22,20,19,15,13,21] has resulted in theoretical security bounds. Feistel constructions of six or more rounds are secure against adaptive chosen plaintext and chosen ciphertext attacks (CPCA-2) when the number of queries $m \ll 2^n$, see [22,13].

There is more related literature on the design of ACs, but to the best of our knowledge there are no proposals for the class of AC schemes that we discuss in this paper. Blundo et al. [4,5,8] introduce an e-coupon which is 420 bytes in size. This scheme uses a message authentication code (MAC) over some characterizing data like the identity of the manufacturer, name of the promoted product, expiry date etc. The resulting e-coupons contain valuable information but are too large to be entered manually by a user. In the work of Kumar et al. [14] and Jakobssen et al. [12] a coupon is basically a digital signature which also means that they describe relatively large e-coupons. Chang et al. [6] recognize the problem of efficiency and describe a scheme that is more suitable for mobile phones that have less processing power. On the one hand, they circumvent the use of public key cryptography which reduces the computational complexity, but on the other hand, their scheme describes relatively long codes. None of the schemes described previously satisfy the requirement of short codes that can be entered manually.

Matsuyama and Fujimura [17] describe a digital ticket management scheme that allows users to trade tickets. The authors discuss an account based and a smart card based approach and try to treat different ticket types that are solely electronically circulated. This in contrast with BEPAC which focuses on codes that can easily be printed on product wrappings. Our intention is not to define a trading system where ACs can be transfered from one person to another. Such contextual requirements are defined in RFC 3506 as Voucher Trading Systems (VTS). Terada et al. [28] come with a copy protection mechanism for a VTS and use public key cryptography. This makes the vouchers only suitable for electronic circulation. Furthermore, RFC 3506 and [17] do not discuss methods on how to generate these vouchers securely. We propose the BEPAC scheme in order to fill this gap.

2   AC Scheme Selection

This section first discusses some examples of AC systems. Then, two different approaches to set up an AC scheme are discussed and their main drawbacks are visited. After this, the Generalized Feistel Cipher of [3] is introduced in Section 2.1 which has some useful concepts that we use in our scheme. The focus of an AC scheme design lays on scalability, cost-efficiency and off-line use. Finally, forgery of ACs should be hard, an adversary is only able to forge ACs with a very small predefined probability.

Examples of Activation Codes. First, we discuss some examples of ACs in real life. A good first example is the *scratch prepaid card* that is used in the telecommunication industry. To use a prepaid card, the customer needs to remove some foil and reveals a code that can be used to obtain mobile phone credits. Then we have the *e-coupon* which is a widely used replacement for the conventional paper coupon. An e-coupon represents value and is used to give financial discount or rebate at the checkout of a web shop. The last example is a *one-time password* that gives access to on-line content. This content should only be accessible to authenticated people who possess this unique password; think of sneak previews of new material or software distribution.

All the aforementioned examples use unique codes that should be easy to handle, that is, people should be able to manually copy ACs without much effort. At the same time, it should be impossible for an adversary to use an AC more than once or autonomously generate a new valid AC. Altogether, ACs are unique codes that have to guarantee authenticity. An AC system provides authenticity when an adversary is not able to forge ACs. It is a misconception that authenticity only is enough for an AC scheme. In the end, most AC systems are used in a competitive environment. When vendor A starts a campaign where ACs are used to promote a product and provide it for free to customers, then it is not desirable that vendor B finds out details about this campaign like the number of released ACs. Other sensitive details might be the value that different ACs represent or the expiry date of ACs. It is for this reason that we need confidentiality, which means that an adversary is not able to recognize patterns or extract any information from a released AC.

Many systems use codes that need to provide the properties discussed above. In this paper we refer to all these codes as ACs. By an AC scheme $\mathcal{S}$ we indicate a tuple $(\mathcal{A}, \mathcal{N}, \mathcal{P}, \lambda)$ where $\mathcal{A}$ is the size of the used alphabet, $\mathcal{N}$ is the number of desired ACs, $\mathcal{P}$ determines the probability $P = \frac{1}{\mathcal{P}}$ of an adversary guessing an AC and λ is the length of the ACs.

Database Approach. The database approach is very straightforward and consists of a database that contains all the released ACs and their current status. The generation of new AC entries is done by a pseudo-random function. When a customer redeems an AC, its status is set to 'used'. An advantage of the database approach is that the randomness of the ACs is directly related to the randomness of the pseudo-random generator. So, it is important to select a good pseudo-random generator, e.g. a FIPS certified one. On the other hand, the protection of this valuable data is still a problem. For instance, if an attacker manages to add entries to the database or is able to change the record status to 'unused', it will be hard to detect this fraud in time. Also, it is necessary to check any new AC against all existing entries since there might be a collision. As a consequence, access to the complete set of ACs is needed on generation of new ACs.

Block Cipher Approach. Another approach is to use a block cipher that gives a random permutation $F : \{0,1\}^n \rightarrow \{0,1\}^n$ from serial numbers to ACs.

The provider maintains a counter i to keep track of the number of generated ACs. This way the authenticity of a serial number can be checked since only ACs that decrypt to a serial $< i$ are valid. A disadvantage of this method is the size of the resulting AC which is 128-bits for AES and 64-bits for 3DES. For AES, this results in a string of about 21 characters when we use numbers, upper- and lowercase characters in our alphabet. For 3DES, this is about 11 characters. Smaller block ciphers do exist, like KATAN [10] which is 32-bits, but are not very well-studied. Furthermore, block ciphers force ACs to have a length that is a multiple of the block size b. An alternative could be the concept of elastic block ciphers [9] which is an extended scheme where variable message sizes are allowed as input. Moreover, this scheme uses well-studied block ciphers. Still, the minimal size of a plaintext message is the block size b of the incorporated block cipher. So, this does not give any advantage and is still too large for our target, which is roughly 20 to 50-bit codes.

2.1   Small Domain Ciphers

Black and Rogaway introduce the Generalized Feistel Cipher (GFC) in [3]. The GFC is designed to allow the construction of arbitrary domain ciphers. Here, arbitrary domain means a domain space that is not necessarily $\{0,1\}^n$. For ACs we want to use a small domain cipher where the domain size can be customized to a certain extent, therefore we look into the proposed method in [3]. Before we describe the Generalized Feistel Cipher, we briefly visit the basic Feistel construction.

Feistel Network. A Feistel network [16] is a permutation that takes an input x of size $2n$, then performs a number of rounds r with round functions $f_1, ..., f_r$, and finally delivers an output y of size $2n$. The input is split into two blocks $\langle L, R \rangle \in \{0,1\}^{2 \times n}$. As shown in Figure 2, every right block is input to a round function f_i. The output of this function is combined with the left block and becomes the new right block, e.g. $L' = f_1(R) + L$ for GFC. The original right block becomes the new left block. For the ease of decryption the last output blocks are swapped in case of an odd number of rounds (which is the case in Fig. 2).

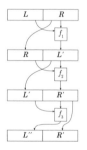

Fig. 2. Feistel

Generalized Feistel Cipher. The GFC of Black and Rogaway [3] was intro- duced to handle flexible domain sizes. Take for example an encryption $E : 5^{14} \to 5^{14}$ which is not a domain that is captured by standard block cipher algorithms. The BEPAC scheme borrows some of the ideas of GFC to be able to construct arbitrarily sized AC configurations.

In GFC the left and right block of the Feistel network are "similarly sized" which means that their domain size may deviate a little. For the particular case of ACs we have looser restrictions on the arbitrariness of our domain and we can increase the guessing probability $\mathcal{P}$ to influence the domain size. As a consequence, the system parameters of BEPAC can be chosen such that the left and right block are equally sized.

An obvious way to use the Feistel network is to create a pseudo-random permutation $F : \mathcal{K} \times \mathcal{M} \rightarrow \mathcal{M}$ where $\mathcal{K}$ and $\mathcal{M}$ are the key space and message space respectively. To generate ACs, we take as plaintext an index i and use the resulting ciphertext as AC α. In order to check α the provider keeps track of the last index i and considers a given α valid when $F^{-1}(\alpha) \leq i$. This construction guarantees:

1. Collision-freeness, since F is a permutation.
2. Valid serial numbers, they cannot be predicted since F is a pseudo-random permutation.

As Black and Rogaway already conclude in [3] the Generalized Feistel Cipher has weak security bounds when used in applications where the message space is roughly from $k = 2^{30}$ up to $k = 2^{60}$. This suggests that our second argument might not be that strong.

Also, the serial i is kept secret and one might argue that this presumes unforgeability. However, the way i is embedded allows an adversary to make useful assumptions about i since the ACs are generated using consecutive numbers. In the GFC, the left block L and right block R are initiated as follows:

$$L = i \bmod 2^n, \qquad R = \lfloor i/2^n \rfloor$$

Here, L represents the least significant bits of i, and the successor of every i always causes a change in L. On the contrary, when i is sequentially incremented, the value of R changes only once every 2^n times. This way, the first 2^n ACs are generated with $R = 0$, the second 2^n ACs with $R = 1$, etc. The problems that this little example already points out are further explained in the next section.

3   Feistel Permutation Recovery Using CPA-2

In this section we present a practical attack on a three-round Feistel construction in order to illustrate the problem of choosing a small number of rounds and using a serial embedding as suggested by Black and Rogaway [3].

Theorem 1. *Consider a three-round $2n$-bit Feistel construction. Then there exists an algorithm that needs at most 2^{n+2} adaptive chosen plain-/ciphertext pairs to compute any ciphertext from any plaintext and vice versa without knowledge of the secret round keys and regardless the used key length.*

Proof. The two ciphertext blocks are defined in terms of the plaintext blocks as follows:

$$\begin{aligned} R' &= f_2(f_1(R) + L) + R \\ L'' &= f_3(f_2(f_1(R) + L) + R) + f_1(R) + L \\ &= f_3(R') + f_1(R) + L \end{aligned} \tag{1}$$

Note that L'' uses R' as input to $f_3(\cdot)$. With L_i we denote $L = i$ and similarly R_j denotes $R = j$. The notation $R'_{(i,j)}$ means the value of R' when L_i and R_j are used as input blocks. We first observe that several triples (f_1, f_2, f_3) lead to the same permutation and show that it is always possible to find the triple with $f_1(0) = 0$. To this end, if we replace the triple (f_1, f_2, f_3) with the triple (f'_1, f'_2, f'_3) defined by Equation (2), this leads to the same permutation (Equation (1)) with the desired property that $f'_1(0) = 0$.

$$f'_1(x) = f_1(x) - f_1(0), \qquad f'_2(x) = f_2(x + f_1(0)), \qquad f'_3(x) = f_3(x) + f_1(0) \quad (2)$$

So, without loss of generality we may assume that $f_1(0) = 0$.

Next, we describe a method to find a triple (f_1, f_2, f_3) with $f_1(0) = 0$. First, we determine f_2, then f_1 and finally f_3.

By Equation (1) we get f_2:

$$f_2(f_1(R_0) + L_i) = R'_{(i,0)} - R_0 = R'_{(i,0)} \qquad \Rightarrow \qquad f_2(L_i) = R'_{(i,0)} \quad (3)$$

Now, to find f_1 observe that $f_1(j)$ is a solution for x in the equation $f_2(x) = R'_{(0,j)} - R_j$. However, this equation does not always have one unique solution since f_2 is a pseudo-random function. In case of multiple solutions we compare the output of successive (wrt. x) function inputs with the values for $f_2(x + i)$ that were found using Equation (3). Then, the correct x is the unique solution to:

$$f_2(x + i) = R'_{(i,j)} - R_j \qquad \text{for } i = 0, \dots, m \quad (4)$$

Sometimes $m = 0$ already gives a unique solution. At the end of this section we show that with very high probability $m = 1$ defines a unique solution. We find:

$$f_1(j) = x \quad (5)$$

When f_1 and f_2 are both determined, L and R can be chosen such that every value for $R' \in \{0, \dots, 2^n - 1\}$ is visited. Since R' functions as direct input to f_3 it is possible to find all input-output pairs for f_3. To visit every possible input value $z = 0, \dots, 2^n - 1$ find a pair L_i, R_j such that $R'_{(i,j)} = z$. First, find an index x such that $f_2(x) = z - R_j$. If such an x does not exist choose a different value for R_j. There is always a solution for x since R_j covers the whole domain of f_2. Second, derive L_i:

$$f_2(f_1(R_j) + L_i) = f_2(x) \qquad \Rightarrow \qquad L_i = x - f_1(R_j) \quad (6)$$

Note that the determination of L_i and R_j does not need any intermediate queries since it is completely determined by f_1 and f_2. Next, we query the system with L_i and R_j and use Equation (3) and (5) to compute f_3 as follows:

$$f_3(x) = L''_{(i,j)} - f_1(R_j) - L_i \quad (7)$$

This completes the solution for a triple (f_1, f_2, f_3) that results in the same permutation as the Feistel construction under attack.

Number of Queries The determination of f_2 is given by Equation (1) and costs 2^n queries. The determination of f_1 is given by Equation (4). The probability p that there exists an $x' \neq x$ for a preselected x such that

$$(f_2(x) = f_2(x')) \wedge \left(\bigwedge_{i=1,\ldots,m} f_2(x + i) = f_2(x' + i) \right) \tag{8}$$

can be split into two parts. First, we have the probability p_1 that there is a collision $f_2(x) = f_2(x')$ with $x \neq x'$. Then, the second probability p_2 covers cases where a preselected position $f_2(x + i)$ has the same value as some other preselected position $f_2(x' + i)$. We take $k = 2^n$ and the two probabilities are then given by $p_1 = 1 - (\frac{k-1}{k})^{(k-1)}$ and $p_2 = \frac{1}{k}$. Now, $p = p_1 \cdot p_2{}^m$ because we need to multiply by p_2 for every other successive match. To conclude, the probability that there is an $x' \neq x$ for a Feistel construction of size $2 \cdot k$ and with m successive queries, i.e. the probability that there is no unique solution x to Equation (4), is the probability

$$p = \frac{1}{k^m} - \frac{1}{k^m} \cdot \left(\frac{k-1}{k} \right)^{k-1} \tag{9}$$

So, $p < \frac{1}{k^m}$ and depending on the size k, $m = 1$ already gives p close to zero. In practice one might sometimes need an additional query ($m = 2$) or only one query ($m = 0$), but on average $m = 1$. This means that the cost for determination of f_1 is $2 \cdot 2^n$ queries on average. Then, the determination of f_3 is given by Equation (7) and costs at most 2^n queries. As a result, the determination of (f_1, f_2, f_3) has an upper bound of 2^{n+2} queries.

4   BEPAC Scheme

In this section we propose our Activation Code Scheme called BEPAC. Its primary objective is to ensure authenticity and its secondary objective is to provide confidentiality. Confidentiality is satisfied up to the security bounds given by Black and Rogaway in [3]. In the BEPAC scheme, loss of confidentiality does not affect the authenticity property.

The authenticity is achieved in an obvious way by the use of an HMAC which is a keyed hash function. We take the truncated HMAC h of a sequence number i and concatenate it to i itself. For this concatenation we use an embedding m like the one used by Black and Rogaway in [3] and Spies in [2]. We rely on the strength of the underlying hash function which covers the *best practice* part of our solution: ACs are not forgeable. The length of an HMAC is usually too long for the ease of use that is demanded for ACs. Therefore we introduce the probability $P = \frac{1}{\mathcal{P}}$ that puts a lower bound on the success rate of guessing correct ACs. We use this parameter to limit the length of the codes, i.e. $\mathcal{P}$ determines the size of the HMAC. A lower success probability for an adversary is achieved by concatenating a bigger part of the HMAC and thus results in a longer AC.

Our solution differs from encryption schemes for small domains [3,18] in the sense that we make a clear separation between the part that provides authenticity and the part that provides confidentiality. The latter is added as an additional operation on the embedding m. We use a balanced Feistel construction as proposed in [3] to create the necessary confusion and diffusion. This separation between authenticity and confidentiality is really different from an approach where the sequence number i is directly fed into a Feistel construction and when it solely depends on this construction for its authenticity. The attack in Section 3 demonstrates that we cannot rely on a Feistel construction for authenticity when it is used on a small domain. These results form the basis of our design decision.

4.1   AC Scheme Setup

The BEPAC scheme setup is a construction (see Fig. 3) where an embedding m of an index i and a part of HMAC(i) are fed into a Feistel network. Since this is a balanced Feistel network, m needs to be divided into two equally sized blocks. When this is not possible a small part h' of HMAC(i) bypasses the Feistel network and is embedded together with the cryptogram c from the Feistel network to form AC α.

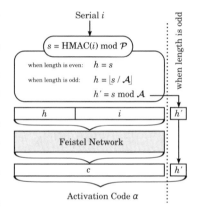

Fig. 3. BEPAC Scheme

The BEPAC scheme $\mathcal{S}$ is a tuple $(\mathcal{A}, \mathcal{N}, \mathcal{P}, \lambda, \omega)$ where $\mathcal{A}$ is the size of the alphabet, $\lambda + \omega$ is the length of the ACs where λ is always even and ω is either 0 or 1. Then, $\mathcal{N}$ is the number of ACs and $\mathcal{P}$ determines the probability $P = \frac{1}{\mathcal{P}}$ of obtaining a valid AC by a random guess, e.g. $\mathcal{P} = 10.000$. We assume $\mathcal{A} < \mathcal{P}$.

Definition 1 (Valid AC Scheme). *An AC scheme* $\mathcal{S} = (\mathcal{A}, \mathcal{N}, \mathcal{P}, \lambda, \omega)$ *is valid when* $\mathcal{A}^\lambda \geqslant \mathcal{N} \times \mathcal{P} \times \mathcal{A}^{-\omega}$ *holds and* λ *is even.*

A valid AC scheme $\mathcal{S}$ can be obtained as follows:

(a) The user chooses the alphabet size $\mathcal{A}$, desired number of ACs $\mathcal{N}$ and some minimal guess probability $\frac{1}{\mathcal{P}}$.

(b) Now the minimal length λ is calculated such that $\mathcal{A}^\lambda >= \mathcal{N} \times \mathcal{P}$ by taking $\lambda = \lceil {}^{\mathcal{A}}\!\log(\mathcal{N} \times \mathcal{P}) \rceil$

(c) $|\mathcal{A}^\lambda - \mathcal{N} \times \mathcal{P}|$ is minimized by taking $\mathcal{P} = \lfloor \mathcal{A}^\lambda / \mathcal{N} \rfloor$

(d) The length λ can be either odd or even:
   - When $\lambda = 2k + 1$ and $\mathcal{A} < \mathcal{P}$ then we adjust $\mathcal{P}$ such that $\mathcal{A}$ is a divisor of $\mathcal{P}$. As a consequence, we might have a larger number of ACs $\mathcal{N}$.

$$\mathcal{P} = \mathcal{P} - (\mathcal{P} \bmod \mathcal{A}), \qquad \mathcal{N} = \lfloor \mathcal{A}^\lambda / \mathcal{P} \rfloor$$

   After these operations we obtain the system $\mathcal{S} = (\mathcal{A}, \mathcal{N}, \mathcal{P}, \lambda - 1, 1)$.
   - When $\lambda = 2k$ we obtain the system $\mathcal{S} = (\mathcal{A}, \mathcal{N}, \mathcal{P}, \lambda, 0)$.

(e) The process is repeated from step (a) when no valid system $\mathcal{S}$ is found.

4.2   Generation

This section describes the generation of new ACs once a valid AC scheme is configured. Algorithm 1 contains the pseudo code for AC generation. The plaintext is an embedding m of a part of $HMAC(i)$ and i itself. In case of an odd AC length ($\omega = 1$) a small part h' of $HMAC(i)$ is excluded from this embedding. The part of $HMAC(i)$ that is used in m is determined by $\mathcal{P}$.

$$s = HMAC(i) \bmod \mathcal{P}, \qquad h = \lfloor s \times \mathcal{A}^{-\omega} \rfloor, \qquad h' = s \bmod \mathcal{A}, \qquad m = h \times \mathcal{N} + i$$

The balanced Feistel construction is defined with:

$$k = \mathcal{A}^{(\lambda/2)}, \qquad L = m \bmod k, \qquad R = \lfloor m\ /\ k \rfloor$$

L and R are input blocks with size k of a balanced Feistel network. We denote the output blocks after r rounds by $L^\star$ and $R^\star$. When the number of rounds r is even the cryptogram c is given by:

$$c = R^\star \times k + L^\star$$

When r is odd, the left and right block are swapped and the cryptogram c is given by:

$$c = L^\star \times k + R^\star$$

This difference between odd and even is there to allow the same construction for encoding and decoding. Finally, the activation code α is given by:

$$\alpha = c \times \mathcal{A}^\omega + \omega h'$$

4.3   Verification

This section describes the verification of previously generated ACs for a valid AC scheme. Algorithm 2 contains the pseudo code for AC verification. Given an AC α and an AC scheme $\mathcal{S}$ the validity can be checked as follows. First compute c and h' from α:

$$c = \lfloor \alpha/\mathcal{A}^\omega \rfloor, \qquad h' = \alpha \bmod \mathcal{A}^\omega$$

The balanced Feistel construction is defined with input block size $k = \mathcal{A}^{(\lambda/2)}$. Now, the input blocks L and R are obtained from c as follows:

$$L = c \bmod k, \qquad R = \lfloor c/k \rfloor$$

L and R are input blocks with size k of a balanced Feistel network. We denote the output blocks after r rounds by $L^\star$ and $R^\star$. In this case we want to decrypt and therefore use the round keys in reverse order. When the number of rounds r is even the plaintext m is given by:

$$m = R^\star \times k + L^\star$$

When r is odd, the left and right block are swapped and the plaintext m is given by:

$$m = L^\star \times k + R^\star$$

Now, we are able to obtain the partial HMAC h and index i from m by:

$$h = \lfloor m/\mathcal{N} \rfloor, \qquad i = m \bmod \mathcal{N}$$

We calculate the partial HMAC h_t and h'_t like in the encoding, but now we use the recovered index i. Finally, we say that α is a valid AC iff $h_t = h$ and $\omega h'_t = \omega h'$.

Algorithm 1. GENERATE(i)

$k \leftarrow \mathcal{A}^{(\lambda/2)}$
$s \leftarrow \text{HMAC}(i) \bmod \mathcal{P}$
$h \leftarrow \lfloor s \times \mathcal{A}^{-\omega} \rfloor$
$h' \leftarrow s \bmod \mathcal{A}$
$m \leftarrow h \times \mathcal{N} + i$
$L \leftarrow m \bmod k; \ R \leftarrow \lfloor m/k \rfloor$
for $j \leftarrow 1$ **to** r **do**
    $tmp \leftarrow (L + f_j(R)) \bmod k$
    $L \leftarrow R; \ R \leftarrow tmp$
end for
if r is odd **then**
    $c \leftarrow L \times k + R$
else
    $c \leftarrow R \times k + L$
end if
$\alpha \leftarrow c \times \mathcal{A}^{\omega} + \omega h'$

Algorithm 2. VERIFY(α)

$k \leftarrow \mathcal{A}^{(\lambda/2)}$
$c \leftarrow \lfloor \alpha/\mathcal{A}^{\omega} \rfloor; \ h' \leftarrow \alpha \bmod \mathcal{A}^{\omega}$
$L \leftarrow c \bmod k; \ R = \lfloor c/k \rfloor$
for $j \leftarrow r$ **to** 1 **do**
    $tmp \leftarrow (L + f_j(R)) \bmod k$
    $L \leftarrow R; \ R \leftarrow tmp$
end for
if r is odd **then**
    $m \leftarrow L \times k + R$
else
    $m \leftarrow R \times k + L$
end if
$h \leftarrow \lfloor m/\mathcal{N} \rfloor; \ i \leftarrow m \bmod \mathcal{N}$
$s \leftarrow \text{HMAC}(i) \bmod \mathcal{P}$
$h_t \leftarrow \lfloor s \times \mathcal{A}^{-\omega} \rfloor$
$h'_t \leftarrow s \bmod \mathcal{A}$
if $h_t = h$ **and** $\omega h'_t = \omega h'$ **then**
    VALID
else
    INVALID
end if

---

5   Example Application: Smart Card

In this section we want to give an example of an Activation Code System (ACS). In an ACS there are a few things that need to be managed. The index i of the latest generated AC and the ACs that have been used so far. Since this information is highly valuable and represents financial value it must be well protected. Think of an application where the ACs are printed on prepaid cards covered by some scratch-off material. The production of these cards is a very secured and well-defined process to ensure that activation codes are kept secret during manufacturing. These cards need to have all kinds of physical properties, e.g. the AC should not be readable when the card is partly peeled off from the back. This can be achieved by printing a random pattern on top of the scratch-off foil.

At some point there is a very critical task to be executed when the ACs need to be delivered to the manufacturer. An obvious method to do this is to encrypt the list of ACs with a secret key. Later on in the process, this list of randomly generated codes needs to be maintained by the vendor who sells the scratch cards. This induces a big security threat since leakage of this list or unauthorized modification results in financial loss. Especially when it directly relates to the core business like in the telecommunications industry.

The use of a secure application module (SAM) significantly reduces this risk. A SAM is typically a tamper-resistant device, often a smart card, which is in

Table 1. BEPAC Configurations

Desired		$\mathcal{A} = 8$				$\mathcal{A} = 20$				$\mathcal{A} = 31$			
$\mathcal{N}$	$\mathcal{P}$	$\mathcal{N}$	$\mathcal{P}(\times 10^3)$	l	Bits	$\mathcal{N}$	$\mathcal{P}(\times 10^3)$	l	Bits	$\mathcal{N}$	$\mathcal{P}(\times 10^3)$	l	Bits
10^1	10^3	10^1	26,214	6	18	10^1	16	4	18	10^1	92,352	4	20
10^2	10^3	10^2	20,968	7	21	10^2	32	5	22	10^2	286,285	5	25
10^3	10^3	10^3	16,777	8	24	10^3	64	6	26	10^3	28,613	5	25
10^4	10^3	10.004	13,416	9	27	10^4	128	7	31	10^4	88,75	6	30
10^5	10^3	100.003	10,737	10	30	10^5	12,8	7	31	10^5	275,125	7	35
10^6	10^3	1.000.006	68,719	12	36	10^6	25,6	8	35	1.000.567	27,497	7	35
10^7	10^3	10.001.379	54,968	13	39	10^7	51,2	9	39	10.000.012	85,289	8	40
10^8	10^3	100.001.057	43,98	14	42	10^8	102,4	10	44	100.010.675	264,368	9	45
10^9	10^3	1.000.010.575	35,184	15	45	10^9	10,24	10	44	1.001.045.818	26,412	9	45

most cases extensively tested and certified in accordance to a standard, e.g. the Common Criteria[1]. The elegance of the solution presented in this paper is that it can be implemented using smart cards. The supplier determines the probability P, number of codes $\mathcal{N}$, size of character set $\mathcal{A}$ and the key K to be used. An obvious approach is to use two smart cards since the production and clearance of activation codes are very likely to happen at two different locations. Both smart cards are initialized using the same AC scheme $\mathcal{S}$ and the same key K. From that moment on the first one only gives out up to $\mathcal{N}$ new activation codes. The second one is used at the clearance house to verify and keep track of traded activation codes. This can be done by a sequence of bits where the i-th bit determines whether the i-th activation code has been cleared. For 1.000.000 activation codes approximately 122 kB of storage is needed. This fits on a SmartMX card [27] which is available with 144 kB of EEPROM. Of course, multiple cards can be used if more ACs are needed.

6 Analysis

In this section we discuss the system parameters of BEPAC and decide on some minimal bounds and algorithms. We tested a 6-round BEPAC scheme for obvious flaws using the NIST random number test [26]. This test implementation also delivered the numbers in Table 1 which give a good indication of the length l of the codes compared to different AC scheme configurations. In the left column the desired values are given for the number of codes $\mathcal{N}$ and the guessing probability $\mathcal{P}$. We tested these different numbers for three different alphabet sizes $\mathcal{A}$.

Number of Rounds We found good arguments to set the minimum number of rounds to six for the BEPAC scheme. The literature shows that Feistel constructions of six or more rounds are secure against adaptive chosen plaintext and chosen ciphertext attacks (CPCA-2) when the number of queries $m \ll 2^n$, see [22,13]. Patarin [21] shows that an adversary needs at least $2^{3n/4}$ encryptions to distinguish a six-round Feistel construction from a random permutation. A six round Feistel network sufficiently covers the risk of leaking serial number information, but this is of course a minimum.

---

[1] http://www.commoncriteriaportal.org

Key Derivation In the BEPAC scheme we need different round keys for every Feistel round and another different key for the calculation of the HMAC on the serial. We propose to derive these keys from an initial randomly chosen key [1] by a key derivation function (KDF). There are several definitions available for KDFs and we propose to use KDF1 which is defined in ISO 18033-2 [11]. Recommendations for KDFs and their construction can also be found in [7]. The first key that is derived is used as the key in the HMAC calculation of h and h' (Section 4). After this the round keys for the Feistel construction are successively derived.

Pseudo-random Functions Furthermore, we need to decide on the pseudo-random functions (PRFs) that are used as round functions of the Feistel network. The pseudo-randomness of the permutation defined by a Feistel network depends on the chosen PRF in each round [15]. It is straightforward to use a cryptographic hash function since we already need a hash function for the HMAC [24] calculation and it keeps our AC scheme simple.

Hash Function In the end, the BEPAC scheme is solely based on a single cryptographic hash function. We follow the secure hash standard FIPS 180-3 [23] and propose to use an approved hash function like SHA-256.

7   Conclusions

In this paper we have introduced activation codes (ACs), short codes of fixed length, that represent value. These ACs should be scalable, cost efficient and forgery resistant. In the literature, several solutions [4,5,8,14,12,6,17,28,17] handle digital coupons or tickets that are somehow reminiscent to our notion of ACs. The difference is that most solutions use public key cryptography or other means that result in lengthy codes. In fact, these solutions come closer to some extended notion of digital cash and are not meant to give a solution on the generation of ACs. To the best of our knowledge there is no scheme that focuses on the class of ACs that are described in this paper (roughly think of 20 to 50-bit codes). Our proposed AC scheme for this class satisfies authenticity and confidentiality in a way that when confidentiality is compromised it does not automatically break authenticity and vice versa.

In order to allow a relatively small and arbitrary message space for our AC scheme we use some of the ideas of Black and Rogaway [3] in their Generalized Feistel Cipher to satisfy the confidentiality in our scheme. Several studies [22,20,19,15,13,21] show that the security bounds of Feistel constructions are not strong enough and thus make the use of Feistel constructions in small domains questionable. To illustrate this, we have demonstrated that CPA-2 allows an adversary to recover the complete permutation from only 2^{n+2} plaintext-ciphertext pairs. Still, the Feistel construction is suitable for the purpose of confidentiality in our AC scheme. Since confidentiality is a secondary goal, it relaxes the demands on the security bounds. Furthermore, in BEPAC the plaintext cannot be predicted which counters the attacks from the literature. And most important of all, a Feistel construction defines a permutation on the AC domain, which means in practice that we do not have to store any additional data in order to remember which ACs are already published and which are not.

To conclude, we found satisfactory system parameters for the minimum number of Feistel rounds and we defined a method to do the key derivation for the round keys. Furthermore, we suggested a specific pseudo-random function (PRF) and hash function for concrete implementations. Finally, we have implemented the BEPAC scheme[2] and performed some statistical tests using the NIST Random Number Test [26]. This test did not reveal any obvious flaws.

It might be interesting for future work to create a smart card implementation of BEPAC as suggested in Section 5.

References

1. Barker, E., Kelsey, J.: Recommendation for Random Number Generation Using Deterministic Random Bit Generators (revised). NIST Special Publication 800, 90 (2007)
2. Bellare, M., Rogaway, P., Spies, T.: Format-Preserving Feistel-Based Encryption Mode (November 2009),
   http://csrc.nist.gov/groups/ST/toolkit/BCM/modes_development.html
3. Black, J., Rogaway, P.: Ciphers with arbitrary finite domains. In: Preneel, B. (ed.) CT-RSA 2002. LNCS, vol. 2271, p. 114–130. Springer, Heidelberg (2002)
4. Blundo, C., Cimato, S., De Bonis, A.: A Lightweight Protocol for the Generation and Distribution of Secure E-Coupons. In: WWW 2002: Proceedings of the 11th International Conference on World Wide Web, pp. 542–552. ACM, New York (2002)
5. Blundo, C., Cimato, S., De Bonis, A.: Secure E-Coupons. Electronic Commerce Research 5(1), 117–139 (2005)
6. Chang, C.C., Wu, C.C., Lin, I.C.: A Secure E-coupon System for Mobile Users. International Journal of Computer Science and Network Security 6(1), 273 (2006)
7. Chen, L.: Recommendation for Key Derivation Using Pseudorandom Functions. NIST Special Publication 800, 108 (2009)
8. Cimato, S., De Bonis, A.: Online advertising: Secure E-coupons. In: Restivo, A., Ronchi Della Rocca, S., Roversi, L. (eds.) ICTCS 2001. LNCS, vol. 2202, p. 370-383. Springer, Heidelberg (2001)
9. Cook, D., Keromytis, A., Yung, M.: Elastic Block Ciphers: The Basic Design. In: Proceedings of the 2nd ACM Symposium on Information, Computer and Communications Security, pp. 350–352. ACM, New York (2007)
10. De Cannière, C., Dunkelman, O., Knežević, M.: KATAN and KTANTAN — A Family of Small and Efficient Hardware-Oriented Block Ciphers. In: Clavier, C., Gaj, K. (eds.) CHES 2009. LNCS, vol. 5747, pp. 272–288. Springer, Heidelberg (2009)
11. ISO/IEC 18033-2:2006. Information Technology - Security Techniques - Encryption Algorithms - Part 2: Asymmetric Ciphers (2006)
12. Jakobsson, M., MacKenzie, P.D., Stern, J.P.: Secure and Lightweight Advertising on the Web. Computer Networks-the International Journal of Computer and Telecommunications Networking 31(11), 1101–1110 (1999)

---

[2] http://www.cs.ru.nl/~gkoningg/bepac

13. Knudsen, L.R.: The Security of Feistel Ciphers with Six Rounds or Less. Journal of Cryptology 15(3), 207–222 (2008)
14. Kumar, M., Rangachari, A., Jhingran, A., Mohan, R.: Sales Promotions on the Internet. In: 3rd USENIX Workshop on Electronic Commerce, pp. 167–176 (1998)
15. Luby, M.: Pseudorandomness and Cryptographic Applications. Princeton University Press, Princeton (1996)
16. Luby, M., Rackoff, C.: How to Construct Pseudorandom Permutations from Pseudorandom Functions. SIAM J. Comput. 17(2), 373–386 (1988)
17. Matsuyama, K., Fujimura, K.: Distributed Digital-Ticket Management for Rights Trading System. In: Proceedings of the 1st ACM Conference on Electronic Commerce, p. 118. ACM, New York (1999)
18. Morris, B., Rogaway, P., Stegers, T.: How to Encipher Messages on a Small Domain. In: Halevi, S. (ed.) CRYPTO 2009. LNCS, vol. 5677, pp. 286–302. Springer, Heidelberg (2009)
19. Naor, M., Reingold, O.: On the Construction of Pseudorandom Permutations: Luby-Rackoff Revisited. Journal of Cryptology 12(1), 29–66 (1999)
20. Patarin, J.: New results on pseudorandom permutation generators based on the DES scheme. In: Feigenbaum, J. (ed.) CRYPTO 1991. LNCS, vol. 576, pp. 301–312. Springer, Heidelberg (1992)
21. Patarin, J.: About Feistel Schemes with Six (or More) Rounds. In: Vaudenay, S. (ed.) FSE 1998. LNCS, vol. 1372, pp. 103–121. Springer, Heidelberg (1998)
22. Patarin, J.: Security of Random Feistel Schemes with 5 or More Rounds. In: Franklin, M. (ed.) CRYPTO 2004. LNCS, vol. 3152, pp. 106–122. Springer, Heidelberg (2004)
23. FIB PUB. FIPS 180-3: Secure HASH Standard (SHS). Federal Information Processing Standards Publication (2008)
24. N.F. PUB. FIPS 198: Keyed-Hash Message Authentication Code (HMAC). Federal Information Processing Standards Publication, 198
25. Quisquater, J.J., Standaert, F.X.: Exhaustive Key Search of the DES: Updates and Refinements. In: Special-Purpose Hardware for Attacking Cryptographic Systems (2005)
26. Rukhin, A., Soto, J., Nechvatal, J., Smid, M., Barker, E., Leigh, S., Levenson, M., Vangel, M., Banks, D., Heckert, A., et al.: A Statistical Test Suite for Random and Pseudorandom Number Generators for Cryptographic Applications. NIST (2000)
27. NXP Semiconductors. P5Cx012/02x/40/73/80/144 Family: Secure Dual Interface and Contact PKI Smart Card Controller. NXP (June 2010)
28. Terada, M., Hanadate, M., Fujimura, K.: Copy Prevention Scheme for Rights Trading Infrastructure. In: Smart Card Research and Advanced Applications: IFIP TC8/WG8, p. 51. Springer, Heidelberg (2000)

Decentralized Generation of Multiple, Uncorrelatable Pseudonyms without Trusted Third Parties

Jan Lehnhardt[1] and Adrian Spalka[1,2]

[1] CompuGroup Medical Software GmbH, Dept. of Data Security and System Architecture,
Maria Trost 23, 56070 Koblenz, Germany
{jan.lehnhardt,adrian.spalka}@cgm.com
[2] University of Bonn, Dept. of Computer Science III,
Römerstr. 164, 53117 Bonn, Germany
adrian@iai.uni-bonn.de

Abstract. Regarding the increasing number of applications provided as external services, the importance of pseudonymous data as a means for privacy protection of user entities is growing. Along with it grows the relevance of secure and accurate generation, use and management of pseudonyms. In particular we consider the involvement of third parties in this process as potentially harmful, and therefore favor a decentralized pseudonym generation approach where the role of central components is reduced to a minimum. In this paper, we propose a pseudonym generation mechanism and focus on its implementation based on elliptic curve cryptography, in which every user entity can generate an arbitrary number of uncorrelatable pseudonyms with minimal effort, initially as well as at any later point in time. Because no sensitive information necessary for pseudonym generation is available on central components, our approach provides security as well as flexibility and usability.

Keywords: Pseudonym generation, trusted third party, decentralized, elliptic curve cryptography.

1 Introduction

The number of applications provided as external services is continuously growing. There also exist more and more applications that deal with sensitive data, on whose security high demands have to be made by their user entities, as well as by application providers. Providers must gain trust and acceptance of possible users of their applications, and may also need to meet further legal requirements in order to comply e.g. with laws of data protection. In this context, the security merit of confidentiality of data handled by external applications is usually in the focus, even more than the security merits of data integrity and availability. After all, the external applications often use the internet as the operating environment, which has to be considered as potentially harmful.

But not only threats of attacks by external adversaries have to be averted; in fact, security measures for transport encryption or data center security are considered as

S. Furnell, C. Lambrinoudakis, and G. Pernul (Eds.): TrustBus 2011, LNCS 6863, pp. 113–124, 2011.
© Springer-Verlag Berlin Heidelberg 2011

highly developed, and are not the target of this paper. The application user entity's informational privacy may also need to be protected from the application providers themselves, if the sensitivity of the managed data demands it, e.g. in the case of medical data underlying the laws of data protection in Germany. The threat of insiders using their assigned privileges in an unintended way like e.g. corrupt data administrators cannot be excluded, no matter how noble the intentions of the application providers are or how deterrent the consequences of privilege abuse are communicated to be.

When looking at user data as a logical pair consisting of the owning user entity's identity (or rather a reference to that identity) and the actual data content, data confidentiality can be ensured by making at least one component of the pair unintelligible to unauthorized entities. It depends on the nature of the application which of the two components is chosen for this, or if it is even necessary to make both components unintelligible. For instance, making the data component unintelligible for unauthorized users (i.e. data encryption) may be the more obvious step, but the nature of the underlying application may demand that the data component remains plaintext in order to be processed by the application provider. Therefore, to ensure privacy, the association with its identity has to be concealed, rendering the data pseudonymous. The unintelligible association with the data owning entity will be referred to as the pseudonym in the following.

We note that in case of pseudonymous data, the plaintext data must not contain any inherent information that allows the association with the data owning entity. However, this is not target of this paper.

We much rather focus on the generation, management and use of pseudonyms; especially who in the system architecture is capable of linking a pseudonym to its owning entity is of interest for us, as it is a key feature in the security architecture of applications dealing with pseudonymous data. Whoever is capable of linking pseudonyms to their owning entities has access to the managed data to the full extent.

However, regardless of this aspect's importance, we identify many architectural shortcomings in its practical use. For instance, in many systems, linking a pseudonym to its owning user entity is performed by a static mapping table, which is operated by a trusted third party, often the same party that also stores the managed data. This is not a desirable solution; as we have pointed out before, we consider the use of trusted third parties as an architectural weakness because they simply can never be fully trusted (one corrupt administrator is enough). Security measures like physical separation of identity/pseudonym mappings on one hand and managed data on the other or strict administrative and jurisdictional regulations may alleviate the threat imposed by the use of trusted third parties, but they can never eliminate it.

There may even exist a further reason against the use of trusted third parties. Under certain circumstances, the user entities may be legally obligated to make their data unintelligible to other entities. For instance, in addition to data protection laws, the German criminal code names occupation groups, e.g. physicians or lawyers, that are responsible for the confidentiality of their data, even if that data are hosted by third parties, known as §203 StGB. According to that, if a corrupt administrator links a physician's managed patient data to the patients' identities and discloses the no more pseudonymous data, the physician is also liable.

We clearly favor a decentralized approach for the generation and management of pseudonyms. More clearly, in the entire lifecycle of a pseudonym from its generation over its normal use to its abandonment, there should be no architectural constraint that the association of a pseudonym with its owning entity can be made by any other entity than the owning entity itself.

A simple solution for a decentralized approach is of course letting the participating user entities choose their own pseudonyms and letting them keep the pseudonyms in their custody. Although this solution might basically work, it suffers from a few drawbacks. For instance, since the pseudonyms are chosen randomly by the user entities, duplicates cannot be ruled out. Another drawback is that entities can impersonate other entities by using their pseudonyms, not to mention that this approach imposes considerable managing effort on the user entities.

We state the following requirements to a decentralized approach for pseudonym generation and management:

1. *Ease of use.* Although the user entity's contribution should be minimal, it should be able to access its pseudonyms at any time.
2. *Confidentiality.* Pseudonym generation should be performed exclusively in the scope of the pseudonym owning entities. Linking a pseudonym to its owning entity should not be possible for any other than the pseudonym owning entity itself, unless it is explicitly permitted. Furthermore, in case user entities can own multiple pseudonyms, it should not be possible to identify different pseudonyms as belonging to the same user entity for any entity other than the pseudonym owning entity itself.
3. *Injectivity.* Although decentralized, the pseudonym generation process should avoid duplicates, even if every user entity may own multiple pseudonyms.
4. *Flexibility.* It should be possible to add new pseudonyms to the user entities with minimal effort at any point in time.

On the following pages, we will propose a pseudonym generation mechanism and its implementation based on elliptic curve cryptography (or a slight variation thereof) that fulfills the requirements stated above. In the following section 2 previous and related work will be discussed; after that, basic notions from the field of elliptic curve cryptography will be introduced in section 3 before our pseudonym generation mechanism will be presented in section 4. Section 5 covers the benefits of our proposed approach to pseudonym generation, before future development is considered in chapter 6. The paper's conclusion is drawn in chapter 7.

Our pseudonym generation mechanism is not only of theoretical relevance, but already in use by CompuGroup Medical AG (CGM), a large producer of healthcare information systems located in Germany. The CGM product family "Software Assisted Medicine" (SAM) comprises systems in which pseudonymous patient data are stored and processed in a central database. The pseudonyms of the SAM participants (physicians and patients) are generated using our mechanism. As SAM comprises multiple modules (e.g. "SAM Diabetes", "SAM COPD" etc), the patients are provided by our pseudonym generation mechanism with different (and not correlatable) pseudonyms for different modules.

2 Previous and Related Work

The authors of [1] propose a pseudonym generation mechanism which makes use of iterative Diffie-Helman (IDH) key agreement schemes, and which is well suited for ad-hoc group communication scenarios. Members agree on a group key using the protocols of the Tree-based Group Diffie-Hellman (TGDH) suite and then compute their own pseudonyms using a newly proposed pseudonym generation scheme, which is an extension of TGDH. Even though the pseudonyms are unlinkable to the user entities owning the pseudonyms in normal operation mode, a subgroup of the user entities can reveal the real identity behind certain pseudonyms after making a democratic decision to do so. The method is based on the idea of generating unique keys (respectively key components like primes) within isolated instances.

In [2], an approach is presented in which user entities generate globally unique pseudonyms locally, which are claimed to be highly random. No information interchange is needed, especially not keys, except for unique identifiers that are issued initially for participating entities. Following the authors' approach, user entities generate RSA key pairs locally at random, encrypt their unique identifier using that random key pair and concatenate the RSA key pair's public key exponent and modulus to the encryption result. The authors claim that the resulting value can be proven to be unique. Proof of ownership for a pseudonym performed by a user entity is implemented by a challenge/response algorithm in which the user entity is proving its pseudonym ownership by using the private key of its generated RSA key pair.

Although [3] deals also with pseudonyms that are cryptographically derived in cooperation with the owning user entity from the entity's identity number, the security architecture of the presented system relies considerably on trusted third parties that are assigned central administration tasks for the pseudonyms. For instance, a proof of pseudonym ownership is performed by certificates that are issued to the users by trust centers.

[4], [5] and [10] are also examples for pseudonym management systems that rely on trusted third parties, although the authors of [5] claim that the involvement of the trusted third party is reduced to a minimum in comparison to previous approaches. Here, the user entities create each an asymmetric key pair, whose private key is kept secret and whose public key is registered with a certification authority (CA). The CA issues credentials that state that the user entities are valid user entities. After that, user entities can register with other organizations and collaboratively compute pseudonyms for interaction with these organizations, after they have authenticated themselves using their CA credential.

The authors of [6] and [7] propose a „privacy manager" applied in the field of Cloud Computing; however, the authors focus rather on encrypted (or "obfuscated", as they call it) data than on pseudonymous data, which forms more or less an additional line of defense. The pseudonym generation mechanism is performed by static mapping tables or by symmetric encryption functions, with no statement being made on key management for the symmetric encryption functions.

The authors of [8] propose a proxy-based public key infrastructure, which is to be applied in the field of Mobile Location-Based Services (LBS). There, users can operate pseudonymously and encrypt their communications using mediated identity-based encryption. Users are claimed to have to own only one private key in order to protect their communications when they access LBS under different pseudonyms, which can be either randomly picked one-time pseudonyms or long-term pseudonyms that are cryptographically computed, albeit this has to be done in collaboration with a trusted third party.

In [9] a novel cryptographic primitive is proposed which is called an "Incomparable Public Key System" in order to protect the anonymity of message receivers while using Multicast. The primitive enables message receivers to create many anonymous identities without disclosing that these identities belong to the same user entity. This is done by creating many different public keys that all correspond to the same private key and that are claimed to be not correlatable. An implementation of the primitive is presented by a variation of the ElGamal cryptosystem.

[11] deals with anonymization of network traffic data, where (source and destination) IP addresses of captured IP packets are anonymized. As the approach is clearly a centralized one and requires secret knowledge by a trusted third party, it is of minor interest for us.

In the field of location based services (LBS), the authors of [12] propose an approach to ensure privacy of LBS users without having to rely on trusted entities, yet without a significant loss in the quality of service. The authors describe a decentralized matching service that unfortunately takes trivially encoded (not encrypted) information from both LBS users and LBS providers (i.e. pseudonymous entity locations and pseudonymous entity identities) and creates triggers that fire when users and their objects of interest are in the vicinity of each other.

3   Basic Notions of Elliptic Curve Cryptography

In this chapter, we recall some basic notions necessary for the description of elliptic curve cryptography and discuss the interpretation of elliptic curve point multiplication as an injective one-way function.

Let:
- p be a prime number, $p > 3$, and F_p the corresponding finite field
- a and b integers

Then the set E of points (x, y) such that

$$E = \{(x, y) \in F_p \times F_p \mid y^2 = x^3 + ax + b \} \tag{F1}$$

defines an elliptic curve in F_p. For reasons of simplicity, we skip the details on E being non-singular and, as well, we do not consider the formulae of elliptic curves over finite fields with $p = 2$ and $p = 3$. The subsequent statements apply to these curves, too. The number m of points on E is its order. Let $P, Q \in E$ be two points on E. Then the addition of points

$$P + Q = R \text{ and } R \in E \tag{F2}$$

can be defined in such a way that E forms an Abelian group, i.e., it satisfies the rules of ordinary addition of integers. By writing

$$P + P = [2]P \qquad \text{(F3)}$$

we define the k-times addition of P as $[k]P$, the point multiplication. Now EC-DLP, the elliptic curve discretionary logarithm problem, states that if

$$Q = [k]P \qquad \text{(F4)}$$

then with suitably chosen a, b, p and P, which are known to the public, and the as well known to the public point Q it is computationally infeasible to determine the integer k. The order n of a point P is the order of the subgroup generated by P, i.e. the number of elements in the set

$$\{P, [2]P, \dots, [n]P\} \qquad \text{(F5)}$$

With all this in mind, we define an elliptic curve cryptographic (ECC) system as follows. Let:

- E be an elliptic curve of order m
- $B \in E$, a point of E of order n, the base point

Then

$$D = \{a, b, p, B, n, co(B)\} \qquad \text{(F6)}$$

with $co(B) = m / n$ defines a set of domain ECC-parameters. Let now g be an integer and

$$O = [g]B \qquad \text{(F7)}$$

Then (g, O) is an ECC-key-pair with g being the private key and O the public key. For we rely on findings of Technical Guideline TR-03111, Version 1.11, issued by the German Bundesamt für Sicherheit in der Informationstechnik (BSI), one of the best accredited sources for cryptographically strong elliptic curves, we can take that $m = n$, i.e. $co(B) = 1$, and hence reduce (F6) to

$$D = \{a, b, p, B, n\} \qquad \text{(F8)}$$

Now we can define our one-way function. Let D be a set of domain parameters concordant with (F7). Then

$$f: [2, n - 1] \rightarrow E, f(k) = [k]B \qquad \text{(F9)}$$

i.e. the point multiplication (F7), is an injective one-way function.

4 The Pseudonym Generation Mechanism

Our pseudonym generation approach will be outlined in this section. First, the basic idea is described before an implementation is presented using elliptic curve cryptography.

4.1 Basic Idea

The basic idea of our pseudonym generation mechanism is that every participating user entity owns a personal secret s which must be unique among the set of participating entities and which must never leave the entity's scope. To perform the pseudonym generation, the user entity adds a public parameter V that may also be in the entity's custody or may be retrieved from a central component.

Note that it is still fair to call our approach decentralized although we do in fact use central components for, like in this case, providing public parameters or for validation of the personal secret's uniqueness, which will be discussed later on. The crucial aspect of a decentralized approach is from our perspective not to place any information on a central component that enables any entities other than the pseudonym owning entity to link a pseudonym to its owning entity.

The user entity's personal secret s and the public parameter are input into an injective cryptographic one-way function h whose output $h(s, V) = PS$ is considered the pseudonym. Because h is injective, the public parameter V is constant and the entity's personal secret is unique, h's output PS is unique as well, though only according to V: If two user entities compute their pseudonyms using their unique personal secrets and two different values for V, it cannot be ruled out that the pseudonyms computed by h are equal.

Hence, by variation of V, referred to as a set of uncorrelated values $V = \{V_1, ..., V_n\}$, a set of pseudonyms $PS = \{PS_1 = h(s, V_1), ... , PS_n = h(s, V_n)\}$ can be generated by the user entity itself in a decentralized manner, as the entity's personal secret s is known by noone except the user entity. Each of the entity's multiple pseudonyms is unique according to the value of V_i used for computation, and it is also unique among the set of the user entity's pseudonyms.

A useful application of the mechanism is to provide a defined set of public parameter values V on a central component from which values V_i can be retrieved by user entities. By doing this, it can be centrally controlled how many pseudonyms each user entity can own.

The uniqueness of the entities' secrets must be ensured, which can be done in an initial step by letting a new user entity choose its secret s, providing the entity with a special public value V_0, letting the user entity compute $h(s, V_0) = PS_0$ and storing the computed pseudonym PS_0 on the central component. If PS_0 is unique according to V_0, the user entity's secret s must be unique as well because of h's injectivity. Now the entity can be provided with any of the actual values V_i in order to compute its own pseudonyms.

4.2 Elliptic Curve Cryptography Implementation

Elliptic curve cryptography is well suited for an implementation of our pseudonym generating mechanism that has been presented in the previous subsection[1]. In the following, the implementation is described in detail.

---

[1] We would like to point out that elliptic curve cryptography is not the only way of an implementation of our pseudonym generation mechanism. An implementation based on element exponentiation on finite, cyclic groups, i.e. an implementation that relies on the intractability of DLP instead of EC-DLP, is also possible. We favored elliptic curve cryptography because it offers more security with smaller key lengths and because we have been using it already in several other projects.

Rather than a personal secret, each user entity owns in this implementation an elliptic curve key pair $K = (g, O)$, with K's private key g being an integer and the corresponding public key O being a point on the used elliptic curve E. The elliptic curve E is defined by a set of public domain parameters $D = \{a, b, p, B, n\}$ (see section 3). Note that the cofactor for the given domain parameter set must equal 1 in order to be suitable for our purpose.

The private key g represents the user entity's personal secret s, and $O = [g]B$ represents the value PS_0 that is used for checking the uniqueness of the user entity secret, while E's base point B corresponds to the initial public parameter value V_0 described in subsection 4.1. Public key O, that has been computed by multiplying base point B by private key g, corresponds to PS_0 and can be checked for uniqueness in a PKI hosted on a central component. By doing this, it can be proven that the corresponding private key g is unique as well, since the point multiplication on the elliptic curve (which corresponds to the cryptographic one-way function h in subsection 4.1) is injective.

The public parameter variation from subsection 4.1 is implemented by a variation of E's base point B, i.e. by replacing B (which is feasible because E's cofactor equals 1) with other base points $B_i \in \mathbf{B} = \{B_1, ..., B_n\}$ picked randomly and uncorrelated from each other from E, which produces different and as well uncorrelated results when an entity multiplies one of the base point variations B_i by its respective private key:

$$[g]B_i = O_i \qquad\qquad (F10)$$

The resulting curve point O_i is considered the user entity's pseudonym according to base point B_i. Because the base point variations B_i are uncorrelated, the pseudonym values are so as well. Furthermore, because of the point multiplication's injectivity, the computed pseudonyms O_i are unique in user entity's pseudonym set, and each pseudonym O_i is unique among all other pseudonyms that have been computed by other user entities using the same base point B_i and their own private key g.

Note that uniqueness of any given pseudonym O_i can only be guaranteed according to the base point B_i that has been used to compute O_i, because it cannot be ruled out that two different base points, multiplied by two different private keys, result in the same curve point.

5   Benefits of the Pseudonym Generation Mechanism

In this section, we will point out the benefits our presented pseudonym generation mechanism offers to the field of applications dealing with pseudonymous data. We will show that the requirements we expressed in section 1 are all met.

5.1   Ease of Use

The efforts of a user entity when accessing a pseudonym are limited to accessing the entity's private key g, retrieving base point B_i from the central component and performing the point multiplication of B_i by g, resulting in pseudonym $O_i = [g]B_i$. The "base point context", i.e. the information to which base point any given pseudonym relates must be clear at all times, so when using a pseudonym, a user entity must provide this information as well.

Note that there is no distinction between a pseudonym O_i's initial generation and accessing it for normal use, because on all occasions, the pseudonym is generated anew by performing the point multiplication $O_i = [g]B_i$. These operations should be easy to implement; if the central component providing the base points is unreachable at times, the user entities can be provided with cached copies of the base points.

5.2 Confidentiality

Our pseudonym generation mechanism offers high confidentiality. Given that all base points B_i provided on the central component, including the original base point B of the used elliptic curve E, are not correlated to each other, and (of course) that the user entity's private key g is kept confidential, there is neither a feasible way to link a user entity to one of its pseudonyms PS nor to identify two pseudonyms O_i and O_j to belong to the same user entity.

Linking a pseudonym $O_i = [g]B_i$ to its owner would mean to link it to the entity's original public key $O = [g]B$. Since B_i and B are uncorrelated, the only way to achieve this would be to somehow determine g from the value pairs (B, O) and/or (B_i, O_i), meaning to solve EC-DLP which is, as of now, computationally infeasible.

5.3 Injectivity

As the user entities' private keys are all distinct (because their initial public keys O that are stored in the central PKI are) and because point multiplication on elliptic curves is injective, the generated pseudonyms are also distinct according to the base point used during their computation.

Regarding the pseudonym set $(PS_1 = [g]B_1, \ldots, PS_n = [g]B_n)$ of a user entity, it is obvious that since all used base points are distinct, the pseudonyms the user entity computes by multiplying each base point by the same private key g must be distinct as well.

5.4 Flexibility

The set of used base points can easily be expanded by adding further base points to the central component. Each new element B_{n+1} added to the set of base points $\{B_1, \ldots, B_n\}$ provided on the central component expands the set of pseudonyms of each user entity by one additional pseudonym for that user entity. Because this can be done any time and not only in the beginning during some registration process, it shows that our pseudonym generation mechanism offers flexibility, as it can be centrally controlled how many pseudonyms each user entity can have, and this number can be adapted at any point in time.

On the other hand, another scenario for the management of base points could be that every user entity generates its own base points, and whenever a user entity communicates a pseudonym, it communicates the base point used to compute it along. However, this approach shows some operational drawbacks. First, if the entity's base points are published on the central component, they have to be linked to their owning entity, and since pseudonyms have to be associated with the base point used for the pseudonym's computation, it would be possible to link a pseudonym to its owning user entity. Thus, all pseudonyms owned by the same entity could be identified as such as well. A second reason is that it would display some kind of redundancy if the user entities have to carry their own base points for pseudonym generation, because they could directly carry their pseudonyms.

6 Future Development

In this section future development of our pseudonym generation mechanism and possible issues are considered.

6.1 Authentication

A useful extension to our approach deals with the mechanism's resistance against spoofing and impersonation of pseudonyms. If an adversary uses a made-up pseudonym or has eavesdropped an actual pseudonym from a regular user entity and uses it to impersonate the user entity, it should be possible for an entity located e.g. in the central component to identify such attempts of unintended behavior.

Every pseudonym $O_i = [g]B_i$ is actually a public key that forms, together with the user entity's private key g, a valid asymmetric key pair according to base point B_i. Hence, when a user entity deploys data linked to a pseudonym O_i, the pseudonym can be authenticated via a challenge/response authentication protocol based on e.g. ECDSA. Although this may be a protection against pseudonym impersonation, it is not against spoofing, because if an adversary just makes up a private key g and computes the corresponding public key O_i (according to a base point B_i) the central component will not be able to distinguish the spoofed pseudonym from a regular one, and the adversary will also be able to authenticate the made up pseudonym against the central component.

So the cost of a functioning authentication mechanism is that all regular pseudonyms have to be cataloged, albeit anonymously, in the central component. Therefore, when a new user entity is introduced to the system and chooses its unique private key, all the entity's pseudonyms must be computed and provided to the central component, which stores these pseudonyms anonymously[2].

Provided with this information, the central component is able to detect spoofed pseudonyms as well as impersonated ones. However, extending the set of base points with additional elements becomes more complicated in such a scenario. The authentication aspect will clearly be target of further investigations.

6.2 Base Point Manipulation

Another possible issue of our approach applies to the choice of the base points. It must be ensured that they are not correlatable to each other, because if they are, the computed pseudonyms are so as well. If e.g. $B_1 = [2]B_2$, then $O_1 = [2]O_2$ holds for all

---

[2] By doing this, the central component would be technically able to correlate all pseudonyms of the user entity, and the user entities would be forced to trust that the central component stores the pseudonyms in a responsible manner.

pseudonyms O_1 and O_2 of all participating user entities, and they are easily correlatable for a dishonest entity located at the central component.

A distributed, collaborative computation of the set of base points outside of the scope of the central component by a group of user entities that each contribute a piece of information, yet are unaware of the pieces of information contributed by the other entities might solve the problem. Another solution for this issue is not only varying the base point on the same curve, but the varying the entire used elliptic curve among a predefined set of publicly accredited elliptic curves that all have about the same order so that it is easy to find an integer g that is a valid private key for all curves. This aspect will too be target of further investigations.

7 Conclusion

In this paper, we proposed a decentralized pseudonym generation mechanism that uses in a general approach injective, cryptographic one-way functions and, in a more concrete implementation, elliptic curve cryptography. Although the mechanism is comfortable and easy to use, it offers high security that is of equal strength as the discrete logarithm problem on elliptic curves, ECDLP.

The mechanism does not have rely on the trustworthiness of third parties in the process, but nevertheless guarantees uniqueness of the pseudonyms generated by the user entities, even when an arbitrary number of pseudonyms is granted to each user entity. By providing user entites with a set of public parameters (base points in the elliptic curve implementation) on a central component when pseudonyms need to be computed, the number of pseudonyms per user entity can be centrally controlled, yet this does not affect the confidentiality of the association between a user entity and its pseudonym. The set of pseudonyms per user entity can be adapted at any point in time by adding further elements to the centrally managed set of public parameters (respectively base points).

Future extensions of the mechanism comprise a pseudonym authentication component, which enables application providers to ensure that no spoofed or impersonated pseudonyms are used, as well as a decentralized base point generation scheme to prevent corrupt entities located on the central component to use manipulated base points that enable adversaries to correlate pseudonyms.

References

1. Manulis, M., Schwenk, J.: Pseudonym Generation Scheme for Ad-Hoc Group Communication Based on IDH. In: Castelluccia, C., Hartenstein, H., Paar, C., Westhoff, D. (eds.) ESAS 2004. LNCS, vol. 3313, pp. 107–124. Springer, Heidelberg (2005)
2. Schartner, P., Schaffer, M.: Unique User-Generated Digital Pseudonyms. In: Gorodetsky, V., Kotenko, I., Skormin, V. (eds.) MMM-ACNS 2005. LNCS, vol. 3685, pp. 194–205. Springer, Heidelberg (2005)
3. Mjølsnes, S.F.: Privacy, Cryptographic Pseudonyms, and The State of Health. In: Matsumoto, T., Imai, H., Rivest, R.L. (eds.) ASIACRYPT 1991. LNCS, vol. 739, pp. 493–494. Springer, Heidelberg (1993)

4. Franz, E., Liesebach, K.: Supporting Local Aliases as Usable Presentation of Secure Pseudonyms. In: Fischer-Hübner, S., Lambrinoudakis, C., Pernul, G. (eds.) TrustBus 2009. LNCS, vol. 5695, pp. 22–31. Springer, Heidelberg (2009)
5. Lysyanskaya, A., Rivest, R.L., Sahai, A., Wolf, S.: Pseudonym systems. In: Heys, H., Adams, C. (eds.) SAC 1999. LNCS, vol. 1758, pp. 184–199. Springer, Heidelberg (2000)
6. Pearson, S., Shen, Y., Mowbray, M.: A Privacy Manager for Cloud Computing. In: Jaatun, M.G., Zhao, G., Rong, C. (eds.) Cloud Computing. LNCS, vol. 5931, pp. 90–106. Springer, Heidelberg (2009)
7. Mowbray, M., Pearson, S.: A Client-Based Privacy Manager for Cloud Computing. In: COMSWARE 2009: Proceedings of the Fourth International ICST Conference on COMmunication System Software and Middleware. ACM, New York (2009)
8. Candebat, T., Dunne, C.R., Gray, D.T.: Pseudonym Management using Mediated Identity-Based Cryptography. In: DIM 2005: Proceedings of the 2005 Workshop on Digital Identity Management, pp. 1–10. ACM, New York (2005)
9. Waters, B.R., Felten, E.W., Sahai, A.: Receiver Anonymity via Incomparable Public Keys. In: CCS 2003: Proceedings of the 10th ACM Conference on Computer and Communications Security, pp. 112–121. ACM, New York (2003)
10. Au, R., Vasanta, H., Kwang, K., Choo, R., Looi, M.: A User-Centric Anonymous Authorisation Framework in E-commerce Environment. In: Janssen, M., Sol, H.G., Wagenaar, R.W. (eds.) ICEC 2004: Proceedings of the 6th International Conference on Electronic Commerce, pp. 138–147. ACM, New York (2004)
11. Schmoll, C., Chatzis, N., Henke, C.: Protecting User Privacy with Multi-Field Anonymisation of IP Addresses. In: SIN 2010: Proceedings of the 3rd International Conference on Security of Information and Networks, pp. 38–45. ACM, New York (2010)
12. Jaiswal, S., Nandi, A.: Trust No One: A Decentralized Matching Service for Privacy in Location Based Services. In: MobiHeld 2010: Proceedings of the second ACM SIGCOMM workshop on Networking, Systems, and Applications on Mobile Handhelds, pp. 51–56. ACM, New York (2010)

Mining Roles from Web Application Usage Patterns

Nurit Gal-Oz[1], Yaron Gonen[1], Ran Yahalom[1], Ehud Gudes[1],
Boris Rozenberg[1], and Erez Shmueli[2]

[1] Deutsche Telekom Laboratories and Department of Computer Science, Ben-Gurion University of the Negev, Beer-Sheva, Israel
{galoz,yarongon,yahalomr,ehud}@cs.bgu.ac.il,
rozenbu@bgu.ac.il
[2] Deutsche Telekom Laboratories and Department of Information Systems Engineering, Ben-Gurion University of the Negev, Beer Sheva, Israel
erezshmu@bgu.ac.il

Abstract. Role mining refers to the problem of discovering an optimal set of roles from existing user permissions. In most role mining algorithms, the full set of user-permission assignments (UPA) is given as input. The challenge we are facing in the current paper is mining roles from actual web-application usage information. This information is collected by monitoring the access of users to application during a period of time. We analyze the actual permissions required to access the application in each user's session, and construct a set of user-permission assignments, which result in an incomplete UPA. We propose an algorithm that uses the session permission information to overcome the deficient data. We show by example how each step of the algorithm overcomes by heuristic instances of higher uncertainty. We demonstrate by simulation the efficiency of our algorithm in handling different levels of deficient data.

1 Introduction

Role-based access control is a common approach for authorization in web applications. The problem is that the roles originally defined are often not the ones actually used. Assume we have a web application accessing some database via a web server. The users of the application perform various actions which are translated to database operations and carried out by the web-server. In this situation the users of the application have access rights to certain modules of the application, however, their rights at the database objects level are not explicitly defined. Tracking the application users' activities allows us to learn the permissions they have in terms of access rights to database objects and create permission-profiles of users or in other words, roles. Such roles can be used to derive the actual access rights of a user or a group of users. A deviation from such a grouping may indicate an attempt for intrusion, thus it can be used for possible intrusion detection.

The challenge we are facing in the current paper is mining roles from actual web-application usage information. We monitor the permission usage habits of

S. Furnell, C. Lambrinoudakis, and G. Pernul (Eds.): TrustBus 2011, LNCS 6863, pp. 125–137, 2011.
© Springer-Verlag Berlin Heidelberg 2011

users during a period of time. Our data is a list of monitored tuples of the type (user, set of permissions) reflecting a user's access to some database objects, possibly within a single application operation or a set of related operations. We refer to such an operation as a logical session. Each set of permissions used together within a logical session is a hint that these permissions should be granted as a group. The data we collect holds a lot of valuable information such as the set of permissions a user has, the set of users that access the same sets of permissions, the frequency of using sets of permissions together, etc.

To align with existing research on the subject of role mining we could simply create a user-permission assignment (UPA) table from all user/permissions tuples in the collected data. Following [5] we may say that this is a UPA with the presence of noise where each permission that was not demonstrated is considered to be noise. From this point on, one could apply an existing role mining algorithm such as Role Miner [6]. However, these algorithms do not take advantage of the knowledge hidden in the monitored data (e.g., session associations). Thus, we propose an algorithm which utilizes this knowledge in order to get a more accurate mapping of users-permissions needs in the application.

Since we are dealing with limited finite samples, it is very likely that rarely used permissions will not be demonstrated by all users who actually have them. This may be seen as a sort of Subtractive noise as defined by [7]. A subtractive noise refers to the case in which a permission could be incorrectly revoked i.e. when a user is only given a subset of the overall permissions he may ultimately need. However it differs from our sampling noise since we may miss permissions that were actually given due to the quality of the sampling.

To the best of our knowledge, our approach differs from the state of the art work on role mining (e.g., [6,1,2,3]) in two aspects: first, the input we use is not a complete UPA but rather a sampled set of user-permissions usage collected from logs of users' actions during system operation. Second, we use the concept of logical sessions to add semantics to the role mining process. Our goal is to reconstruct the roles which best match the monitored data taking into account the above special characteristics.

The rest of this paper is organized as follows. In section 2 we discuss related work that serves as the background for our work. In section 3 we describe the Smart Database Audit (SDA) role mining problem and in section 4 we present our approach for solving it. In section 5 we present experimental results and in section 6 we conclude and discuss further research directions.

2   Related Work

The role mining problem (RMP) was defined by Vaidya et al. [4] as the problem of discovering an optimal set of roles from existing user permissions. Their definition of RMP bound the approximation produced by an inaccurate number of roles found: Given a set of users U, a set of permissions P, and a user-permission assignment UPA, find a set of roles, R, a user-to-role assignment UA, and a role-to-permission assignment PA $\delta - consistent$ with UPA and minimizing the number of roles, k.

In most role mining researches the user-permission assignments (UPA), are the basic information given as input to any RMP algorithm. This information is derived from actual permissions given at the database level and the task of RMP is to find the optimized set of roles that can cover the UPA. Vaidya et al. [5] have defined a noise model for the role mining problem which refers to errors in the UPA table as noise. Additive noise which refers to permissions incorrectly given (e.g., a permission given to a user to accomplish some task, but was not revoked after the task/duration is complete). The second is Subtractive noise which refers to permissions incorrectly revoked e.g., a user is only given a subset of the overall permissions he may ultimately need. To minimize the effect of noise, instead of bounding the approximation, and minimizing the number of roles in RMP, they suggest doing the reverse - bound the number of roles, and minimize the approximation- Minimal Noise Role Mining Problem (MinNoise RMP). CompleteMiner algorithm [6] starts by creating an initial set of roles from a known set of User-Permissions. Then it computes all possible intersection sets which results exponential running time algorithm. A more practical algorithm presented in is FastMiner algorithm which identifies only a subset of the potential roles, very fast (complexity is only n^2). The authors argued that the roles discovered by this algorithm are sufficient for practical purposes.

A key challenge that has been raised by Molloy et al. [2] is how to discover roles with semantic meanings. They argue that roles that are discovered by existing role mining approaches are no more than a set of permissions and it is unclear whether such roles correspond to any real-world concepts, such as a job position or a work location. Without semantical meanings, such roles may be hard to use and maintain in practice. Molloy et al. [2] study the problem in two settings with different information availability. When the only information is user-permission relation, they propose to discover roles whose semantic meaning is based on formal concept lattices. When user-attribute information is also available, they propose to create roles that can be explained by expressions of user-attributes. Since an expression of attributes describes a real-world concept, the corresponding role represents a real-world concept as well. Our approach is somewhat similar to [2] in that we use the concept of a session as representing the semantics of a role.

3   The SDA Role Mining Problem

The information we have for constructing a UPA is derived from monitoring user activities for a period of time. In contrast with [4] there is no guarantee that the data we have actually demonstrates each and every permission that should be granted to a user in the application. It is possible for example, that users will have the permission to view information related to their employment but only some of them actually access this information regularly. A few others prefer to call the HR department and ask for the information by phone. In this case we will not be able to capture the fact that the latter have the required permission since they don't use it. The subtractive noise in our problem is much more difficult to realize as it is highly dependent on the quality of the sampled data.

Given a deficient dataset our task is to come up with assignments that were not explicitly observed, but are implied from the data. However an assignment of a role to a user can be a mistake if this role grants the user a permission that is not truly hers. Thus, inferring the user roles is prone to error due the subtractive noise in the input data and we define its effect on the resulting roles in terms of possible mistakes. We aim at minimizing the set of resulting roles while also minimizing the effect of noise, i.e., the amount of mistakes.

3.1   Semantic Information and Logical sessions

A logical session is part of a user login session in which the user performs a single logical operation. For example a student may ask to register to a course. The registration is a single logical operation although it may consist of several database actions such as: check if the student is allowed to register this course academically, check if the student has payed the registration fees in the current semester, etc. These actions may access several database objects and require various permissions related to these objects. One may think of a logical session as an operation a user may carry out using her permissions in a specific role. In this sense the semantics are hidden behind the gathering of actions within a single unit.

Following [2], we adopt the idea of a lattice however we do not use the concept lattice since concepts relates to maximal itemsets and we are looking for the information hidden in the usage of partial sets of items. In the next section we describe the initial lattice and our heuristic approach to mine roles from it.

4   The SDA Role Mining Solution

One of the major goals of the SDA project is to identify logical sessions by monitoring web applications (the session identification problem is out of the scope of this paper). The input we get from the logical session identified, consists of a set of tuples (one for each session), containing a session number, a user id and a set of permissions. We represent this input in a table in which each row represents a session and there is a column for each permission identified in the system. The cell representing session i and permission j contains the value 1 if the permission was used within this logical session and 0 otherwise. Figure 1 describes an example input table. Due to space limitations we grouped together sessions in which the same user used the same permissions. Table (a) is sorted by users and the support column states the number of times a session of this type occurred. Table (b) is sorted by the size of the permissions set used within the sessions. Our solution is composed of several stages. In each stage we attempt to reduce the number of roles while trying to minimize the amount of potential mistakes. In the first stage we construct the *Permission Usage Lattice (PUL)*. A node in a PUL represents a set of permissions that appeared within a session. Each node in the lattice is attached with a usage-table that details the users that had such logical sessions and the number of times they had it, i.e. support. A node SN in the lattice is a sub-node of another node N if

User	P1	P2	P3	P4	P5	P6	Support
1	x						1
1				x			2
1	x	x					6
1	x	x	x	x			3
2	x						2
2	x	x					2
2	x				x		2
2	x	x			x		3
2	x	x	x	x			2
3	x						1
3				x			1
3	x				x		1
3				x	x		2
3	x	x	x	x			2
4	x						1
4				x	x		2
4	x	x				x	5
5				x			1
6				x			2
7				x			5
7	x	x					3
7			x	x			3
7	x	x				x	6

(a)

User	P1	P2	P3	P4	P5	P6	Cardinality
1	x						1
3	x						1
4	x						1
2	x						1
3				x			1
1				x			1
5				x			1
6				x			1
7				x			1
2	x	x					2
7	x	x					2
1	x	x					2
3	x				x		2
2	x				x		2
3				x	x		2
4				x	x		2
7				x	x		2
2	x	x				x	3
4	x	x				x	3
7	x	x				x	3
2	x	x	x	x			4
3	x	x	x	x			4
1	x	x	x	x			4

(b)

Fig. 1. Permission usage: (a) sorted by users (b) sorted by the cardinality of permissions in a session

$setofPermissions(SN) \subset setofPermissions(N)$. A node N of cardinality i is connected to its sub-node SN of cardinality $j < i$ if there is no other sub-node SN' of N with cardinality k, $j < k < i$ s.t, N is connected to SN' and SN' is connected to SN. In this case SN is a *DirectSon* of N.

Figure 2 presents the PUL created from the input in Figure 1 (b). The usage table in each node lists the users that had sessions represented by this node and for each user it stores two values: original support and dynamic support. Original support counts the number of times (sessions) the user used the set of permissions represented by this node. Dynamic support represents the updated support in later stages of our role mining process. There are two measures we define in this respect. The first is *Total Role Support*, which sums up the total actual support of the role. The second is *Users per Role* which counts the number of active users (users with support > 0) that appear in the node's usage table. For each of the two measures we set a threshold: *MinSupport* which defines the minimum required value of *TotalRoleSupport*, and *MinUsers* which defines the minimum required value of *UsersperRole* for any given node. These thresholds will serve us in the role mining process to determine the importance of keeping a node as a role on its own. Algorithm 1 describes the lattice construction phase.

A node in the PUL represents an *Initial Role Candidate*. In rare cases the PUL can represent the optimal set of Roles. In most cases an operation requires part of the set of permission in a role. Therefore, our goal is to use some statistical measures to determine which nodes in the lattice should become permanent roles and which nodes should be eliminated or incorporated in other nodes.

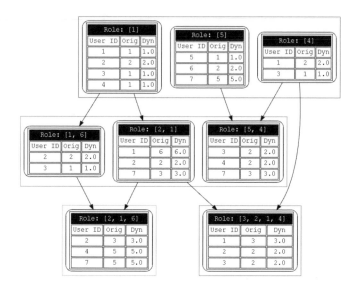

Fig. 2. Permission Usage Lattice (PUL)

4.1   Generalizing Initial Roles

Preserving all sets of permissions that appeared in the application log data may result with a large number of initial role candidates. In the worst case it may lead to a PUL with 2^n nodes, where n is the total number of permissions. However, aiming at a significantly smaller number of roles, our first steps is towards reducing the number of partial roles which are roles whose set of permissions is contained in the set of permissions of some other, more general role. For example, a teaching assistant would require a subset of the permissions that a professor requires. To do this we eliminate nodes that represent partial roles, i.e. nodes that capture a subset of permissions of other nodes. The roles represented by these nodes are *generalized* into wider roles. Intuitively it means that a user may not always use the complete set of permissions enabled by a role she own but only a subset of these permissions. This will result in two initial roles where one of them is a subset of permissions of the other one, while in fact the latter is sufficient. We say that eliminating the former is a legal operation since it does not grant the user any additional permission.

The generalization stage is a BFS scan of the lattice. The *Level* of a node is defined by the cardinality of its permission set, e.g., a node that consists of two permissions $\{P1, P2\}$ will be of level 2. We start with nodes of the lowest level and attempt to move the support of each user in this node to nodes of higher level which are ancestors of this node. Once we find the set of ancestor nodes which contain the user in their usage table, we divide the support of the user in the original node among them according to the relative support that user has in each ancestor node (the support of each ancestor node is proportional to the

---

Algorithm 1. Constructing the Permission Usage Lattice
Input
Partial User Permission Assignment Table pUPA
Output Permission Usage Latice PUL

1: sort pUPA by the cardinality of the permissions set in the sessions
2: **for** i=1 to MaxCardinality **do**
3:   level(i)= createLatticeLevel(i)
4:   **for** each session s of cardinality i, associated with user u and permission set p
     do
5:     **if** there is no node N s.t. N.setofPermissions $= p$ **then**
6:        Node $=$ level(i).AddNewNode
7:        Node.setofPermissions $= p$
8:        Node.usageTable.insertUser(u)
9:        Node.usageTable.users(u).support $= 1$
10:       Connect Node to all of its direct sons
11:     **else**
12:        {A node for the set of permissions p already exists}
13:        **if** $u \notin$ Node.usageTable **then**
14:           Node.usageTable .insertUser(u)
15:           Node.usageTable.users(u).support+=1

---

probability that the user used this role). Nodes left with a usage table having
a total support of 0 may be ignored. The generalization process is described in
Algorithm 2.

The example in figure 3 demonstrates the result of the generalization stage
of the PUL described in figure 3. The usage table has two columns, the left
column keeps the original support values and the right column keeps the current
dynamic support for each user, that is, it takes into account the support added
upon user node generalization.

4.2   Eliminating Redundant Roles

While generalization stage may eliminate a lot of roles, some roles may be left
with a few users or a very low node support. To decide whether a node should be
kept to represent a role we have to define some reasonable thresholds. Assume we
have a node N representing permissions P1 and P2 and its usage table containing
user u with support 2. All other users has support 0 (they were assigned a wider
role in the generalization stage). User u does not appear in any other node's usage
table. Is it reasonable to have node N representing a role for just one person?
Should we assign user u to a wider role even if we have no explicit evidence that
the user has the extra permissions in the wider role? Although there is no one
clear answer to these questions we know that keeping roles that are too specific
for one or even a few persons can cause over fitting and we may end up with a
lot of roles($2^{|permissions|}$). In addition we know that it is very likely that some
users will not use all of their permissions within the monitored period of time.

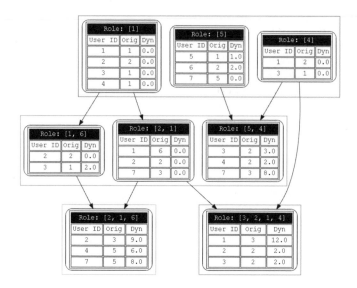

Fig. 3. Generalized Lattice

In this stage we attempt to eliminate redundant roles. A *Redundant Role* is a node in the PUL for which $UsersPerRole < MinUsersPerRole$ or $RoleSupport < totalRoleSupport$. Once we have identified a node N to be a redundant role we search for the best wider roles to assign the users left in the redundant role.

The best wider role for a user u must be an immediate ancestor of N (a node in the closest level that exists for N) to ensure minimum extra permissions assigned to u. In addition it should be a role that is most likely to be assigned to the user. The *Common Node Users (CNU)* of u is the set of users that appeared together with u in the same nodes denoted

$CNU(u) = \{u_i | \exists \text{ node } N \text{ s.t. } u \in N \text{ and } u_i \in N\}$

A *MatchingLevel* of N_{super}, an ancestor of node N with respect to user u, is the number of users of N_{super} that appear in $CNU(u)$. Intuitively it defines to what extent we are implied that node N_{super} represents a role that should be granted to u. We take this strategy one step further and search for the MatchingLevel of the the sub-lattice whose root is N_{super} with respect to u. This extension allows us to learn the matching level of a node from a more global view of the lattice. A formal definition follows. A *MatchingLevel* of two sets of users A,B is $MatchingLevel(A, B) = |A \cap B|$. A *MatchingLevel* of a node N to its ancestor node N_{super} with respect to user u that appears in N's usage table is expressed by:

$MatchingLevel(N, N_{super}, u) = |users(Lattice(N_{super})) \cap CNU(u)|$

where $Lattice(N_{super})$ is the sub-lattice whose root is N_{super} and $users(Lattice)$ is the union of all the users appearing in nodes of Lattice. Let $SN(N) = \{SN_1, SN_2, ..., SN_n\}$ be a set of ancestors of node N, the $BestWiderRole(u, N)$ for user u in node N is a node $SN_i \in SN$ with the minimal node level that

---

Algorithm 2. Generalizing Initial Roles
Input
Initial PUL
Output
Generalized PUL

---

    for i=1 to MaxLatticeLevel-1 **do**
      for each node N of level i **do**
        for each user u of N.usageTable **do**
          for j=i+1 to MaxLatticeLevel **do**
            setOfAncestros = $\{N_s | N_S \in N.ancestors.level(i)\ and\ u\ \in\ N_s.users\}$
            if setOfAncestros $\neq$ empty **then**
               assignDynamicSupportByProbability(N,u,setOfAncestros)
               N.usageTable.users(u).dynamicSupport= 0
               break

---

has the maximal MatchingLevel with N with respect to u. A formal definition follows:

$BestWiderRole(N, u)$ $=$ $\{SN_i | MatchingLevel(N, SN_i, u)$ $>$ $MatchingLevel$ (N, SN_k, u)

$\forall SN_i, SN_k \in MinAncestorLevel(N)\}$

where $MinAncestorLevel(N) = \{SN_i | level(SN_i) \leq level(SN_j)\ \forall SN_i, SN_j \in SN(N)\}$

If we have more than one best wider role candidate we randomly select one of them according to the distribution of their matching levels. The stage of eliminating redundant roles is also a BFS scan of the PUL but it only scans active nodes that is nodes that have dynamic support greater than zero 0. Algorithm 2 describes this stage in details. Figure 4 describes the result PUL of our example after eliminating the redundant roles. Note that now the left most role in the middle row can be eliminated, however user 3 now was assigned to his ancestor

---

Algorithm 3. Eliminating Redundant Roles
Input
Generalized PUL
Output
Reduced PUL

    BFS scan of Generalized PUL
    for i=1 to MaxLatticeLevel-1 **do**
      for each node N of level i **do**
        if redundantRole(N) **then**
          for each user u of N.usageTable **do**
            widerNode=findBestWiderRole(N,u)
            widerNode.usageTable.insertUser(u)
            widerNode.usageTable.users(u).originalSupport= 0
            widerNode.usageTable.users(u).dynamicSupport=
            N.usageTable.users(u).dynamicSupport
            N.usageTable.users(u).dynamicSupport= 0

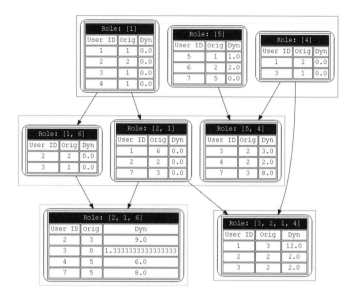

Fig. 4. Reduced Lattice

node resulting with extra permission 2. This may or may not be a potential mistake.

Within the redundant roles that we could not eliminate at the previous stages we distinguish roles that had high support in the original PUL from the others. The former roles became redundant due to our attempt to generalize them. However, the fact that we could not completely generalize them or eliminate them, and the high support they had in the initial PUL, increase the confidence that they can become permanent. In our example, if *MinSupp* is set to 4, the role containing permission 5 meets this criteria. In the final stage we add these roles to the set of permanent roles. The set of redundant roles left consists of roles that have no justification in terms of support to become permanent.

5   Evaluation

We have developed the Session Generator, a simulation tool that generates user sessions. The session generator gets as an input a file containing roles (sets of permissions) and *maxNumOfUsers* - the number of users in the experiment; *maxRolesPerUser* - the highest number of roles assigned to each user; *maxSessionsPerUser* - the highest number of sessions produced per user and *BernoulliProb* - the probability for a permission that belongs to a role to appear in a session of this role (conforms to the Bernoulli sampling).

Using the input file, the session generator produces sessions as follows: For each user it selects a random number of roles and a random number of sessions.

It then creates a user session by randomly selecting the active role for this session from that user's roles. For each permission of the active role it uses the Bernoulli Prob parameter to decide if the permission is used in the session or not. The algorithm produces an output file containing the permissions that a user used in each session. A complete UPA (user permission assignment) matrix can be obtained by listing the permissions of each user as derived from the roles assigned to the user. Assigning a value of p to the BernoulliProb parameter in the experiment, we get an output file that covers approximately p of the permissions in the complete UPA matrix. Thus the deficiency measure (noise) is approximately $1 - p$. The session generator output file along with the threshold parameters $MinSupport$ and $MinUsers$ are the input file for the role mining algorithm. The roles dataset we use is a synthetic dataset based on a template used in [2]. We generated a session dataset based on this template by creating users and assigning roles to them using the session generator described above. The dataset contains 7 roles and 12 permissions. We generated datasets of sessions for 100 users with different values of the Bernoulli parameter ranging from 1-0.6 (constructing datasets of approximately 0 - 40% deficiency level respectively). We also used different values of the generalization threshold minNumOfUsers, minSupp ranging from 2 -20.

5.1   Evaluation Results

The results are summarized in figure 5. In this chart the horizontal axis represents the level of deficiency of the dataset. The vertical axis represents the average error measured by the ratio of the number of discovered roles with respect to the number of original roles. Each column in the chart represents an error with respect to a threshold levels.

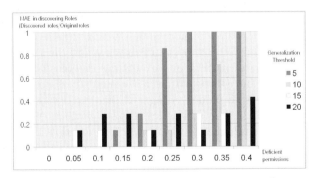

Fig. 5. MAE in discovering roles from noisy data

The majority of the tests that discovered more than 7 roles, the 7 actual original roles were discovered. Only in 4% of these tests - one of the original roles was absent. In all tests that discovered less than 7 roles, the set of discovered roles was a subset of the original roles. The 7 roles were identified from large amounts of initial role candidates for example: For 10% deficiency: 92 initial roles (1020 sessions) For 20% deficiency: 131 initial roles (989 sessions) A

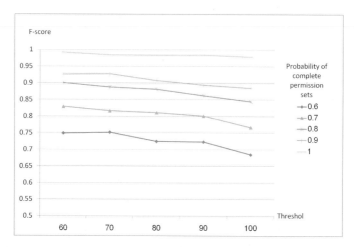

Fig. 6. F-score with respect to threshold and probability of complete permission sets

lower Bernoulli parameter = a lower coverage of the UPA, required higher levels of minNumOfUsers minSupp to discover the exact roles. Next, we used the F-score, which is defined as the the harmonic mean of precision and recall measure, to evaluate the ability of our algorithm to discover roles with respect to the original roles. Figure 6 demonstrates the correlation between the deficiency of the dataset and the Generalization threshold required to discover the original roles. This is explained as follows. The role miner algorithm generalizes redundant roles by unifying them with wider roles that contain them. A Redundant Role is a node in the Lattice for which $UsersPerRole < minNumOfUsers$ or $RoleSupport < minSupp$. If a role was not generalized although there is a wider role that contains it, it implies that $UsersPerRole >= minNumOfUsers$ and $RoleSupport >= minSupp$. By increasing the generalization thresholds, minNumOfUsers and minSupp, we allow more nodes to be generalized. The permission sets deficiency increases as the bernoulliProb parameter decreases and as a result more combinations of permission subsets are created for each role. Thus, the role mining algorithm starts with a large number of initial roles (nodes). According to the algorithm, nodes of high cardinality (relatively high number of permissions), generalize their sub-nodes of lower cardinality and get their relative support. However a higher level of generalization threshold is required to guarantee generalization. The threshold parameter in this experiment was more significant when we examined deficient permission data.

6   Conclusions

We introduced an algorithm for mining roles from data gathered by monitoring users access to a web application. The algorithm is carried out in three stages:

construction of user permission lattice, generalizing initial roles and eliminating redundant roles. We demonstrated the ability of the algorithm to overcome the major problem we have with such data, a deficient user permission assignment data. While most of the roles are discovered after the third stage applying an additional stage of accepting redundant roles with initial high support improves the results. Examining the additional roles generated beyond the original ones, we found out that these are of high cardinality. They were not generalized since they had relatively high values of support due to the many nodes generalized to them in the earlier steps of the algorithm. This implies that the support should not be unified for the nodes in the lattice and should be adjusted to the state of the lattice in each step of the algorithm. In future work we intend to examine the use of dynamic threshold values that are determined according to the state of each node traversed in the lattice.

References

1. Steffens, U., Schlegelmich, J.: Role mining with orca. In: SACMAT 2005: Proceedings of the Tenth ACM Symposium on Access Control Models and Technologies. ACM Press, Stockholm (2005)
2. Molloy, I., Chen, H., Li, T., Wang, Q., Li, N., Bertino, E., Calo, S.B., Lobo, J.: Mining roles with semantic meanings. In: SACMAT, pp. 21–30 (2008)
3. Molloy, I., Li, N., Qi, Y. (A.), Lobo, J., Dickens, L.: Mining roles with noisy data. In: SACMAT, pp. 45–54 (2010)
4. Vaidya, J., Atluri, V., Guo, Q.: The role mining problem: finding a minimal descriptive set of roles. In: Proceedings of the 12th ACM Symposium on Access Control Models and Technologies, pp. 175–184. ACM, New York (2007)
5. Vaidya, J., Atluri, V., Guo, Q., Lu, H.: Role mining in the presence of noise. In: Foresti, S., Jajodia, S. (eds.) Data and Applications Security and Privacy XXIV. LNCS, vol. 6166, pp. 97–112. Springer, Heidelberg (2010)
6. Vaidya, J., Atluri, V., Warner, J.: RoleMiner: mining roles using subset enumeration. In: Proceedings of the 13th ACM Conference on Computer and Communications Security, pp. 144–153. ACM, New York (2006)
7. Vaidya, J., Atluri, V., Guo, Q.: The role mining problem: A formal perspective. ACM Trans. Inf. Syst. (2010)

A Mobility and Energy-Aware Hierarchical Intrusion Detection System for Mobile Ad Hoc Networks

Eleni Darra, Christoforos Ntantogian, Christos Xenakis, and Sokratis Katsikas

Department of Digital Systems, University of Piraeus, Greece
{edarra,dadoyan,xenakis,ska}@unipi.gr

Abstract. This paper presents a hierarchical cluster-based IDS architecture for Mobile Ad-hoc NETworks (MANETs) that considers the mobility and energy of nodes in the cluster formation in order to improve detection accuracy and reduce energy consumption. The proposed architecture adopts and enhances the Mobility and Energy Aware Clustering Algorithm (MEACA), which is the most appropriate for IDS in MANETs, since it aims at forming mobility aware and energy efficient 1-hop clusters. The algorithm maximizes the clusters' stability by choosing nodes with relatively low mobility and high energy to be the cluster-heads and keeping the constructed clusters unchanged to the extent of their maximum possible lifetime. The key advantage of the proposed IDS is that its detection accuracy is not affected from nodes mobility, since each cluster includes nodes with similar direction and speed. Thus, mobile nodes of the same cluster appear more static to each other eliminating cluster reformation, which negatively affects the detection accuracy. Moreover, the distribution of the detection load is based on the remaining energy in each node. Thus, nodes with adequate energy undertake more detection responsibilities than nodes with low power. In this way, the proposed IDS balances the energy consumption in a fair and efficient manner.

Keywords: Intrusion Detection System, IDS, mobile ad hoc networks, MANETs, hierarchical architecture, clustering algorithm, mobility, energy.

1 Introduction

A mobile ad hoc network (MANET) is an autonomously formed collection of mobile nodes without the involvement of any established infrastructure or centralized control. In MANETs, the nodes themselves communicate with each other creating dynamic network topologies. Due to their unpredictable topology, wireless shared medium, heterogeneous resources and stringent resource constraints, MANETs are vulnerable to a variety of attacks (i.e., target routing, cooperation, confidentiality, integrity, etc.) and thus, sufficient protection from them is fundamental requirement. The implementation of an Intrusion Detection System (IDS) can identify such attacks and trigger the appropriate protection mechanisms [1].

An IDS for MANETs can be divided into two parts: (i) the architecture which explicates its operational structure and (ii) the detection engine that is the mechanism used to detect malignant behaviors. The existing IDS architectures for MANETs fall

S. Furnell, C. Lambrinoudakis, and G. Pernul (Eds.): TrustBus 2011, LNCS 6863, pp. 138–149, 2011.

under three main categories [2 - 4]: stand-alone, cooperative and hierarchical. As hierarchical IDSs apply multiple levels of detection, they present increased detection accuracy compared to others (i.e, stand alone and cooperative). They mainly bring about low processing and communication overhead by employing voting schemes to elect cluster-heads (CH), which monitor large portions of the network reaching more accurate decisions [13]. Moreover, they attempt to distribute fairly the processing workload among the nodes, considering the remaining energy power. Finally, effort has been put to create more robust hierarchies under high node's mobility, by selecting CHs with the objective of lasting longer [9].

A limitation of the existing IDSs for MANETs is that they do not consider the negative impacts of mobility on the detection accuracy [13]. More specifically, in various mobility scenarios the changes in topology and routing tables are rapid and inconsistent. These changes may occur also from malicious behaviors that attempt to disrupt the network operation and routing process. An IDS should distinguish which changes are legitimate, caused by nodes mobility and which are the results of abnormal behaviors, provoked by malicious nodes. Nevertheless, IDSs may erroneously indentify legitimate changes as attacks and vice versa, increasing in this way the ratio of false positives and negatives (i.e., detection accuracy). Moreover, the creation and maintenance of clustered/hierarchical structures adds extra processing load to the network nodes, which also increases under conditions of relatively high nodes' mobility. This overhead is produced by the continuous execution of the clustering functionality, due to the constant change of clusters. Finally, the majority of the existing IDS do not take into account that the detection process should not increase significantly the energy consumption at the level of nodes. Especially, in cooperative IDS architectures, where each node runs a detection engine, the energy consumption may be significantly high, reducing the lifetime of nodes in the network.

Driven by the above observations, this paper presents a hierarchical cluster-based IDS architecture for MANETs that considers the mobility and energy of nodes in the cluster formation in order to improve detection accuracy and reduce energy consumption. The proposed IDS architecture adopts and enhances the mobility and energy aware clustering algorithm (MEACA) [12], which aims at forming mobility aware and energy efficient 1-hop clusters. The algorithm maximizes the clusters' stability by choosing nodes with relatively low mobility and high energy to be the CHs and keeping the constructed clusters unchanged to the extent of their maximum possible lifetime. The key advantage of the proposed IDS is that the detection accuracy is not affected from the nodes mobility, since each cluster includes nodes with similar direction and speed. Thus, mobile nodes of the same cluster appear more static to each other eliminating cluster reformation, which negatively affects the detection accuracy. Moreover, the distribution of the detection load is based on the remaining energy in each node. Thus, nodes with adequate energy undertake more detection responsibilities than nodes with low power. In this way, the proposed IDS balances the energy consumption in a fair and efficient manner. Finally, the proposed IDS minimizes the communication overhead as there is 1-hop distance between a CH and its cluster members (CMs).

The rest of this paper is organized as follows. Section 2 presents the related work. Section 3 elaborates on the proposed IDS architecture and the MEACA algorithm.

Section 4 evaluates the proposed IDS architecture focusing on its advantages and disadvantages and, finally, section 5 draws the conclusions.

2 Related Work

There is a rather limited literature of IDS for MANETs that copes with the impact of mobility on the detection accuracy, while at the same time takes into account the energy consumption at the level of nodes. The hierarchical IDS architecture, proposed by Ma and Fang [5], follows a modular approach based on clusters and presents a number of strengths including: (i) the nodes with the highest battery power are elected to serve as CHs, (ii) it supports two layers of detection (i.e., local and network) providing increased detection accuracy, and (iii) the CH monitors the network packets exchanged thus, there is no extra communication overhead between the CH and the CMs. The major drawback is that high nodes' mobility may reduce the detection accuracy of the IDS and increase the ratio of false positives, since a number of nodes may move out of the range of a CH. This limits the information that the network detection module may use to perform detection.

Otrok et al. have proposed a hierarchical approach [6] that attempts to balance the consumption of resources (which results from intrusion detection tasks) among the nodes of a cluster. It encourages network nodes to participate in the election of CHs and tries to prevent elected CHs from misbehaving. One of the main operational strengths of this architecture is that the nodes with the highest battery power are elected to serve as CHs. On the other hand, there is no discussion regarding the mobility of nodes and its implications in the detection accuracy.

Marchang and Datta [7] have proposed two IDS architectures that rely on a voting scheme to perform intrusion detection, instead of employing an anomaly or signature based intrusion detection engine. The main disadvantages of these two are: (i) high ratio of false alarms, since they do not take into account mobility, and (ii) they do not consider energy consumption.

H. Deng et al. in [8] have proposed a clustered IDS architecture in which only the CHs carry out intrusion detection. It focuses on detecting attacks that target the routing infrastructure of a network and forms clusters using the "Distributed Efficient Clustering Approach" protocol. Although this architecture distributes fairly the processing workload among the nodes, as the CHs rotate after a certain period of time, there is no analysis of the mobility implications in the detection accuracy.

Manousakis et al. [9] have proposed a hierarchical IDS architecture that uses a dynamic tree-based structure in which detection data are aggregated upwards, from leaf nodes to authoritative nodes at the root of the hierarchy (i.e., upper layer nodes), and the latter dispatch directives down to the former (i.e., lower-level nodes). The tree-based structure is established and maintained using two algorithms: the initial solution generation and the state transition mechanism. The main drawback of this algorithm is that the election process of CHs does not consider the energy of nodes.

Finally, Sun et al. [10], [11] have proposed a cooperative IDS architecture that focuses on routing disruption attacks using an intrusion detection engine based on statistical methods with adjustable threshold values. The technique of adjustable thresholds ensures that periodical changes in routing information, caused by nodes' mobility, remain under the detection threshold, while malicious behaviors that are persistent exceed the thresholds indicating the occurrence of attacks. This addresses the negative impacts of mobility on the detection accuracy. However, the simulation analysis revealed that the decrease in the ratio of false positives was relatively low.

3   The Proposed IDS

3.1   IDS Architecture

The proposed IDS architecture is organized into autonomous and distributed multi-leveled hierarchies. Each level of them consists of several clusters in which specific nodes act as CHs gathering local audit data from its CMs, analyzing them and extracting conclusions about the integrity of the nodes in the cluster. The autonomous clusters-based hierarchies are formed using the MEACA algorithm [12] which can be applied in dynamically changed network topologies.

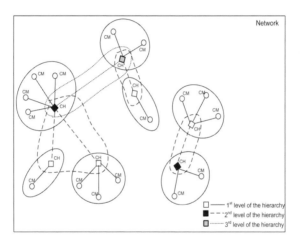

Fig. 1. Graphical example of the proposed IDS architecture

Initially, the algorithm creates the first level of hierarchies by forming autonomous clusters. Afterwards, the CHs of the previously formed clusters are selected to participate in the next level of hierarchies. Some of them will keep their attributes acting as CHs in the new level, while many others will act as CMs. Generally, the algorithm is repeated until the higher level of each hierarchy consists of a single node (i.e., hierarchy CH). It is important to note that in each layer the nodes that participate in a cluster should have 1-hop distance among them. A graphical example of the proposed IDS architecture is represented in **Fig. 1**. Intrusion detection occurs at the CH of each cluster by aggregating data from the CMs in order to have increased detection accuracy. If the responsible CH cannot detect an attack accurately, it forwards the detection data to the CH of the upper level, if such exists.

3.2 Algorithm Description

The multi-level hierarchies of the proposed IDS have the following characteristics: (i) every node in the network becomes either a CH or a CM, (ii) every node is associated with only one cluster in each level of the hierarchy, and (iii) every CM is 1-hop distance from its CH. During the algorithm execution, every node sends attribute values to its neighbor nodes (i.e., nodes that have 1-hop distance). Each node keeps a neighborhood table that includes information regarding A_m (i.e., mobility attribute), A_e (i.e., energy attribute) and the related node *ID*. When an attribute's value is received, the corresponding entry of the sending node in the table is updated. If a node no longer receives any value from a neighbor node then, the related entry in the neighborhood table is cleared. A_m and A_e are required to determine a node's priority to become a CH. A_m measures the mobility stability of a nodes and A_e measures the remaining time of a node before its energy is ended.

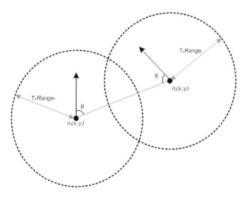

Fig. 2. LET parameters between two nodes

The mobility stability is defined by the Link Expiration Time (LET) [9], [14], [15]. By predicting the LET for any link on a route R, the route's R expiration time is estimated as the least of the LET values of all links on R. Based on this prediction, routes are reconfigured before they disconnect [16]. In [15] a mobility prediction method is presented for estimating the expiration time of the wireless link between two ad hoc nodes. The estimation of the LET, or in other words the time period T that two ad hoc nodes being within mutual transmission range (i.e., remain connected) is done as follows: If the motion parameters of two neighbors (such as speed, direction, and radio propagation range) are known, we can determine the duration of time these two nodes will remain connected. Assume two nodes i and j. Let (x_i, y_i) be the coordinates of mobile host i and (x_j, y_j) be that of mobile host j. Also let v_i and v_j be the speeds, and θ_i and θ_j (*where* $0 \le \theta_i, \theta_j < 2\pi$) be the moving directions of the nodes i and j, respectively. Also, $TxRange_i, TxRange_j$ are the transmission ranges of nodes i and j. In this situation, the $TxRange_i, TxRange_j$ is the same. So, the LET_{ij} for the direct link between nodes n_i and n_j is defined in **Fig. 2**:

$$LET_{ij} = \begin{cases} \dfrac{-(ab+cd)+\sqrt{(a^2+c^2)r^2-(ad-bc)^2}}{a^2+c^2}, & nodes\ i,j\ are\ in\ range \\ 0 & ,\ nodes\ i,j\ are\ not\ in\ range \\ \infty & ,\ nodes\ i,j\ are\ relatively\ static \end{cases}$$

where:

$a = v_i \cos\theta_i - v_j \cos\theta_j$, $b = x_i - x_j$, $c = v_i \sin\theta_i - v_j \sin\theta_j$, $d = y_i - y_j$, $r = TxRange_{i,j}$

The host with a large value of average LET is able to maintain relatively long connection with their neighbor hosts [15] [16]. Therefore, the average LET of each host, which can be calculated in a distributive manner, can be used as mobility metric for the CH selection.

Table 1. Pseudo code of the proposed algorithm for the formation of the hiearchies

N: *Node*, T: *Attributes' table*, A_e: *Energy attribute*, A_m: *Mobility attribute*, **ID**: *identity of a node*
Step I: *N receives A_e, A_m, ID from its neighboring nodes*
Step II: *N creates table T with A_e, A_m, ID of its own and its neighboring nodes*
Step III: *N selects the highest value of A_m in T, defined as max (A_m)*
Step IV: *N determines threshold A_m* = a × max (A_m), where a ∈ (0, 1)*
Step V: *N removes from T the nodes with A_m < A_m*. Let T' be the remaining nodes in T.*
Step VI: *N chooses from T' the node with the highest A_e. Let C be this node.*
{
*   if node C is the node N*
*   then N becomes CH*
*   else*
*   N sends a registration request message to C. If the latter accepts,*
*   then C becomes CH and N becomes CM of C*
}
Step VII: *Steps I to VI are repeated from the elected CHs to create the next level of the hierarchy*

At the initialization of the algorithm, all nodes are in an undecided role state, where they do not know yet which is the CH or CM. When a node N executes the algorithm to determine whether it will become a CH or CM, first it requests from its neighboring nodes (i.e., nodes with 1-hop distance) their attributes values (i.e., *Step I*). Next, the node N creates an attributes' table T with the received *ID*, A_m and A_e including its own attribute values (i.e., *Step II*). Then, N selects the node with the highest value of A_m defined as *max (A_m)* (i.e., *Step III*). In the next step (i.e., *Step IV*), N determines a mobility threshold defined as A_m* $= a \times max (A_m)$, where $a \in (0, 1)$. The parameter a is selected randomly from node N. Based on the mobility threshold value, the node N excludes the nodes from the attributes' table that have A_m lower than A_m*. In this way, it achieves to eliminate the unstable nodes. Let T' be the remaining nodes after the elimination of unstable nodes. After this, node N selects, from the remaining nodes in table T', the node with the highest A_e (i.e., *Step V*). Let C be the node with the highest A_e from the remaining nodes. If C is the same node as node N, then it becomes a CH. Otherwise, N sends a registration request message to C. If the latter accepts it, then C becomes a CH and node N becomes a CM of node C (i.e., *Step VI*). The process continues until all the nodes define their CH. Note that each node that becomes a CM sends to its neighboring nodes advertisements with *ID*, A_m, A_e values equal to NULL to acknowledge that it cannot be a CH. For the creation of the next levels of the hierarchy, steps I to VI are repeated between the CHs (i.e., *Step VII*). After the creation of all the hierarchies, each node periodically broadcasts their *ID*, A_m and A_e values to its neighbor nodes to acknowledge any changes in the registration tables (see section 3.3). **Table 1** gives the pseudo code of the algorithm for the formation of the hierarchies.

3.3 Case Study

For a better understanding of the presented notions, in this section we apply the aforementioned algorithm in a MANET comprised of 15 nodes (see **Fig. 3**).

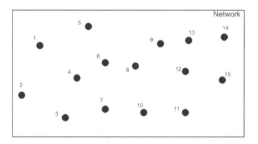

Fig. 3. The structure of the network

For the presented example we set various values of the mobility A_m and energy A_e attributes measured in seconds. Moreover, node 1 receives attributes values from nodes 2, 3, 4 and 5 which has 1-hop distance with them.

Table 2. Example of attributes' tables of nodes 1, 2 and 4

Node 1	ID	Am	Ae
	1	742	4097
	2	826	2539
	3	560	6088
	4	663	4772
	5	368	5982

Node 2	ID	Am	Ae
	2	826	2539
	3	560	6088
	4	663	4772

Node 4	ID	Am	Ae
	3	560	6088
	4	663	4772
	6	632	4700
	7	392	3909

As shown in **Table 2**, in the attributes' table of the node 1, node 2 has the greatest value of A_m and thus, *max* $(A_m) = 826$. Assuming now that node 1 selects $\alpha=0,7$, the mobility threshold is calculated as $A_m^* = 0,7 \times 826 = 578,2$. Thus, node 5 is excluded from the process as its mobility attribute is lower than A_m^*. From the remaining nodes (1, 2, 3 and 4), node 1 selects the node with the highest A_e, that is node 3 (see **Table 2**). Since node 3 is not the node executing the algorithm (i.e., node 1), a registration message is sent from node 1 to node 3. If the latter accepts, then it becomes CH while node 1 becomes its CM.

Next, node 2 receives attribute values from nodes 3 and 4. Observing **Table 2**, it is evident that node 2 has the greatest A_m and, therefore $max\ (A_m) = 826$. Next, node 1 selects $\alpha=0,57$ and the mobility threshold is derived as $A_m{}^* = 0,57 \times 826 = 470,82$. Since all nodes have mobility attribute A_m higher than the mobility threshold, none of these nodes are excluded. Next, node 2 selects node 3 with the highest A_e. Node 3 is not the one executing the algorithm, and therefore, node 2 sends a registration message to node 3. The latter has previously accepted this message and node 2 becomes its CM. Since nodes 1 and 2 have the same CH (i.e., node 3) they belong to the same cluster.

Then, node 4 receives attributes values from nodes 3, 6 and 7. Observing **Table 2**, node 4 has the greatest A_m value with $max\ (A_m) = 663$. Node 4 selects $\alpha=0,9$ and thus, $A_m{}^* = 0,9 \times 663 = 596,7$. Nodes 3 and 7 are excluded, since their mobility attributes have smaller values than $A_m{}^*$. From the remaining nodes, node 4 has the highest A_e. Since node 4 is the same as the one executing the algorithm, it becomes a CH.

The algorithm is executed from all nodes to become either CHs or CMs. At the end of the formation of the first level of the hierarchy, nodes 3, 4, 5, 6, 12 and 15 are CHs. More specifically, nodes 1 and 2 have node 3 as CH; node 4 and 5 CHs, node 7 and 8 have node 6 as CH; node 9, 10 and 13 have node 12 as CH; and nodes 11 and 14 have node 5 as CH. This is also depicted in **Fig. 4**.

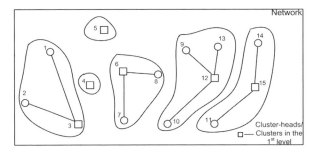

Fig. 4. 1st level of the hierarchy

The second level of hierarchies is formed by the elected CHs of the first level of hierarchy by executing the proposed algorithm again. The nodes that participate in the next level are: 3, 4, 5, 6, 12 and 15. After the algorithm execution, the formation of new clusters is depicted in **Fig. 5**.

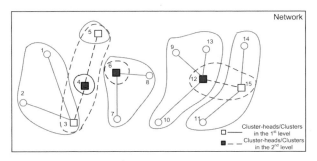

Fig. 5. 2nd level of the hierarchy

For the next level, the CHs of the previous level are selected, that is node 4, 6 and 12. From these, node 6 does not participate, since in the previous level it created a cluster with only itself. In this case, the specific hierarchy has already been completed. Each of the participating nodes receives attribute values from others. However, this is not possible in the considered case because the distance between nodes is greater than 1-hop. Therefore, node 4 and 12 are root CHs of the related hierarchies, as depicted in **Fig. 6**.

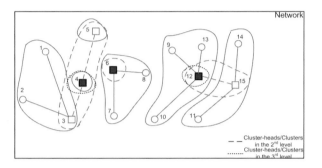

Fig. 6. 3rd level of the hierarchy

After determining roles, each node maintains registration tables, one for every level of hierarchy that participates. If a node is a CH, the registration table keeps the *IDs* of its CMs. If a node is a CM, the registration table keeps the *ID* of its CH. If a node creates a cluster by itself then, the table keeps its *ID*. **Table 3**, **Table 4** and **Table 5** present the registration table of the 1st, 2nd and 3rd level of the hierarchy.

Table 3. 1st level of hierarchy

N1	ID: 3	N2	ID: 3	N3	ID: 1 ID: 2	N4	ID: 4	N5	ID: 5
N6	ID: 8 ID: 7	N7	ID: 6	N8	ID: 6	N9	ID:12	N10	ID:12
N11	ID:15	N12	ID: 9 ID:10 ID:13	N13	ID:12	N14	ID:15	N15	ID:11 ID:14

A node uses its registration table to decide when it needs to re-cluster. Re-clustering takes place in case that the registration table of a node becomes empty. This means that if a node is CH, it re-clusters only when it loses contact with all its CMs. On the other hand, if it is a CM, it re-clusters when it loses contact to the CH. In any case, re-clustering is performed, locally, in the nodes neighborhood.

Table 4. 2nd level of the hierarchy

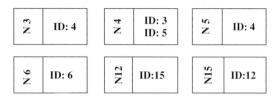

Table 5. 3rd level of the hierarchy

4 Evaluation

The proposed IDS architecture considers nodes' mobility in the formation of clusters in order to improve detection accuracy. In general, nodes' mobility decreases the detection accuracy by increasing false positives and negatives. This happens because an IDS cannot distinguish which changes in the network topology and routing tables are legitimate, caused by nodes mobility and which are the results of abnormal behaviors, provoked by malicious nodes. The proposed IDS tries to minimize these by creating clusters that includes nodes with similar direction and speed. Thus, mobile nodes of the same cluster appear more static to each other, eliminating in this way the negative effects of mobility in the detection accuracy.

Moreover, the distribution of detection load is based on the remaining energy in each node. Thus, nodes with adequate energy undertake more detection responsibilities than nodes with low power. In this way, the proposed IDS balances the energy consumption in a fair and efficient manner.

The proposed IDS also attempts to minimize the imposed communication and processing overhead, which disrupts the network operation. More specifically, it minimizes the processing overhead by employing detection engines only at some key nodes (i.e., CHs), while the remaining nodes do not use any detection engine. Although, in general, the creation and maintenance of clusters add extra processing workload to the network nodes, the clusters created by the proposed algorithm are as stable as possible and do not change frequently. In our approach the communication overhead is limited to the minimum since every CM is 1-hop away from its CH. The 1-hop distance is also valid in each level of the hierarchy among the CMs.

Another advantage of the proposed IDS is that it attempts to reduce the bandwidth consumption in each level of the hierarchy. As data travel up the levels of hierarchy, significant data reduction/aggregation may be possible at intermediate levels, reducing the bandwidth consumed in transit. Finally, the proposed IDS architecture tries to perform detection at the lower possible level of the hierarchy if sufficient audit data exist. In this way, it minimizes the bandwidth consumption and communication overhead by avoiding sending audit data to the higher levels.

On the other hand, a critical issue that should be investigated further lies in the fact that the proposed hierarchical IDS architecture may impose unfair workload distribution among the network nodes, since the nodes elected as CHs are overloaded with detection responsibilities. Another issue is that a malicious node or set of nodes may be elected as CHs hindering or misleading intrusion detection.

5 Conclusion

This paper presents a hierarchical cluster-based IDS architecture for MANETs that considers the mobility and energy of nodes in the cluster formation, in order to improve detection accuracy and reduce energy consumption. The proposed IDS architecture adopts and enhances the MEACA [12] algorithm which maximizes the clusters stability by choosing nodes with relatively low mobility and high energy to become CHs. The key advantage of the proposed IDS is that the mobile nodes of the same cluster appear more static to each other, eliminating in this way the negative effects of mobility in the detection accuracy. Moreover, the distribution of the detection load is based on the remaining energy of each node. Thus, nodes with adequate energy undertake more detection responsibilities than nodes with low power. In this way, the proposed IDS balances the energy consumption in a fair and efficient manner. Finally, it minimizes the communication overhead due to the 1-hop distance between a CH and its CMs. As a future work, we will conduct simulations to estimate the detection accuracy (also false positive, false negative) of the proposed IDS under various mobility and attacks scenarios.

References

1. Mishra, A., Nadkarni, K., Patcha, A.: Intrusion Detection in Wireless Ad Hoc Networks. IEEE Wireless Communications 11(1), 48–60 (2004)
2. Rafsanjani, M., Movaghar, A., Koroupi, F.: Investigating Intrusion Detection Sys-tems in MANET and Comparing IDS for Detecting Misbehaving Nodes. Proceeding of the World Academy of Science, Engineering and Technology 34, 351–355 (2008)
3. Anantvalee, T., Wu, J.: A survey on intrusion detection in mobile ad hoc networks. In: Xiao, Y., Shen, X., Du, D.-Z. (eds.) Wireless/Mobile Network Security, pp. 170–196. Springer, Heidelberg
4. Panos, C., Xenakis, C., Stavrakakis, I.: A Novel Intrusion Detection System for MANETs. In: Proc. of International Conference on Security and Cryptography (SECRYPT 2010), Athens, Greece (2010)
5. Ma, C., Fang, Z.: A Novel Intrusion Detection Architecture Based on Adaptive Selection Event Triggering for Mobile Ad-hoc Networks. In: Proc. IEEE Second International Symposium on Intelligent Information Technology and Security Informatics, pp. 198–201 (2009)
6. Otrok, H., Mohammed, N., Wang, L., Debbabi, M., Bhattacharya, P.: A game-theoretic intrusion detection model for mobile ad hoc networks. Elsevier Computer Communications 31(4), 708–721 (2008)
7. Marchang, N., Datta, R.: Collaborative techniques for intrusion detection in mo-bile ad hoc networks. Elsevier Ad Hoc Networks 6(4), 508–523 (2008)

8. Deng, H., Xu, R., Li, J., Zhang, F., Levy, R., Lee, W.: Agent-based cooperative anomaly detection for wireless ad hoc networks. In: Proc. of the 12th Conference on Parallel and Distributed Systems, pp. 613–620 (2006)

9. Manousakis, K., Sterne, D., Ivanic, N., Lawler, G., McAuley, A.: A stochastic approximation approach for improving intrusion detection data fusion structures. In: Proc. of IEEE Military Communications Conference (MILCOM 2008), San Diego, CA, pp. 1–7 (2008)

10. Sun, B., Wu, K., Xiao, Y., Wang, R.: Integration of mobility and intrusion detec-tion for wireless ad hoc networks. Wiley International Journal of Communication Systems 20(6), 695–721 (2007)

11. Sun, B., Wu, K., Pooch, U.W.: Routing anomaly detection in mobile ad hoc networks. In: Proc. of IEEE International Conference on Computer Communications and Networks (ICCCN 2003), pp. 25–31 (2003)

12. Xu, Y., Wang, W.: MEACA: Mobility and Energy Aware Clustering Algorithm for Constructing Stable MANETs. In: Proc. of IEEE Military Communications Conference (MILCOM 2006), Washington, D.C., pp. 1–7 (2006)

13. Xenakis, C., Panos, C., Stavrakakis, I.: A Comparative Evaluation of Intrusion De-tection Architectures for Mobile Ad Hoc Networks. Computers & Security 30(1), 63–80 (2011)

14. Leng, S., Zhang, Y., Chen, H., Zhang, L., Liu, K.: A Novel k-Hop Compound Met-ric Based Clustering Scheme for Ad Hoc Wireless Networks. IEEE Transactions On Wireless Communications 8(1), 367–375 (2009)

15. Lee, S.-J., Su, W., Gerla, M.: Ad hoc Wireless Multicast with. Mobility Prediction. In: Proc. of IEEE ICCCN 1999, Boston, pp. 4–9 (1999)

16. Gavalas, D., Konstantopoulos, C., Pantziou, G.: Mobility Prediction in Mobile Ad Hoc Networks. In: Pierre, S. (ed.) Next Generation Mobile Networks and Ubiquitous Compu-ting, ch. 21, pp. 226–240. IGI Global, USA (2010) ISBN10: 160566250X

An Evaluation of Anomaly-Based Intrusion Detection Engines for Mobile Ad Hoc Networks

Christoforos Panos[1], Christos Xenakis[2], and Ioannis Stavrakakis[1]

[1] Department of Informatics & Telecommunications, University of Athens, Greece
[2] Department of Digital Systems, University of Piraeus, Greece
{cpanos,ioannis}@di.uoa.gr, xenakis@unipi.gr

Abstract. Mobile Ad Hoc Networks are susceptible to a variety of attacks that threaten their operation and the provided services. Intrusion Detection Systems may act as defensive mechanisms, since they monitor network activities in order to detect malicious actions performed by intruders. Anomaly-based detection engines are a topic of ongoing interest in the research community, due to their advantage in detecting unknown attacks. However, this advantage is offset by a number of limitations such as high rates of false alarms, imposition of processing overhead, lack of adaptability under dynamic network conditions etc. This paper presents a comprehensive evaluation and comparison of the most recent literature in the area of anomaly detection for MANETs. The provided weaknesses and limitations, which are thoroughly examined in this paper, constitute open issues in the area of MANET security and will drive future research steps.

Keywords: Intrusion detection system, IDS engines, mobile ad hoc networks, MANETs, security, security attacks, anomaly-based detection, security vulnerabilities.

1 Introduction

A mobile ad hoc network (MANET) is a collection of autonomous nodes that form a dynamic, purpose-specific, multi-hop radio network in a decentralized and cooperative fashion. Their wireless and mobile nature in conjunction with the absence of access to a centralized authority makes them susceptible to a variety of attacks [1]. An effective way to identify whether an attack occurs in a MANET is the deployment of an Intrusion Detection System (IDS). An IDS monitors network activities and utilizes one or more detection engines, which determine if the monitored activity corresponds to a malicious or legitimate behavior. The detection engines can be classified into three main categories [2]: (i) signature-based engines, which rely on a predefined set of patterns to identify attacks; (ii) specification-based engines, which rely on a set of constrains (i.e., description of the correct operation of programs/protocols) and monitor the execution of programs/protocols with respect to these constraints; and (iii) anomaly-based engines, which rely on particular models (i.e., normal profiles) of nodes' behavior and mark nodes that deviate from these models as malicious.

S. Furnell, C. Lambrinoudakis, and G. Pernul (Eds.): TrustBus 2011, LNCS 6863, pp. 150–160, 2011.
© Springer-Verlag Berlin Heidelberg 2011

In general, anomaly-based detection consists of two phases: the training phase and the monitoring phase. During the training phase, which can be performed either offline (i.e., the network operation is simulated in a controlled environment, without actually deploying a MANET) or online (i.e., during the actual deployment of the MANET), the normal profile is created. Subsequently, during the monitoring phase, the engine monitors a set of carried activities (i.e., features) and compares them against the normal profile. The variation between them (i.e., monitored features and normal profile) is usually determined by utilizing statistical analysis, machine learning, or data mining techniques.

The majority of IDS literature in MANETs focuses on anomaly-based detection, due to its advantage in detecting unknown attacks. However, this advantage is offset by a number of limitations such as high rates of false alarms, imposition of processing overhead, lack of adaptability under dynamic network conditions, etc. These limitations stem from the fact that these engines were primarily inherited from static or mobile networks, which differ radically from MANETs. A number of recent publications attempt to address these limitations, through the introduction of several new mechanisms. On the other hand, little work has been done in evaluating and comparing these new approaches in anomaly detection. Existing surveying papers such as [16][17][18][19][20][21], either focus on outdated solutions, or mainly examine the architectural part of the studied IDSs and do not provide an analysis or evaluation of the deployed detection engines.

This paper presents a comprehensive analysis and evaluation of the most recent literature in the area of anomaly-based detection for MANETs. The works selected for evaluation introduce new mechanisms in anomaly-based detection, aiming to resolve existing limitations. For each evaluated detection engine, its functionality is considered and outlined as well as its advantages and weaknesses are elaborated. Furthermore, a comparison of the evaluated engines is performed using some critical evaluation metrics. These metrics derive from: (i) the deployment, architectural, and operational characteristics of MANETs; (ii) the functionality of anomaly-based detection; and (iii) the carried analysis that reveals the most important strengths as well as the limitations and weaknesses of the considered engines. The provided weaknesses and limitations, which are thoroughly examined in this paper, constitute open issues in the area of MANET security and will drive next research steps.

The rest of this article is organized as follows. In section 2, the selected anomaly-based detection engines for MANETs are analyzed and commented. Section 3, presents a comparative evaluation of the considered engines and finally, section 4 contains the conclusions.

2   Anomaly-Based Detection Engines for MANETs

This section presents and analyses the most recent anomaly-based detection engines that have been proposed for MANETs. For each engine, the basic functionality is outlined as well as the provided advantages and weaknesses are elaborated.

2.1 A Dynamic Anomaly Detection Scheme for AODV-Based MANETs

Nakayama et al. [3] have proposed an anomaly-based engine for detecting malicious actions that target the Ad-hoc On-demand Distance Vector (AODV) [14] routing protocol. The proposed engine utilizes machine learning in order to generate and maintain a normal profile and relies on principal component analysis (PCA) [4] for resolving malicious behaviors. PCA has been widely used in image compression and pattern recognition. It transforms n correlated random variables into $d \leq n$ uncorrelated variables. The uncorrelated variables (i.e., principal components) are linear combinations of the original variables and can be used to express the data in a reduced form.

In the proposed engine, an offline training phase is required to generate the initial normal profile. During this phase, N simulated nodes are monitored and a set of training data is collected, which subsequently forms the normal profile. Then, during the monitoring phase, the engine records a set of features (i.e., monitored data) from the network layer (e.g., route control packets, sender and destination information, etc.) in fixed-time intervals of five seconds. The recorded data are transformed into a $p -$ *dimension vector*, where p is the number of monitored features. In the sequel, using PCA on the normal profile, the first principal component is calculated, which reflects an approximate distribution of the normal profile. The first principal component is the linear combination of the original variables with the largest variance. On the other hand, by applying PCA on the collected data of the first monitored time slot, the deviation from the first principal component can be estimated. If this deviation exceeds a threshold M, the engine assumes that an attack takes place. Otherwise, the recorded data from the monitored time slot becomes the new normal profile. According to the authors, the computational complexity of this engine is $O(m_n \times p^2)$, where m_n represents the training data set for n monitored nodes and p is the number of monitored features.

The most important strength of this engine is the low rate of false positive alarms caused by dynamic network changes. This is achieved by dynamically updating the normal profile at runtime. However, this strength also causes the most important limitation of the engine. If, for example, in a monitored time slot the engine fails to detect a malicious behavior, while an attack(s) takes place (i.e., false negative) then, the attack(s) will become part of the normal profile. As a result, the attack(s) will remain undetected until the normal profile is updated again. In addition, updating the normal profile induces extra processing overhead, since the PCA has to be re-applied to the new normal profile. Another limitation results from the use of fixed-time monitoring slots, since the engine does not take advantage of correlations between features at nearby time slots. Finally, the proposed engine cannot be used to detect all the types of possible attacks, as it monitors features only at the network layer.

2.2 Cross-Layer Detection of Sinkhole Attacks in MANETs

J. Felix et al. [5] have proposed an anomaly-based engine for detecting sinking attacks (i.e., nodes that do not cooperate in the routing and forwarding operations of a network) in MANETs. The proposed engine utilizes a support vector machine (SVM) [6] classifier in order to distinguish malicious behaviors. SVM is a non-probabilistic binary linear classifier, which, given a training sample, builds a model that decides whether a new example falls within the same category as the training sample or not. According to the authors, the training process of the SVM has a computational complexity of $O(N^3)$, where N represents the number of training samples [5].

During the training phase, which takes place offline at a system with abundant resources [5], data are collected from the physical, medium access control (MAC) and network layers. Then, the collected training data are pre-processed using a data reduction process, which aims at reducing their size in order to be processed by SVM. The employed data reduction process includes three steps:

1. *Association*: collected data from different layers are correlated for associations, so that the number of features can be reduced.
2. *Feedback-Based Filtering*: uninformative and redundant features are removed.
3. *Feedback-Based Sampling*: data are further reduced by randomly selecting a subset of the original training data.

The training phase concludes with the application of SVM classifier on the reduced training data set. This produces a linear decision function, which is then used during the monitoring phase to resolve if a monitored event is legitimate or the result of a sinking attack.

The most important strength of this engine is the use of features from multiple layers, which may lead to increased detection accuracy. However, the application of data reduction process outweighs this advantage, since only 5 – 9 % of the original data features are used for training [5]. Usually, data reduction is used in engines that include online training, in order to conserve resources. On the contrary, the proposed engine uses offline training, which means that there are no limitations of resources. During training, the considered engine employs data reduction in order to make computationally feasible the use of the SVM classifier in MANETs, limiting in that way the information gain from the collected multi-layer data and thus, the associated advantages.

2.3 A Two-Stage Anomaly Detection Engine for MANETs

Adrian Lauf et al. [7] have proposed a two-stage, anomaly-based detection engine that aims at operating in resource-constrained environments such as MANETs. The proposed engine can be divided into two stages: in the first stage detection is performed by the maxima detection system (MDS), while in the second by the cross-correlative detection system (CCDS). MDS is used to rapidly identify a potential threat as well as to calibrate a threshold for CCDS, while CCDS is used to accurately detect the source(s) of threat, as well as to detect multiple attacks simultaneously.

During the training phase, a normal profile is created offline. The monitored set of features consists of a set of application-level interactions, each of which corresponds to a specific function or behavior of the normal network operation. In the monitoring phase, MDS is deployed initially, which monitors and logs all application interactions in a history table. Then, MDS performs an analysis of global and local maxima in the probability density functions (PDF) of the monitored behaviors to isolate deviations from the normal profile. If a deviation is detected, MDS traverses the history table to locate the node that statistically has the greatest contribution to the local maximum in the PDF and then calls CCDS.

CCDS performs detection by calculating individual PDFs for each node (based on data from the history log) and comparing them to a threshold. However, the threshold must be first calibrated through a transition period, before accurate detection can be performed. Initially, (transition period) the threshold of CCDS is set up to represent 100% deviation and then, both MDS and CCDS run simultaneously. If a suspected node is detected by MDS, CCDS check whether this node is included in the set of deviant nodes it detects too. If it is not, the corresponding threshold for the CCDS is reduced. This calibration procedure (i.e., indication of malicious behaviors, check MDS and CCDS results, and threshold adjustments) is repeated until there is a match between MDS and CCDS. If this is the case, the transition period (threshold calibration) ends, and the CCDS, properly calibrated, starts operating as described by the engine's specifications.

The proposed engine minimizes the consumption of resource, as it mainly employs the lightweight MDS detection mechanism, while the more computationally demanding CCDS is only executed when needed. It may also provide increased detection accuracy, compared to other single detection engines, because the two employed detection mechanisms supplement each other. However, the MDS feedback in the calibration of the CCDS threshold may result in improper threshold's tuning and thus, reduced overall detection accuracy. This is due to the fact that different attacks may present different application-level behaviors and thus, a single attack detected by MDS cannot be used to set up a generic/cumulative threshold in CCDS. Finally, the proposed engine is prone to high rates of false positives in cases that dynamic changes on the network occur, since the normal profile of MDS is static.

2.4 Anomaly Detection Engine with Optimal Features

P. Kabiri et al. [8] have proposed an anomaly-based engine that focuses on detecting denial of service attacks (DoS). The proposed engine shares a number of similarities with [3] analyzed in sect. 2.1. More specifically, it utilizes machine learning to generate and maintain a normal profile, and relies on PCA for resolving malicious behaviors. However, in the considered engine, the training phase (which takes place online) builds one normal profile for each neighboring node. Furthermore, the monitored features used by the engine are selected after evaluation, which reveals the features with the highest information gain in detecting DoS attacks.

The most important strength of this engine is that it limits the overhead of gathering and processing data, by using a set of optimal features, since it performs the training process online. However, the authors do not clarify how those data, which are collected during the training process, represent a node's normal operation. If dynamic changes in the network occur, the engine is prone to high rates of false positives (or even no detection at all) as well as presents increased processing and memory overhead. This is because the list of neighbors constantly changes, forcing the detection engine to build a new normal profile for each new neighboring node, without enough time to complete the training phase. Another limitation results from the use of fixed-time monitoring slots, and thus, the engine does not take advantage of correlations between features at nearby time slots.

2.5 Adaptive Anomaly Detection of Denial of Service Attacks

A. Nadeem and M. Howarth [9] have proposed an anomaly-based engine for detecting DoS attacks in MANETs. The proposed engine utilizes a dynamic normal profile and relies on statistical analysis for resolving malicious behaviors. In the training phase, which takes place after network initialization, the engine counts incoming route request packets and calculates the probability distribution of the collected data. The authors assume that during training the behavior of a newly created network is free of anomalies. Subsequently, during the monitoring phase, the engine: (a) logs incoming route request packets, in five-second intervals; (b) calculates the probability distribution of the collected data; and (c) compares it with that of the normal profile, using the chi-square test [10]. If the distribution of the collected data does not fit the normal profile then, the observed behavior is considered suspicious. Whenever a suspicious behavior is detected, a counter is incremented and the node responsible for the symptom is marked as suspicious. If the incident repeats and the counter exceeds a threshold value within a fixed time window, the node from where the incident originates is labeled as malicious. Finally, if no suspicious behavior is detected within the monitored time interval, the collected data become the new normal profile.

The most important strength of this engine is the low rate of false positive alarms caused by dynamic network changes. This is achieved by dynamically updating the normal profile at runtime and employing a threshold mechanism in which only recurring malicious behaviors are considered as attacks. However, similarly to [3] (see sect. 2.1), if in a monitored time slot the detection engine fails to detect a malicious behavior, while an attack(s) takes place (i.e., false negative) then, the attack(s) will become part of the normal profile. As a result, the attack(s) will remain undetected until the normal profile is updated again. The authors assume that during initialization the network is free of attacks, but this assumption can be considered misleading. Furthermore, the online execution of the training phase induces extra processing overhead. Malicious nodes may attempt to exploit the threshold mechanism by performing sporadic attacks considering not exceeding the threshold values and raising alarms. Another limitation arises from the use of a fixed-time monitoring slot, since the engine does not take advantage of correlations between features at nearby time slots. Finally, the proposed engine is only capable of detecting DoS attacks.

3 Comparative Evaluation

This section provides a comparative evaluation of the studied anomaly-based detection engines for MANETS using some critical evaluation metrics. These metrics derive from: (i) the deployment, architectural, and operational characteristics of MANETs; (ii) the functionality of anomaly-based detection; and (iii) the carried analysis that reveals the most important strengths, weaknesses and limitations of the latest anomaly-based detection engines for MANETs (see table 1).

MANETs retain a number of differences from traditional wireless networks. First, MANET nodes can be a variety of mobile devices (such as laptops, handheld devices, or mobile phones), which typically rely on the use of battery power and present various computational, memory, and bandwidth capabilities. The mobile nature of those nodes creates dynamic network topologies, in which nodes may independently join, leave or change their position. Moreover, the absence of access points that connect the nodes to any centralized authority does not leave much room for a clear line of defense or for a high level of trust between nodes. As a result, MANET nodes are susceptible to a variety of attacks, which mainly target the transport, network and data-link layers of the protocol stack, since these layers are responsible for the most critical functionality of MANETs (i.e., one-hop/multi-hop communication, routing, etc.) [2].

On the other hand, anomaly-based detection requires the execution of: (i) a training phase in which the normal profile is created; and (ii) a monitoring phase in which malicious behaviors are resolved. The training phase can take place either online or offline and the resulting normal profile can be static or dynamic. During the monitoring phase, the features, collected in fixed-time intervals, indicate the type and range of malicious behaviors and actions, detected by the engine.

It is evident that anomaly-based detection engines for MANETs have to be *adaptable to dynamic network changes*, which means that their normal profile should always represent the normal network operation. However, in [7] and [9] the normal profile is static including only the initial conditions of the network when the normal profile is created. This may lead to high rates of false positives when dynamic changes on the network occur, since these changes are not incorporated into the normal profile and therefore, are falsely considered as results of malicious behaviors. In order to address this limitation, several detection engines [3][5][8] utilize dynamically updated normal profiles, which attempt to reduce the rate of false positive alarms, caused by dynamic network changes. However, this approach also creates an important limitation: if in a monitored time slot the detection engine fails to detect a malicious behavior, while an attack(s) takes place (i.e., false negative) then, the attack(s) will become part of the normal profile. Thus, these attack(s) will be undetected.

Table 1. A summary of the studied anomaly-based detection engines

IDS engine	Methodology	Strengths	Weaknesses
Dynamic detection for AODV	Dynamic profile using PCA analysis	Adaptability to network changes	False negatives become part of the normal profile
			Induces extra processing overhead
			Monitors a fixed time slot
			Cannot detect all possible attacks
Cross-layer detection of sinkhole attacks	Cross-layer data reduction and use of SVM classifier	Cross-layer monitoring	No benefits from the data reduction process
			Can only detect sinking attacks

Table 1. (*continued*)

Two-stage IDS	Scalable use of two detection engines (MDS and CCDS)	Increased detection accuracy by employing two detection engines	The ratio of false positives and detection accuracy are negatively affected by high nodes' mobility
		Scalability	
		Incurs less processing overhead	There is no way to adjust an improperly tuned threshold
Optimal feature based IDS	Dynamic profile using PCA analysis	Uses an optimal set of features	The ratio of false positives and detection accuracy are negatively affected by high nodes' mobility
		Incurs less processing overhead	Monitors a fixed time slot
			Can only detect DoS attacks
Adaptive IDS	Dynamic profile using statistical analysis	Adaptability to network changes	False negatives become part of the normal profile
			Monitors a fixed time slot
			Malicious nodes may attempt to exploit the threshold mechanism
			Incurs extra processing overhead
			Can only detect DoS attacks

Another approach to address the limitation of the static normal profiles is through the use of thresholds [7][9]. In this approach, periodic symptoms of suspicious behaviors, mainly caused by network topology changes, remain under the detection thresholds; while malicious behaviors that are constant exceed the thresholds indicating the occurrence of attacks. Nevertheless, the use of thresholds introduces new security weaknesses, since malicious nodes may exploit this mechanism by performing an attack(s) considering not exceeding the threshold values and raising alarms.

Since MANETs are typically formed by devices with limited processing and communication capabilities, the *processing overhead* imposed by the detection engines to the underlying network nodes should be kept to a minimum. However, the majority of the evaluated detection engines induce computational overhead of approximately polynomial-time complexity [3][5][8]. Therefore, their deployment is computationally feasible only if the set of monitored features is extensively reduced. As a result, the detection engines are only *capable of detecting a limited set of possible attacks*, and thus, do not constitute comprehensive security solutions. An exception is the two-stage detection engine [7], which attempts to minimize the processing overhead through a scalable detection mechanism. Finally, an approach to further reduce the computational overhead of the detection engine is proposed in [8]. In this approach, the set of monitored features is reduced through an evaluation process, which reveals the features with the highest information gain in detecting DoS attacks.

Summarizing, we can deduce that that the considered anomaly-based detection engines for MANETs share a number of limitations (see table 1). In particular, the majority of them have not resolved the issue of high rates of false positives under conditions of high nodes' mobility. Furthermore, in all of them (except for [7]) it is computationally infeasible to process a broad set of features, and thus, they are only capable of detecting a limited type and range of attacks. Finally, the engines that employ online training impose computational overhead to the network nodes.

In future work, more research effort should be given in the optimization of existing anomaly detection algorithms, as well as the introduction of new ones, which will enable the monitoring of larger sets of features. Furthermore, a number of limitations presented in detection engines might be addressed by utilizing the characteristics of the employed IDS architectures. For example, in a signature-based detection engine, the distribution and maintenance of a signature database under a MANET environment is a difficult task, due to the network's unique characteristics. However, Sterne et al. [22] have proposed an IDS, based on a hierarchical architecture, that addresses this limitation. In the proposed scheme, the detection engine takes advantage of the hierarchical IDS architecture in order to efficiently distribute and update signatures.

Specification-based detection engines constitute another promising alternative to anomaly-based detection. They are capable of detecting both known and unknown attacks, and they avoid high rates of false alarms, since they do not rely on normal profiles, as happens in anomaly detection. However, the development of specifications for an engine might be a lengthy and convoluted process, since the developer has to determine what is the expected behavior of each individual application and protocol, and then, develop constrains that characterize this behavior. Therefore, specification-based engines for MANETs have seen limited use, as they are employed to monitor only the network layer for routing attacks [11][12][13]. Nevertheless, the required overhead of developing specification can be reduced, since the un-hindered operation of MANETs relies on a specific set of protocols at the transport, network and data-link layer, where the majority of security attacks occur [1]. Moreover, aggregated specifications may be developed exploiting cross-layer features among the transport, network and link layer that provide the main functionality of MANETs. Finally, another possibility that should be explored is the development of hybrid detection engines that combine the advantages of more than one type of engines, aiming to eliminate the related drawbacks. This will be facilitated if we consider the special deployment and operational characteristics of MANETs, as well as the attacks that target them.

4   Conclusions

Intrusion detection algorithms for MANETs have attracted much attention recently and thus, there are many publications that propose new IDS solutions or improvements to the existing. This paper presented a comprehensive evaluation of the most recent literature in the area of anomaly detection for MANETs. For each of the considered engines, its functionality was outlined as well as its advantages and weaknesses were elaborated. Furthermore, the studied detection engines were comparatively evaluated based on the following evaluation metrics: (i) the adaptability to dynamic network changes, (ii) the imposition of processing overhead, and (iii) the type and range of possible attacks that they detect. These metrics were derived from the deployment, architectural, and operational characteristics of MANETs; the functionality of anomaly detection; and the carried analysis. The evaluation revealed that the most recent anomaly-based detection engines for MANETs still present significant limitations and weaknesses. In particular, the majority of them rely on a limited set of features in order to make their deployment computationally feasible on MANETs. Therefore, they detect a limited type and range of attacks. The detection accuracy of several proposed engines is negatively affected by nodes' mobility, encountered in MANETs. This can be addressed through the use of dynamic normal profiles and thresholds. However, these solutions may be exploited by malicious nodes allowing for attacks to remain undetected. Future research endeavors might address these limitations if they achieve a reduction in the computational complexity of anomaly detection algorithms. Other directions that can be followed include the utilization of the employed IDS architectures, the shift of development to other promising detection approaches (such as specification-based detection), and the use of hybrid detection schemes that attempt to combine the advantages of different detection engines.

References

[1] Djenouri, D., Khelladi, L., Badache, N.: A Survey of Security Issues in Mobile Ad Hoc Networks. IEEE Communications Surveys 7(4) (Fourth Quarter 2005)

[2] Xenakis, C., Panos, C., Stavrakakis, I.: A comparative evaluation of intrusion detection architectures for mobile ad hoc networks. Computers & Security 30(1) (January 2011)

[3] Nakayama, H., Kurosawa, S., Jamalipour, A., Nemoto, Y., Kato, N.: A Dynamic Anomaly Detection Scheme for AODV-Based Mobile Ad Hoc Networks. IEEE Transactions on Vehicular Technology 58(5), 2471–2481 (2009)

[4] Duda, R., Hart, P., Stork, D.: Pattern Classification and Scene Analysis. Wiley, New York (1973)

[5] Joseph, J.F.C., Lee, B.-S., Das, A., Seet, B.-C.: Cross-Layer Detection of Sinking Behavior in Wireless Ad Hoc Networks Using SVM and FDA. IEEE Transactions on Dependable and Secure Computing 8(2), 233–245 (2011)

[6] Nello, C., John, S.-T.: An Introduction to Support Vector Machines and Other Kernel-Based Learning Methods. Cambridge Univ. Press, Cambridge (2000)

[7] Lauf, A., Peters, R.A., Robinson, W.H.: A Distributed Intrusion Detection System for Resource-Constrained Devices in Ad Hoc Networks. Elsevier Journal of Ad Hoc Networks 8(3), 253–266 (2010)

[8] Kabiri, P., Aghaei, M.: Feature Analysis for Intrusion Detection in Mobile Ad-hoc Networks. International Journal of Network Security 12(2), 80–87 (2011)

[9] Nadeem, A., Howarth, M.: Adaptive intrusion detection and prevention of denial of service attacks in MANETs. In: International Conference on Wireless Communications and Mobile Computing: Connecting the World Wirelessly, Leipzig, Germany, pp. 926–930 (2009)

[10] Lancaster, H.O.: The Chi-Squared Distribution. Wiley Publications in Statistics (1969)

[11] Tseng., C.-Y., et al.: A specification-based intrusion detection system for AODV. In: Proc. Of ACM Workshop on Security of Ad Hoc and Sensor Networks (2003)

[12] Tseng, C.H., Song, T., Balasubramanyam, P., Ko, C., Levitt, K.N.: A specification-based intrusion detection model for OLSR. In: Valdes, A., Zamboni, D. (eds.) RAID 2005. LNCS, vol. 3858, pp. 330–350. Springer, Heidelberg (2006)

[13] Hassan, H., Mahmoud, M., El-Kassas, S.: Securing the AODV protocol using specification-based intrusion detection. In: Proceedings of the 2nd ACM International Workshop on Quality of Service & Security for Wireless and Mobile Networks, Terromolinos, Spain (2006)

[14] Perkins, C., Belding-Royer, E., Das, S.: Ad hoc On-Demand Distance Vector (AODV) Routing. IETF RFC 3561 (July 2003)

[15] Sun, B., Wu, K., Xiao, Y., Wang, R.: Integration of mobility and intrusion detection for wireless ad hoc networks. Wiley International Journal of Communication Systems 20(6), 695–721 (2007)

[16] Sun, B., Osborne, L., Yang, X., Guizani, S.: Intrusion Detection Techniques in Mobile Ad Hoc and Wireless Sensor Networks. IEEE Wireless Communications 14(5), 56–63 (2007)

[17] Mishra, A., Nadkarni, K., Patcha, A.: Intrusion Detection in Wireless Ad Hoc Networks. IEEE Wireless Communications 11(1), 48–60 (2004)

[18] Azer, M.A., El-Kassas, S.M., El-Soudani, M.S.: A Survey on Anomaly Detection Methods for Ad hoc Networks. Ubiquitous Computing and Communication Journal 2(3), 67–76 (2005)

[19] Li, Y., Wei, J.: Guidelines on Selecting Intrusion Detection Methods in MANET. In: The 21st Annual Conference for Information Systems Educators (ISECON), Rhode Island, USA, November 4-7 (2004)

[20] Sen, S., Clark, J.A.: Intrusion Detection in Mobile Ad Hoc Networks. In: Misra, S., Woungang, I., Misra, S.C. (eds.) Guide to Wireless Ad Hoc Networks. Springer, Heidelberg (2009)

[21] Anantvalee, T., Wu, J.: A Survey on Intrusion Detection in Mobile Ad Hoc Networks. In: Wireless/Mobile Network Security, ch. 7, pp. 170–196. Springer, Heidelberg (2006)

[22] Sterne, D., Balasubramanyam, P., Carman, D., Wilson, B., Talpade, R., Ko, C., Balupari, R., Tseng, C.-Y., Bowen, T., Levitt, K., Rowe, J.: A General Cooperative Intrusion Detection Architecture for MANETs. In: Proceedings of the Third IEEE International Workshop on Information Assurance, pp. 57–70 (2007)

Privacy Measures for Free Text Documents: Bridging the Gap between Theory and Practice

Liqiang Geng, Yonghua You, Yunli Wang, and Hongyu Liu

National Research Council of Canada, Institute for Information Technology,
46 Dineen Drive, Fredericton, Canada E3B 9W4
{Liqiang.Geng,Yonghua.You,Yunli.Wang,
Hongyu.Liu}@nrc.gc.ca

Abstract. Privacy compliance for free text documents is a challenge facing many organizations. Named entity recognition techniques and machine learning methods can be used to detect private information, such as personally identifiable information (PII) and personal health information (PHI) in free text documents. However, these methods cannot measure the level of privacy embodied in the documents. In this paper, we propose a framework to measure the privacy content in free text documents. The measure consists of two factors: the probability that the text can be used to uniquely identify a person and the degree of sensitivity of the private entities associated with the person. We then instantiate the framework in the scenario of detection and protection of PHI in medical records, which is a challenge for many hospitals, clinics, and other medical institutions. We did experiments on a real dataset to show the effectiveness of the proposed measure.

Keywords: Privacy compliance, ontology, privacy measure, personal health information.

1 Introduction

Privacy compliance has been an important issue that faces most organizations, as more and more privacy legislation and organizational privacy policies became mandatory. It is especially difficult, yet important, for organizations to reinforce privacy compliance on free text documents due to the following reasons. First, approximately 80% of corporate data is in free text format. Secondly, the free text documents are more easily accessed and transmitted than structured data stored in databases. Thirdly, technically it is more challenging to deal with privacy in free text documents where no data schema is available.

Natural language processing and machine learning techniques can be used to identify private entities, such as persons' names, email addresses, telephone numbers. heath records, and credit card numbers. Korba et al. proposed to use named entity recognition to identify private entities and use machine learning method to extract relations between the private entities [1]. That solution is based on the assumption that if one or more of the private entities and their proprietor's name are found in a

S. Furnell, C. Lambrinoudakis, and G. Pernul (Eds.): TrustBus 2011, LNCS 6863, pp. 161–173, 2011.

document, the document is considered as containing private information. A drawback of this method is that it may retrieve huge number of documents as containing private information as long as these documents contain a person's name and his/her private entities. However, among the retrieved documents, only a small proportion may be practically considered as real private information. Furthermore, this method only classifies the documents into two categories: containing private information and not containing private information. Sokolova and Emam did a similar work that proposed a two-phase approach to identify personal health information (PHI). In the first phase, personally identifiable information (PII) is detected. In the second phase, the PHI is detected. They also proposed two measures to evaluate their approach. [2]. However, the method does not measure the degree of private information contained in the medical documents either.

Defining privacy measures to evaluate privacy levels in documents has several advantages. First, privacy measures can be used as a standard for de-identification and de-sensitivity. De-identification and de-sensitivity require that privacy should be protected while as much information can be released for data analysis as possible, i.e., to balance the private information protection and the quality of information released for data analysis. For example, the user may set a privacy degree threshold to determine if a document may be released. If the value of the privacy measure for a document is above the threshold, the system should remove some private entities until the privacy measure of the document is below the threshold. Second, when huge numbers of documents containing privacy are detected, privacy measures can rank them so that the privacy experts may focus on documents with more serious private information.

In this paper we present a method to measure the private information in free text documents and to address the above-mentioned difficulties in practice. Section 2 reviews the related work. Section 3 presents the theoretic framework for measuring privacy in free text. Sections 4 uses PHI as a case study to show how this framework can be implemented in the case of personal health records. Section 5 presents preliminary experimental results. Section 6 concludes the paper.

2 Related Work

Much work has been done on privacy compliance for structured data, i.e., databases. In the scenario of databases, each record in a data table corresponds to the personal information for an individual person. The attributes of the table are classified into quasi-identifying attributes (QIA) and sensitive attributes (SA). QIAs are those that can be used to identify a person, for example, a person's name, address, and so on. SAs are those that contain sensitive information for a person, the disclosure of which may result in harm to the person. SAs include diseases a person has, credit rating a person receives, and so on. The concepts of K-anonymity and L-diversity were proposed as the standards for privacy information release. K-anonymity requires generalization of each record such that it is not distinguishable with at least K other records in terms of QIAs [3]. L-diversity requires that each equivalence class in terms of the QIAs contains at least L "well represented" SA values, so as to reduce the probability of a person's sensitive information disclosure [4]. An alternative standard to deal with sensitive values is called *t*-closeness, which requires that the distance between the distribution of sensitive attribute values in each equivalence class and that of the attribute values in the entire table is no more than a threshold *t* [5]. Although these studies are focused on the procedures of de-identification and de-sensitivity, and did not explicitly mention the privacy measures, the number of the records in each equivalence class and the diversity of sensitive values in each equivalence class can be considered as factors to measure privacy content for each record in the databases.

In the case of free text, Al-Fedaghi proposed a theoretical definition for measuring private information [6]. In that framework, every assertion involving a person is considered as a unit of private information. The privacy index regarding each person then is defined as $\dfrac{priv\_u + 1}{priv\_k * pers}$, where *priv_u* denotes the number of units of the person's private information unknown to others, *priv_k* denotes the number of units of his/her private information known to others, and *pers* denotes the number of the persons that know his/her information. This measure is not suitable for practical implementation, since it is impossible to estimate what portion of a person's private information is known or unknown to other people, and how many people know his/her private information.

Fule P. and Roddick proposed a practical method to evaluate the sensitivity of the privacy in the rules obtained from data mining [7]. They specify a sensitivity value for each attribute or attribute-value pair in the rules and proposed various combination functions to calculate the sensitivity values for the rules. However, their approach requires that the sensitivity value for each attribute or attribute-value pair must be specified by users. This is not practical for domains with huge number of attribute-value pairs. Also it does not consider the semantic relationship between the attribute-value pairs.

Literature survey shows that far less research has been done for measuring privacy in free text than in databases. This may be due to the difficulties for measuring privacy in free text documents. First, in databases, the probability of identifying a person in a table is solely based on the information within the table itself. In the case of free text, we have to resort to external sources to determine this probability. Secondly, in the databases, the data is structured and the QIAs and the SAs are already known. In the free text, the sensitive information has to be identified first using some technologies, such as information extraction. Thirdly, sensitive information in free text may involve different entity types, and more sensitive values may be derived based on the information occurred in the documents. For example, with some basic medical knowledge, adversaries can infer that a person is infected with AIDS if cocktail treatment is mentioned in his/her medical record, even if AIDS is not explicitly mentioned.

3   Framework for Privacy Measures

As in the database scenario, we identified two factors for determining privacy degree in free text: quasi-identifying entities (QIE) and sensitive entities (SE). The QIEs refer to the entities that can be used to identify a specific person. They include persons' names, genders, ages, races, weight, height, addresses, and so on. The more likely a set of QIEs can uniquely identify a person, the more privacy these QIEs contain. For example, the statement "Tom is HIV positive" has lower privacy degree than "Tom, who lives in Yonge Street, Toronto, is HIV positive", because the second statement has one more QIE "Yonge Street, Toronto" which may reduce the scope of the candidates and further help identify the person "Tom". Similarly, the statement "David is HIV positive" has lower privacy degree than "Burt is HIV positive" because fewer people are named Burt than those named David.

Formally, let n denote the number of the persons in the universe matching the QIEs in a document. The probability of identifying a particular person satisfying the QIEs is $1/n$. The difficulty in calculating this probability is that there is not a table available that contains all personal information for all the individuals in the world. In the next section, we propose to use web search engines to obtain an estimate for this probability.

The SEs may include diseases, medication, bank account numbers, bank account passwords, religions and so on. The degree of sensitivity for SEs entities can be both objective and subjective. For example, the statement "John is diagnosed with heart disease" is more sensitive than "John suffers from a cold" in the sense that the former statement may incur more personal loss for the individual, such as the increased life insurance premiums and reduced employment opportunities. In this sense, the sensitive degree can be evaluated with objective measures. On the other hand, whether the statement "John was put into the prison" is more sensitive than "John suffers from AIDS" depends on social and cultural factors that may not be objectively measured. In our framework, we consider the degree of sensitivity to be subjective and determined by the privacy experts, since it is difficult to define comprehensive objective measures on different types of SEs. To overcome the bias of the subjective sensitivity values from an expert, a practical way is to let a few privacy experts assign the values to the SEs independently and resolve the inconsistency through discussion.

When the number of SEs in a domain is huge, it is not practical to ask the experts to manually assign the sensitivity values for all the SEs, therefore an ontology is desirable to provide the degree of sensitivity for each SE and to conduct inferences among these entities.

Although the sensitivity values for the SEs are to be determined by the users, the assignment of these values should not be arbitrary due to the semantic relationship between these entities. We propose some principles for ensuring consistency between the SEs.

Let A, B, and $C \in SE$ denote the SEs, which are organized in an ontology. Let S denote the degree of sensitivity, which is a function $S: 2^{SE} \rightarrow [0, 1]$. We define five principles for assigning sensitivity values as follows.

1. $0 \leq S(A) \leq 1$
2. $A \leq B \Rightarrow S(A) \geq S(B)$
3. $\max(S(A), S(B)) \leq S(A, B)$
4. $A \leq B \Rightarrow S(A, B) = S(A)$
5. $A \leq B \Rightarrow S(A, C) \geq S(B, C)$

Principle 1 specifies that a sensitivity value should be a normalized positive real value between 0 and 1, with 0 representing no privacy and 1 representing highest degree of privacy. Principle 2 states that if entity A is more specific than B in the ontology, A is considered to be more sensitive than B. For example, date of birth is more sensitive than the year of birth. Principle 3 says that the combination of two sensitive entities is more sensitive than or equally sensitive with the maximum sensitivity of each of them considered alone. For example, the combination of the bank account number and password are far more sensitive than each of the two entities alone. Principle 4 states that if between two entities, one is more general than the other, the former does not contribute to the overall sensitivity. Principle 5 states that a more general entity introduces less sensitivity than a more specific one when combined with other entities.

Principles 1 and 2 specify the consistency among the entities defined in ontology, which may be represented in a tree or a graph. The other three principles are useful in deriving sensitivity values for compound entities. A composition function f is needed to calculate the sensitivity values for compound entities. For example, suppose we set $S(diabetes) = 0.6$, $S(heart\ attack) = 0.9$. Then $S(diabetes,\ heart\ attack) = f(S(diabetes), S(heart\ attack))$ may yield a sensitivity value of 0.95.

Adversaries usually have background knowledge and could conduct inferences on the SEs in the documents. For example, if *cocktail treatment* is mentioned as a medical procedure for a person, it is highly likely that this person was infected with *AIDS*.

Let D denote a document and $Ent(D)$ denote the SEs contained in the document. By applying inference rules, we can get the closure of $Ent(D)$, denoted as $Closure(D)$. Then we can calculate the sensitivity value $S(Closure(D))$ for the document D.

The procedure for calculating the privacy measure for a free text document is as follows.

1. Preprocess: Extract QIEs and the SEs in the document, identify relations between entities.
2. Calculate the probability p that a person can be identified with the QIEs.
3. Use inference rules and ontology to obtain the closure of SEs for the document.
4. Remove the entities that are a more general entity of another entity in the closure.
5. Calculate the sensitivity value s for the closure
6. The privacy measure is calculated with $privacy = p * s$.

It should be noted that theoretically the QIEs and SEs are not necessarily exclusive to each other. For example, *date of birth* may be used as a QIE to identify a person and it also can be considered as a SE that may be used for fraud.

4   Calculating Privacy Measures for PHI

In this section, we use PHI as an example to illustrate the implementation of the proposed framework for calculating privacy measures.

4.1 Using WEB Search Engine to Estimate the Probability of Identifying a Person

When we calculate privacy measures, a difference between the database scenario and the free text scenario is that the former (for example, *l*-diversity for database) assumes that the adversary has the background knowledge about QI information of the target person, and also knows that the person's information is stored in the database table, while the latter assumes that the adversary only knows some QI information of the target person and does not know whether the file matching the QI information refers to the target person. Therefore, we need to model the adversary's background knowledge about the demographic statistics for the free text scenario. This is one of the challenging tasks for defining the privacy measures for free text documents. Using published demographic database for the modeling may be a solution. However, there are two problems. First, the published demographic databases are usually generalized. If we use them, we have to calculate the estimates of the real distributions at the more detailed level. For example, in [8], distribution over date of birth is estimated based on the real distribution over year of birth. However, this calculated distribution may be distorted from the real one. Secondly, no tables contain all kinds of QI information that can be identified from a free text document, such as color of hair.

Inspired by [9], [10], we adopt the Web as a knowledge base to estimate the probability of uniquely identifying a person given QIEs. First, the QIEs are identified. Then all the QIEs are concatenated as a string delimited by spaces. Finally it is submitted as keywords to a search engine, such as Google, to retrieve the number of the web pages containing these keywords. We use the inverse of the number as the estimate of the probability. This probability is not accurate for any inference, but would be enough to represent the relative strength to rank the QI information.

At the current stage, we do not take into account the information in the related documents when we calculate the privacy measure for a document.

In our study, we consider the following QIEs which are directly associated with a person: *name, age, date of birth, telephone number, email address, address* and *gender*. Other entities that may help identify the person, but are not directly associated with the person, including person's parents' names, spouse's name, time of admission to a hospital, travel date, and so on, are not considered in our work.

4.2 Calculating Sensitivity of Diseases

Some studies use information gain obtained by information disclosure to measure the sensitivity of privacy. For example, Lonpre and Kreinovich [11] used the financial loss to measure the sensitivity of diseases. However, in order to calculate the information gains and utility losses, we must know the related probability distribution for all diseases and financial losses due to disclosure of the diseases. This is practically impossible. Kobsa argues that the further a value is from the normal value, the more privacy the value contains [12]. Also he argues that entities with lower probabilities are more sensitive than the entities with higher probabilities because they can be considered as anomalies [12]. However, this model also needs all probability distributions among each kind of the entities, and hence it is not practical for implementation.

In this study, we consider sensitivity levels of SEs as subjective because it is determined by social, economic, and cultural factors. For example, a person's age is considered as privacy in North America, but maybe not in some Asian countries. Therefore, we ask the user to specify the sensitivity values for each disease. Our solution consists of three steps. First, the user specifies the sensitivity values to medical terms in an ontology. Then the system extracts medical terms from a document and maps them to the ontology to get the sensitivity values for the terms. Next, the system uses inference and aggregation to calculate the sensitivity value for the document. We used MeSH in our case study. MeSH is a medical ontology that records terms for diseases, medications, procedures, etc. and shows the relationship between them [13]. The terms in MeSH are organized in a tree with root node representing the most general concept and the leaf nodes representing the most specific ones. Our goal is to associate a sensitivity value for each disease in MeSH. Since currently there are more than 10,000 concepts representing diseases in MeSH, it is tedious to assign the values for all diseases. We first specify the default values for all the disease to 0. Then the user can change the default settings for the diseases that are more important from privacy perspective. For example, the user may change the sensitivity value for AIDS to 1.0 and that for lung cancer to 0.9. After the new values are specified, they will be propagated to other concepts. The propagation of sensitivity values should observe the principles proposed in Section 2. We propose an algorithm for sensitivity value propagation, which is shown in Figure 1.

The algorithm first checks the consistency of the initially assigned sensitivity values, i.e., the sensitivity value of a parent node should not be greater than that of a child node. Then the algorithm propagates the sensitivity values upward. Finally, it propagates the sensitivity values downward to populate the entire tree.

We can prove that if the initial assignment is consistent (satisfying principle 1 and 2), the sensitivity values obtained from our propagation algorithm will also satisfy principles 1 and 2. It is straightforward that downward propagation observes principles 1 and 2. We only need to prove that two principles also hold for upward propagation.

Proof using induction:

It is straightforward that the first propagation observes principles 1 and 2.

Suppose that the first k propagations observe principles 1 and 2. For the $(k+1)$th propagation, we only need to prove that in the chosen path, the top node t's sensitivity value is less than its bottom node p's sensitivity value (Figure 2). Suppose t's sensitivity value was obtained by propagation from another node s to node q, which means that t is between s and q. Since path $(s\ q)$ was chosen over path $(p\ q)$, according to the algorithm, the increment in the path $(s\ q)$ is smaller than the increment over the path $(p\ q)$. We have $\dfrac{s_p - s_q}{d(p,q)} \geq \dfrac{s_s - s_q}{d(s,q)}$. We also have

$\dfrac{s_t - s_q}{d(t,q)} = \dfrac{s_s - s_q}{d(s,q)}$ when it propagates sensitivity values from s to q. Combining these

observations, we have $\dfrac{s_p - s_q}{d(p,q)} \geq \dfrac{s_t - s_q}{d(t,q)}$. Since $d(p, q) > d(t, q)$, we have $s_p > s_t$, hence

principles 1 and 2 are satisfied.

```
PrivacyValuePropagation(T: a MeSH tree; N: nodes in T. S:
nodes that have obtained sensitivity values){
  if (ConsistencyCheck( )){
    UpwardPropagation( );
    DownwardPropagation( );
  }
}
UpwardPropagation(){
  For each s ∈ S
    Find ancestors sa ∈ S such that there is at least one
    node sp∉S between s and sa and there is no sp ∈ S
    between s and sa
  Put all the pairs (sa, s) in set R
  while R is not empty
    For each pair (sa, s) ∈ R
      Inc(sa,s) = (s.sensitivity - sa.sensitivity)/length(sa, s)
    Inc  = min(Inc(sa,s) )
    (sa₁, s₁) = argmin(Inc(sa, s))
    For each sp₁ between sa₁ and s₁,
      sp₁.sensitivity = sa₁.sensitivity + Inc * length(sa₁,
      sp₁)
    R = R - {(sa₁, s₁)}
    For each pair (sa₁, s) ∈ R
      Find sa₂ between sa₁ and s₁ to replace sa₁ in (sa₁, s)
      such that sa₂ is a newly labeled node and sa₂ is the
      closest labeled ancestor of s.
  }
}
DownwardPropagation(){
  Traverse the tree in a breadth first fashion.
  For each non-updated node
    update sensitivity value with the value of its parents
      node
}
CheckConsistency(){
  consistency = true
  Traverse the tree in a breadth first fashion
  for each node p, find its child node c{
    if c is labeled with a sensitivity value
      if p.sensitivy ≥ c.sensitivy
        consistency = false
    Else
        c.sensitivy = p.sensitivity
  }
  return consistency
}
```

Fig. 1. Propagation of sensitivity values in MeSH

Fig. 2. Proof of conformance to Principles 1 and 2

We use an example in Figure 3 to illustrate the propagation steps

Initially we set sensitivity values for nodes A, B, C to 0.8, 0.6, and 0.8 respectively (Figure 3(a)). First, node B was chosen for upward propagation (Figure 3(b)), then node A and node C were chosen in a sequence (Figures 3(c) and 3(d)). Finally, the downward propagation was done (Figure 3(e)).

To make the propagated values accurately reflect the real sensitivity levels for the user, the rule of thumb on which nodes the user should assign initial sensitivity values is that the nodes with significant difference with parent or sibling nodes should be specified.

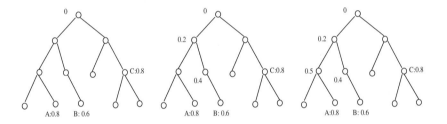

(a) Initial assignment   (b) Upward propagation from node B (c) Upward propagation from node A

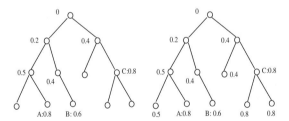

(d) Upward propagation from node C (e) Downward propagation

Fig. 3. A propagation example

PHI may contain other medical terms in addition to diseases. If some medical documents contain medical procedures or medication, it is easy for the adversaries to infer the diseases that are closed related to these procedures and drugs. Using web search engine to find correlation between sensitive keywords [10] provides a solution for inference between medical procedures, medication, and diseases. However, in the PHI scenario, ontologies are readily available. Using an ontology for inference can provide more accurate results than using web search. In MeSH, the entities are classified into different categories, which include *Disease*, *Medication*, and *Procedure*. In this study, we only take into account these three categories. We only assign sensitivity values to the disease in the ontology. The medication and procedure are used to infer diseases.

Let R_i denote a medication or procedure and D_i denote a disease

From MeSH, we can obtain rules in the following format

$$R_i \rightarrow \{(D_{i1}, p_{i1}),...\{D_{in_i}, p_{in_i})\}$$

This rule states that medication or procedure R_i may infer diseases D_{i1} with probability p_{i1}, and so on. Suppose disease D_{ij} has sensitivity value S_{ij}. The sensitivity value for R_i is determined by

$$S(R_i) = \sum_{j=1}^{n_i} S_{ij} * p_{ij}$$

When multiple medications and procedures are found in a document, we need an aggregation method to calculate the sensitivity value for the set of terms.

The method we used to calculate the aggregation is shown in Figure 4. It is straightforward that this aggregation algorithm satisfies the Principle 3.

```
Input: n rules  R_i → {(D_{i1}, p_{i1}),...{D_{in_i}, p_{in_i})} , where 0 < i ≤ n
Rank pairs (D_{ij}, p_{ij}) according to S(D_{ij}) in a descending order
Prob = 0
Num = 0
While prob <1, in the ordered list do{
   prob = prob + D_{ij}
   num = num +1
}
Adopt the top-num pairs for aggregation
Adjust the num-th probability with 1-prob

Calculate sensitivity value with  S(R_i) = Σ_{j=1}^{n_i} S_{ij} * p_{ij}
```

Fig. 4. Sensitivity value aggregation method

5   Experimental Results

We conducted our experiments on a dataset downloaded from an online health discussion forum Dipex (http://www.dipex.org.uk/), which consists of 250 messages. The messages posted on this forum do not have real names of patients, but they have nicknames such as "Paul123" and other identifiers such as locations, email addresses, phone numbers, posted dates and times. The advantages of using this real dataset are that the data is anonymous and they are publically available.

We used the PHI detection system described in [14] to pre-process the data, i.e., to identify personally identifiable information and the medical terms. Then we manually checked and rectified the results that became the input for our method.

Then we set the sensitivity values for 5 diseases in MeSH as shown in Table 1.

Table 1. Sensitivity values assigned to five diseases

Disease	Sensitivity Value
Infection	0.2
Arthritis	0.5
Sarcoma	0.9
Cough	0.3
Anaemia	0.6

The system propagated these values in MeSH and calculated the privacy measures for all the 250 messages. We set the threshold to 5×10^{-5} to classify the messages into 175 PHI and 75 non-PHI. We also manually reviewed and classified the messages into 155 PHI and 95 non-PHI as golden standard. Then we compared the results from the system with the golden standard. Table 2 shows the confusion matrix.

Table 2. Confusion matrix

	Positive Identified	Negative Identified
Real Positive	131	24
Real Negative	44	51

We have Precision = 0.749, Recall = 0.845, and F = 0.794.

We then took a look at the ranked messages and found that the top ranked messages indeed contain more privacy information than the other messages. For example, the message ranked first contains the disease names such as *ovarian cancer* and *tumors*. It also contains medication terms such as *Doxil* and *Gemcitabine*. This leads to a high aggregated sensitivity value of 0.99. The author of this message had used a very uncommon nickname which generated the probability that the person can be identified to be 6.6×10^{-4}. This probability value was calculated by calling the Google search engine.

The experiment was conducted on a PC with Intel Core 2 duo CPU of 2.20GHz and memory of 3.25GB. The sensitivity value propagation in MeSH took 69 minutes and 8 seconds. The privacy index calculation for 250 files took 185 minutes and 6 seconds.

6 Conclusion

We proposed a general framework for defining privacy measures for free text documents. We also proposed principles for evaluating sensitivity levels of private information. We then proposed a practical solution to estimate the privacy levels in the PHI scenario. Preliminary experimental results show the effectiveness of our approach.

For the database scenario, there is no problem about correlation between QIEs and SEs, because each row in a table refers to one person and the relationship is already embodied in the tables. However, in the case of free text, correlations between QIEs and SEs are a practical problem. In our experiments, we assumed that the correlations between QIEs and SEs have been perfectly identified. Identifying the correlations between these entities is our future work.

We also assume that each file contains PHI or PII for only one person. This is the case for many health records. However, in a more general scenario, one document may contain privacy for several persons. Defining privacy degree for this situation is also a future work.

Another future work is to detect correlation for different documents that may contain private information for one person. In this scenario, the combination of the private information in different documents may disclose more private information.

References

1. Korba, L., Wang, Y., Geng, L., Song, R., Yee, G., Patrick, A.S., Buffett, S., Liu, H., You, Y.: Private Data Discovery for Privacy Compliance in Collaborative Environments. In: Luo, Y. (ed.) CDVE 2008. LNCS, vol. 5220, pp. 142–150. Springer, Heidelberg (2008)
2. Sokolova, M., Emam, K.: Evaluation of Learning from Screened Positive Examples. In: Proceedings of the 3rd Workshop on Evaluation Methods for Machine Learning, in Conjunction with the 25th International Conference on Machine Learning (ICML 2008), Helsinki, Finland (2008)
3. Sweeney, L.: K-Anonymity: a Model for Protecting Privacy. International Journal on Uncertainty, Fuzziness, and Knowledge-Based Systems 10(5), 557–570 (2002)
4. Machanavajjhala, A., Gehrke, J., Kifer, D.: l-Diversity: Privacy Beyond k-Anonymity. In: Proceedings of the 22nd International Conference on Data Engineering (ICDE 2006), Atalanta, USA, p. 24 (2006)
5. Li, N., Li, T., Venkatasubramanian, S.: Privacy Beyond k-Anonymity and l-Diversity. In: Proceedings of the 23rd International Conference on Data Engineering (ICDE 2007), Istanbul, Turkey, pp. 106–115 (2007)
6. Al-Fedaghi, S.S.: How to Calculate the Information Privacy. In: Proceedings of the Third Annual Conference on Privacy, Security and Trust, St. Andrews, Canada, pp. 12–14 (2005)
7. Fule, P., Roddick, J.F.: Detecting Privacy and Ethical Sensitivity in Data Mining Results. In: Proceedings of the Twenty-Seventh Australasian Computer Science Conference (ACSC 2004), Dunedin, New Zealand, pp. 159–166 (2004)
8. Golle, P.: Revisiting the Uniqueness of Simple Demographics in the US Population. In: Workshop on Privacy in the Electronic Society (WPES 2006), Alexandria, USA, pp. 77–80 (2006)
9. Chow, R., Golle, P., Staddon, J.: Detecting Privacy Leaks Using Corpus-based Association Rules. In: Proceedings of KDD 2008, Las Vegas, Nevada, pp. 893–901 (2008)
10. Staddon, J., Golle, P., Zimny, B.: Web-Based Inference Detection. In: Proceedings of the 16th UNENIX Security Symposium, Boston, MA, pp. 71–86 (2007)

11. Lonpre, L., Kreinovich, V.: How to Measure Loss of Privacy,
    http://www.cs.utep.edu/vladik/2006/tr06-24.pdf
12. Kobsa, A.: Privacy-Enhanced Web Personalization. In: Brusilovsky, P., Kobsa, A., Nejdl,
    W. (eds.) Adaptive Web 2007. LNCS, vol. 4321, pp. 628–670. Springer, Heidelberg
    (2007)
13. U.S. National Library of Medicine, http://www.nlm.nih.gov/mesh/
14. Wang, Y., Liu, H., Geng, L., Keays, M.S., You, Y.: Automatic Detecting Documents
    Containing Personal Health Information. In: Combi, C., Shahar, Y., Abu-Hanna, A. (eds.)
    AIME 2009. LNCS, vol. 5651, pp. 335–344. Springer, Heidelberg (2009)

Towards Legal Privacy Risk Assessment and Specification

Ebenezer Paintsil

Department of Applied Research in ICT
Norwegian Computing Center
Oslo, Norway
paintsil@nr.no

Abstract. This article focuses on privacy risk assessment from a legal perspective. We focus on how to estimate legal privacy risk with legal norms instead of quantitative values. We explain the role of normative values in legal risk assessment and introduce a specification for legal privacy risk using a modal language. We examine the difference between legal privacy risk assessment and Information Technology (IT) security risk assessment. IT security risk assessment supports the decision-making processes of system stakeholders - individuals, managers, groups or organizations. It supports both quantitative and qualitative risk analyses and may rely on the knowledge of security experts to estimate the risk. The application of an IT security risk assessment method for legal privacy risk assessment may lead to poor communication and high uncertainties in the risk estimation because legal reasoning is based on normative values and requires legal knowledge. This article proposes legal privacy risk assessment in the knowledge domain of a legal risk assessor.

1   Introduction

An Information Technology (IT) risk assessor can facilitate communication and reduce uncertainty in IT risk assessment if the assessment is done in the risk assessor's knowledge domain [1]. Traditional IT security risk assessment may employ quantitative, qualitative or semi-quantitative values to estimate or report risk [1], [2]. The risk estimation techniques may reflect the goal of an organization [3], [4] or the experience of the security risk assessor since IT risk assessment depends on the risk assessors' experience [1]. For example, the Risk IT [4] management framework relies on the COBIT Information Criteria, Balanced Scorecard Criteria, COSO and Westerman techniques to communicate risk impact to system owner - the organization. These communication techniques are organization-focused because they express risk impact in business and financial terms. They intend to communicate risk to the policy makers or the system owners but not to others system stakeholders.

Similarly, the AS/NZS:4360 [5] risk management standard (now ISO 31000), the NIST [6], OCTAVE [7], CORAS [8] and ISO27005 [9] are mainly security-focused, assets driven, organization-oriented [3] and use qualitative, quantitative or semi-quantitative values to estimate risk (see [1], [2]).

S. Furnell, C. Lambrinoudakis, and G. Pernul (Eds.): TrustBus 2011, LNCS 6863, pp. 174–185, 2011.

However, privacy has security as well as legal perspective. We may effectively communicate and estimate the legal privacy risk with normative values rather than quantitative values. This is because quantitative values may not make legal sense in legal risk assessment since legal decision-making is based on normative values rather than quantitative values. Moreover, they may not effectively communicate risk or uncertainty to a lawyer who may assess the legal aspect of the privacy risk.

The objective of this article is to explain the importance of legal norms in privacy risk assessment and to examine the difference between legal privacy risk assessment and IT security risk assessment. Further, we introduce a conceptual model for legal privacy risk assessment leading to an attempt towards logical formalizations of legal privacy risk.

The rest of the article is organized as follows. In Section 2, we introduce existing works on privacy risk assessment. We examine other approaches to privacy risk assessment and protection. Section 3 is the overview of the legal risk assessments' concepts focusing on how the legal aspect of privacy contributes to privacy risk assessments. We introduce a conceptual model for legal privacy risk assessment in section 4 and the language for the legal risk specification in section 5. Section 6 is the legal privacy risk specification. Finally, section 7 states the conclusion and future work.

2 Related Work

The Platform for Privacy Preferences (P3P) is a protocol for expressing privacy policy in both a machine and human readable way using a standard XML schema [10]. The standard schema allows the service provider to use a set of predefined terms to describe their privacy policy. The privacy policy may specify the kind of data the web site collects, dispute resolution procedure, how long data will be retained and how the personal data will be used. Furthermore, the World Wide Web Consortium (W3C) designed a Platform for Privacy Preferences Preference Exchange Language (APPEL) to enable individuals to express their privacy preferences, to query the data represented by P3P, and to make decisions accordingly [10]. However, P3P and APPEL focus on privacy policies, but not legal reasoning.

Furhermore, Ardagna et al. introduced the PrimeLife policy language for privacy enforcement [11]. The language uses modalities such as temporal constraints, pre-obligations, conditional obligations, and repeating obligations to model different types of obligations. It uses authorization modality to specify data transfer competence. Rules have two modalities, permit or deny. The language uses the concept of trusted credentials and specifies the agreement between a data controller and a data subject as a promise. The language focuses on empirical specification instead of legal specification. The obligation and authorization modalities used in the language are not expressive enough to embrace all aspect of legal reasoning. Legal reasoning has several modalities including right, permission, obligations, exceptions, rule, power and commitment.

Berthold [12] introduces the language for privacy options which is an adaptation of the financial contracts language proposed by Peyton Jones and Eber [13]. Similarly, Mahler introduces a legal risk assessment approach focusing on legal contract and communication [14]. Yet, legal privacy risk is not necessarily contractual; it depends on the nature of the applicable law. A regulatory framework permits both norm of conduct (command or permission) and competence (power) [15], [16]; however, mandatory law may permit no competence norm. Hence, it is not clear that a contractual risk model is appropriate for legal privacy risk assessment. Another limitation of the contractual approach to privacy risk modeling is that the approach focuses on those who explicitly declare their consent or enter into a contractual agreement with a data controller regarding the protection of their personal data. This means, where there is no contractual agreement, such model may fail to apply.

Wang introduces five requirements for security metrics including the requirement for quantitative metric [2]. Quantitative metrics reduce subjectivity and increase the level of trust. However, Aven disagrees with these assertions. He argues that the arbitrariness in quantitative risk estimation ""could be significant, due to the uncertainties in the estimates or as a result of the uncertainty assessment being strongly dependent on the assessors" [1]. He introduced a mixed approach called the semi-quantitative approach which combines both quantitative and qualitative estimation techniques in order to assess the risk. The approach is intended to reduce the uncertainties in quantitative risk analysis (QRA). Nevertheless, Aven did not consider the effect of semi-quantitative approach on legal risk communication and reasoning since legal risk depends on normative values instead of semi-quantitative values.

CORAS [17] uses the unified modeling language (UML) to model a targeted system. It then employs complementary risk management methods to assess different models of the targeted system. CORAS risk management method facilitates communication and interaction among stakeholders. However, CORAS is asset or security-oriented, focusing on asset protection and estimates legal risk based on quantitative values [8, p.327-337] instead of normative values.

3   Legal Risk Assessments and Privacy

Legal propositions or norms and ""normative values" are central to legal risk assessment. We regard normative values as standards for assessing legal reasoning. They include obligation, permission, exception and right. We refer to them as legal modalities. Normative values may be referred to as norms [15], [16]. A legal norm consists of facts (legal antecedents or something that must happen before) and consequences [18]. The antecedent describes which factual circumstances have to be present for a normative value to apply. The consequent indicates the legal implications of the applicable normative value. Thus, normative values may connect a legal antecedent to a legal consequent or determine the transition from legal antecedent to legal consequent.

Legal antecedent is either a fact or a proposition. A fact is something that is established to be true and may not be disputed. A proposition is something that is true, believed to be true, known to be true, ought to be true, eventually true or is necessarily true. We refer to the words "ought to, believe, known, eventually and necessary" as the modalities of the proposition.

We refer to legal modalities as normative values and categorize them as normative values for conduct, competence and right. The normative values for conduct (command) require a stakeholder to conditionally perform an action [19]. The competence normative values confer public or private power, immunity, subjection, disability etc. on a legal person [15], [16]. They may determine the validity of legal power or capacity. Legal competence may grant the capacity to create legal rules binding others or oneself. Legal right permits a stakeholder to conditionally perform an action that may advance his/her interest or the interest of others.

The normative values are obligation, permission, prohibition, commitment, rule, authority, power, right, responsibility, and exception [20], [16]. "Facultative" is a special kind of normative value which permits an action and its negation [16]. Unlike traditional risk assessment, normative values may play an important role in legal risk assessment. Nevertheless, their thorough analysis and relationships are beyond the scope of this article. However we provide the Black Dictionary definitions as follows[1]:

- **Obligation:** a legal or moral duty to do or not to do something
- **Permission:** a license or liberty to do something
- **Prohibition:** a law or order that forbids a certain action
- **Commitment:** an agreement to do something in future
- **Rule:** to command or require to do something
- **Authority:** the right or permission to act legally on someone's behalf
- **Power:** the ability to act or not act
- **Right:** a power, privilege or immunity secured to a person by law
- **Responsibility:** liability or the quality, or state of being legally obligated or accountable
- **Faculty:** an authorization granted to someone to do what otherwise would not be allowed

How we choose an applicable legal norm depends on the applicable law. The mandatory or regulatory character of the rules laid down in the applicable privacy law determines the applicable legal norm. Rules of mandatory law are generally rules from which the parties cannot derogate by contract [23],[24]. Generally, the right to withdraw from a contract and protection against unfair contractual terms are mandatory rules.

Similarly, the applicable normative values for privacy risk depend on the nature of the privacy law or regulation. Deciding the nature of an applicable privacy law is not a straightforward matter. For instance, it is not clear that the nature

---

[1] For more information on norms refers to [21],[22], [15], [16].

of rules laid down in the European Union (EU) data protection directive (DPD) [25] is rules of mandatory law.

Cuijper [24] argues that the EU DPD does not require implementation into mandatory rules of law. The objectives focus on individual protection with regard to processing of personal data and free movement of personal data. She emphasized the latter as more important. The regulation for free movement of personal data does not mandate the implementation of the DPD into mandatory rules of law. In addition, Cuijper stressed that the directive contains no clause requiring mandatory law and DPD article 7 [25] leaves room for processing of personal data based on contract. She concluded that, ""it will be a step too far to denounce judicial effect to all contracts between data controllers and data subjects in which the data subject willingly gives up part of the rights granted to him on the basis of this directive".

However, Bergkamp argues otherwise. According to Bergkamp the ""DPD establishes a public law regime that cannot be varied by a private law contract" [26, p. 123]. Even Cuijper [24] noted that, the argument for private law regime depends on whether the data subject has a strong bargaining power. In cases where the data subject is the weaker party, the law may have to give the subject a strong protection. In addition, the data controller may process personal data under the EU DPD without a contractual agreement [27]. The lack of legal consensus between the public and private law character of the DPD represents legal uncertainty that can contribute to legal privacy risk. Furthermore, the nature of the applicable privacy law is an important modality to consider in legal privacy risk assessment because it determines the applicable normative values.

4   Legal Privacy Risk Assessments Conceptualization

Currently, there are over 200 risk management methods with no adequate selection criteria [28]. We selected the CORAS [8] because it is a well-documented risk assessment method, has straightforward risk assessment concepts and attempts to model legal risk. CORAS manages risk in eight steps but the central concepts revolve around the combined effect of threat, vulnerability, threat scenario, unwanted incident on an asset [8]. A threat exploits vulnerabilities in an asset, leading to a chain of events called threat scenario that may lead to unwanted incident that may in turn cause loss to a system owner or a stakeholder.

Figure 1 depicts a risk assessment conceptual model based on the CORAS risk assessment concepts. It also depicts one of the fundamental differences between legal risk assessment and information technology (IT) security risk assessment. Figure 1(a) represents a simple IT security risk assessment scenario and 1(b) is the legal risk assessment scenario. Quantitative values determine the transitions in Figure 1(a) reflecting a good security risk assessment [2]. Nevertheless, the transitions in Figure 1(b) are determined by normative values (obligations) reflecting legal decision-making. Legal decision-making depends on normative values rather than quantitative values and transition decisions depend on the legal rule(s).

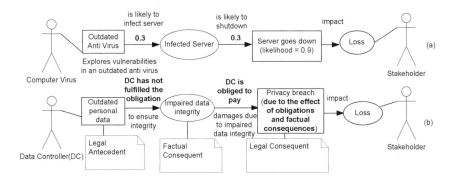

Fig. 1. Diagram (a) Represents a Simple Security Risk Assessment Scenario and (b) is a Simple Legal Privacy Risk Assessment Scenario

Unlike IT security risk assessment, legal risk assessment relies on legal antecedents, normative values and legal consequents to determine the effect of a legal breach [18], [14]. Therefore a risk assessment method based on quantitative values may not make legal sense. We determine the risk by measuring the extent by which the legal breach impact on the objectives of a stakeholder. This is referred to as risk tolerance [4]. We have privacy risk if the loss is higher than the acceptable risk level or risk tolerance. The risk tolerance and the decision to arrive at the loss should be deduced from the legal rules and applicable case laws.

In Figure 1(b) a legal antecedent may lead to a factual consequence. Legal antecedents may consist of one or more facts that may lead to a factual consequent. They have both legal propositions and factual propositions. This conceptualization highlights one of the possible ways of reasoning about legal privacy risk. The directed graph and the normative values could make it possible to use hybrid modal logics for the legal privacy risk specification leading to a possible automation. Consequently, we model legal privacy risk as a directed graph with normative values that determine the transitions leading to a loss.

5   The Privacy Risk Specification Language

We introduce a language for privacy risk specification language. The language is based on deontic, hybrid modal and propositional dynamic logics. Modal logics are highly expressive and suitable for directed graph (see [29]). They provide a good balance between expressiveness and complexity. Most importantly modal logics are syntactically simple language and mathematically rich [30, p. xii-x].

We model the privacy risk as a directed graph. A directed graph or a relational structure is a set of nodes and edges between them [29]. It is defined as $\langle W, R \rangle$ where W is non-empty set of vertices of the relational structure called the worlds or a states. The members of W represent the states, points, nodes, instants or situations of the relational structure. The R is the set of edges of the relational structure representing the accessibility relation between worlds. The cross product $\{W \times W\}$ stands for $\{(w_1, w_2)|w_1 \in W, w_2 \in W\}$ is the set of all ordered pairs (w_1, w_2) where w_1 and w_2 are members of W. The set $R \subseteq W \times W$ is the binary or accessibility relation over W. A model in modal logic is a relational structure with valuation i.e. $M = (W, R, V)$ where V is the valuation. The valuation determines the truth or falsity of a proposition or a formula.

Hybrid modal logic extends the traditional modal logic. In addition to the set of proposition at each world, hybrid modal logic introduces special propositional symbol known as nominal. A nominal is true at exactly one world of a model [31]. Hence, we can use it to name a state. Further, hybrid modal logic introduces a state variable. A state variable is an atomic formula denoting a state. Hybrid logic has additional operators: @ and $\downarrow$. The $\downarrow$ is known as the binder. It is possible to express irreflexivity of a state with the binder. Using $\downarrow$ allows one to name a world where a formula $\downarrow x\Psi$ will be evaluated. The x is a state variable or a nominal and Ψ is a formula. $\downarrow x\Psi$ binds all the occurrences of x in Ψ to the current state where the evaluation is occurring [31]. The @ operator allows a "jump" from the current world to another world or a state in a frame. For example, the formula $@_x\Psi$ is true if Ψ is true at the world denoted by x.

Modal logics express modalities. The basic modalities are necessarily and possibly. The necessarily modality is represented by a box []. Also, the possibly modality is represented by a diamond $\langle\rangle$. The symbols for the modalities can be empty or non-empty. The empty box [] (necessarily or obligation) means the evaluation statement is true in every one-step successor of the current world of the model. Similarly, empty diamond $\langle\rangle$ symbol modality (possibly modality or permission) means the evaluation of the modal formula is possible in some one-step successor of the current world of the model [31], [32], [33].

Propositional dynamic logic is another kind of modal logics. It may be used to express action. The actions are included in the necessary or the possibly box. The non-empty necessarily box $[\pi]\beta$ in propositional dynamic logic means every execution of π from the current state leads to the states bearing the information β [30, p. 13]. Similarly, the non-empty possibly modality $\langle\pi\rangle\beta$ means some terminating execution of π from the current state leads to the states bearing the information β. Also, we can refer to β as a formula or a proposition that hold in a necessary or possible world or the consequence of an action (proposition or legal rules) π.

We note that the following complex relations hold:

- If π_1 and π_2 are programs, then so is $\pi_1 \cup \pi_2$ – executes π_1 or π_2
- If π_1 and π_2 are programs, then so is $\pi_1; \pi_2$ – executes π_1 and then π_2
- If π is a program then so is π^* – executes π zero or finite number of times
- If π_1 and π_2 are programs, then so is $\pi_1 \cap \pi_2$ – executes π_1 and π_2 in parallel
- If β is a formula, then β? is a program that test whether β holds, if so the execution continues; else it stops

We use Deontic logic [20], [16] to express the legal rules that may determine the effect of an action or a fact and dynamic proposition logic for the actions or factual propositions. We can express a proposition in a form of an action and vice versa. Deontic logic is used to express legal obligations. In order to express the legal modalities in deontic logic, we group the normative values into three groups (legal competence, conduct and legal right) and introduce the notation $PL^A_{(C,D,R)}$ to express the legal rules or propositions. The modality C represents a set of competence norms; D is a set of conduct norms, and R is a set of right norms. The notation $PL^A_{(r)}(\beta)$ represents legal right, meaning the stakeholder P may perform the action β in order to advance the interest of A, where $r \in R$. P is the same as A when one performs an action to advance his/her own interest.

The following are the syntax and semantic of the specification language.

- Let the basic unanalyzed proposition or atomic formula
  $prop := p, q, r...$ and $\top$ $"always\ true"$, $\bot$ $"always\ false"$.
- Let the set of nominal $NOM = \{n1, n2, n3...\}$.
- Let the set of state variables $SV = \{s1, s2, s3...\}$.
- The binary connective $\wedge$.
- The unary connective $\neg$.
- Let the finite set of programs or propositions $PI = \{\pi_1, \pi_2, \pi_3...\pi_n\}$.
- The unary operator $[\pi]$ where $\pi \in PI$.
- The unary operator $\langle\pi\rangle$ where $\pi \in PI$.
- The binder operator $\downarrow$.
- The $@_x$ where x is a state variable or nominal.

$\theta := prop|\neg\varphi|(\varphi \wedge \phi)|(\varphi \vee \phi)|(\varphi \rightarrow \phi)|[\pi]\varphi|\langle\pi\rangle\varphi|[]\varphi|^PL^A_{(C,D,R)}(\pi)$ where $\pi \in PI$
We write a formula that is true at a world w of a model $M = (W, R, V)$ as $M, w \models \varphi$. It follows that

- $M, w \models p$ iff $w \in V(p)$ where $p \in prop$
- $M, w \models \neg\varphi$ iff not $M, w \models \varphi$
- $M, w \models \varphi \wedge \phi$ iff $M, w \models \varphi$ and $M, w \models \phi$
- $M, w \models @_x\varphi$ iff $M, x \models \varphi$ where $x \in SV$
- $M, w \models \varphi \rightarrow \phi$ iff not $M, w \models \varphi$ or $M, w \models \phi$

We refer to this as Kripke semantics, named after Saul Kripke [29].

6   Legal Privacy Risk Specification

We consider an example of the application of the language in this section. We consider the DPD article 6 (data quality) and article 23 [25] with reference to Figure 2. We manually extract the normative values following the example in [19]. The result of the simplified extraction is shown in Table 1.

The normative phrase determines the normative values. The extraction program will extract the normative values depending on the normative phrase. For example the normative phrase ""Must" implies obligation and ""May or Can" implies right (see [19]). We specify the legal privacy risk with the language described in section 5 with reference to the model in Figure 2.

Fig. 2. A Simple Legal Privacy Risk Assessment Scenario

Table 1. Extracted Legal Normative Values

Rule No.	Norm Proposition (Rule)	Normative Phrase	Normative Value
R1	Personal data must be collected for specified, explicit and legitimate purposes and not further processed in a way incompatible with those purposes	must	obligation
R2	Further processing of data for historical, statistical or scientific purposes shall not be considered as incompatible provided that Member States provide appropriate safeguards	Shall not	not obligation
R3	Personal data must be adequate, relevant and not excessive in relation to the purposes for which they are collected and/or for which they are further processed	must	obligation
R4	DPD aricle 23: Member States shall provide that any person who has suffered damage as a result of an unlawful processing operation or of any act to this Directive incompatible with the national provisions adopted pursuant is entitled to receive compensation from the controller for the damage suffered	shall	obligation

In modal logics, a world has a set of propositions and is accessible from another world. We assume that each of the entities Legal Antecedent, Factual Consequent, Legal Consequent and Loss in Figure 2 are accessible from other worlds. Therefore, they are the possible worlds or states which we represent by w_{la}, w_{fc}, w_{lc} and w_l respectively. The set of the possible worlds or the universe is $W = \{w_{la}, w_{fc}, w_{lc}, w_l\}$. The analysis of a scenario or a legal proposition may lead to a program execution that may in turn lead to a new state or world. We assume that it is possible to access the Loss state from the Legal Consequent state in both directions as in Figure 2. We represent each state w_{la}, w_{fc}, w_{lc} and w_l with a set of nominal, $\{la, fc, lc, l\}$ respectively. Each state has a set of legal and factual propositions. Let C, D, R represent the set of competence, conduct and legal right norms respectively. Table 2 presents the analysis of factual prepositions and legal rules.

Table 2. Legal Privacy Risk Assessment

ID	Legal Assessment	Normative Value	Formula
L1	is outdated data leads to impaired data integrity (According to DPD article 6(e) (R4 in Table 1) personal data must be accurate and, where necessary, kept up to date)	Obligation	$^P L^A_{(o_1)}(\pi_1)$ π_1 is "accurate and up to date data" $o \in D$ where D is the set of conduct norms
L2	is impaired data integrity is illegal (According to DPD article 23 (R4 in Table 1) violations shall lead to damages)	Obligation	$^P L^A_{(o)}(\pi_2)$ π_2 is ""stakeholder entitled to receive compensation from the controller for the damage suffered" $o \in D$ where D is the set of conduct norms

$$PossibleRisk := @^P_{la} L^A_{(o_1)}(\pi_1) \wedge \langle \pi_1(F_1)? \rangle \wedge^P L^A_{(o_2)}(\pi_2) \wedge \langle \pi_2(F_2)? \rangle$$
$$\downarrow_x (^P L^A_{(C,D,R)}(\pi_3) \wedge \langle \pi_3(F_3)? \rangle \alpha \wedge \langle tolerate(\alpha)? \rangle_x) \dots (1)$$

Where F_1, F_2, F_3 are the facts, π_1, π_2 and π_3 are functions, $o_1, o_2 \in D$, α is the consequences of the legal rules and facts, $tolerate(\alpha)$ is a test program for risk tolerance.

Equation (1) is a legal privacy risk specification. We begin the legal privacy risk assessment at the state w_{la} (the Legal Antecedent state). The formula $@_{la}^P L_{(o_1)}^A(\pi_1) \wedge \langle \pi_1(F_1)? \rangle$ evaluates at the Legal Antecedent's state. The formula $^P L_{(o_1)}^A(\pi_1)$ expresses the legal proposition for the available fact. The formula $\langle \pi_1(F_1)? \rangle$ checks if the fact F_1 violates the legal rule (π_1) and makes a transition to the factual consequent's state otherwise the execution is stopped. We repeat a similar process at the Factual Consequent state. The formula $(^P L_{(C,D,R)}^A(\pi_3) \wedge \langle \pi_3(F_3)? \rangle \alpha)$ estimates the consequence α based on the appropriate privacy legal rules. The formula $\downarrow_x (^P L_{(C,D,R)}^A(\pi_3) \wedge \langle \pi_3(F_3)? \rangle \alpha \wedge \langle tolerate(\alpha)? \rangle_x)$ is a test program. It returns to the current state or the Legal Consequent's state(w_{lc}) if the stakeholder can tolerate the loss. The transition $\langle \pi_3(F_3)? \rangle$ leads to the Loss state. The Loss state then evaluates the impact for the possible loss and return to the Legal Consequent state if the stakeholder can tolerate the loss.

The possible legal privacy risk is the transition from the Legal Antecedent's state to the Loss state. We represent the transition by the formua (1) or *PossibleRisk*. The formula *PossibleRisk* is satisfied if the stakeholder can tolerate the legal privacy risk, otherwise the estimated loss is inconsistent with the objectives of the stakeholder and therefore we may transfer, avoid, mitigate or share the risk. We can generalize the *PossibleRisk* formula by understanding the effects of possible combinations of legal norms and facts. The formula *PossibleRisk* is an example of a simple logical specification of legal privacy risk.

7   Conclusion

Legal privacy risk depends on the applicable normative values determined by the nature of rules of the legal provision (regulatory or mandatory rules of law). It is not concerned with the protection of physical assets and estimation of quantitative values but considers the effect of normative values on facts or legal antecedents. In this article, we focus on making legal privacy risk assessment more meaningful to information technology (IT) professional by introducing a legal privacy risk assessment conceptual model. Further, we propose a language based on hybrid modal logic, propositional dynamic logic and deontic logic as a possible tool for legal privacy risk specification. We exemplify legal privacy risk specification with the language. Although the specification is simple and case specific, it highlights one of the possible ways of assessing legal privacy risk and how legal privacy risk assessment differs from IT security risk assessment. We can build on this initial insight to automate legal privacy risk assessment. Our future work will investigate how to improve the specification by relaxing some of the assumptions. We will focus on the complexities of combining facts and legal norms in legal privacy risk estimation and the effect of legal uncertainty on legal privacy risk estimation. We will provide a general specification for legal privacy risk automation.

Acknowledgment. The work reported in this paper is part of the PETweb II project sponsored by the Research Council of Norway under grant 193030/S10.

References

[1] Aven, T.: A semi-quantitative approach to risk analysis, as an alternative to qras. Reliability Engineering & System Safety 93(6), 790–797 (2008)

[2] Wang, A.J.A.: Information security models and metrics. In: ACM-SE 43: Proceedings of the 43rd Annual Southeast Regional Conference, pp. 178–184. ACM, New York (2005)

[3] Strecker, S., Heise, D., Frank, U.: Riskm: A multi-perspective modeling method for it risk assessment. Information Systems Frontiers (2010)

[4] ISACA: The Risk IT Practitioner Guide. ISACA, 3701 Algonquin Road, Suite 1010 Rolling Meadows, IL 60008 USA (2009) isbn: 978-1-60420-116-1

[5] Committee, A.Z.S.: Risk management as/nzs4360:1999. Technical report, Standards Australia (1999)

[6] Gary, S., Goguen Alice, F.A.: Nist special publication 800-30 risk management guide for information technology systems. Technical report, National Institute of Standards and Technology (2002)

[7] Christopher, A., Dorofee Audrey, S.J.W.C.: Introduction to the octave approach, vol. 37. Carnegie Mellon Software Engineering Institute (2003)

[8] Lund, M.S.: Bjørnar Solhaug, K.S.: Model-Driven Risk Analysis, The CORAS Approach, 1 edn. Springer, Heidelberg (2011) 978-3-642-12322-1

[9] ISO: Iso 27005 information security risk management. Technical report, International Organization for Standardization (2008)

[10] Cranor, L., Langheinrich, M., Marchiori, M., Presler-Marshall, M., Reagle, J.: The platform for privacy preferences 1.0 (p3p1.0) specification (2002), http://www.w3.org/TR/P3P/

[11] Ardagna, C., Bussard, L., De Capitani di Vimercati, S., Neven, G., Paraboschi, S., Pedrini: PrimeLife Policy Language. In: W3C Workshop on Access Control Application Scenarios, Luxembourg (2009)

[12] Berthold, S.: Towards a formal language for privacy options. In: Fischer-Hübner, S., Duquenoy, P., Hansen, M., Leenes, R., Zhang, G. (eds.) Privacy and Identity 2010. IFIP Advances in Information and Communication Technology, vol. 352, pp. 27–40. Springer, Heidelberg (2011) 10.1007/978-3-642-20769-3_3

[13] Jones, S.E.P.: How to write a financial contract. Macmillan Publishers Limited, Palgrave Macmillan, Oxford (2003)

[14] Mahler, T.: Legal Risk Management Developing and Evaluating Elements of a Method for Proactive Legal Analyses, With a Particular Focus on Contracts. Monograph, The Faculty of Law, University of Oslo, Postboks 6706 St Olavs Plass, 0130 Oslo Norway (2010)

[15] Bulygin, E.: On norms of competence. Law and Philosophy 11(3) (1992)

[16] Sartor, G.: Fundamental legal concepts: A formal and teleological characterisation. Artificial Intelligence and Law 14, 101–142 (2006)

[17] Stølen, K., Braber, F.D., Dimitrakos, T., Fredriksen, R., Gran, A., hilde Houmb, S., Lund, M.S., Stamatiou, Y.C., Aagedal, J.Ø.: Model-based risk assessment the coras approach. In: Presented at the 1st Itrust Workshop (2002)

[18] Vraalsen, F., Lund, M.S., Mahler, T., Parent, X., Stølen, K.: Specifying legal risk scenarios using the CORAS threat modelling language. In: Herrmann, P., Issarny, V., Shiu, S.C.K. (eds.) iTrust 2005. LNCS, vol. 3477, pp. 45–60. Springer, Heidelberg (2005) 10.1007/11429760_4

[19] Kiyavitskaya, N., Zeni, N., Breaux, T.D., Antón, A.I., Cordy, J.R., Mich, L., Mylopoulos, J.: Extracting rights and obligations from regulations: toward a tool-supported process. In: Proceedings of the Twenty-Second IEEE/ACM International Conference on Automated Software Engineering, ASE 2007, pp. 429–432. ACM, New York (2007)

[20] Encyclopedie, D.L.I.: Deontic logic. IVR Encyclopedie (2010)

[21] Jones, A.J.I., Sergot, M.J.: A formal characterisation of institutionalised power. Logic Journal of the IGPL 4(3), 427–443 (1996)

[22] Hart, H.: The Concept of Law, 2nd edn. Clarendon Press, Oxford (1994) isbn:0-19-876123-6.

[23] Edwards, L.: The New Legal Framework for E-Commerce in Europe. Hart Publishing, Oxford (2005) ISBN 13:978-1-84113-451-2

[24] Cuijpers, C.: A private law approach to privacy; mandatory law. SCRIPTed 4:4(318) (2007)

[25] Commission, E.: Directive 95/46/EC of the European Parliament and of the Council of 24 October 1995 on the protection of individuals with regard to the processing of personal data and on the free movement of such data. Technical report, European Parliament (1995)

[26] Bergkamp, L.: European Community Law for the New Economy. Intersentia Publishers, Antwerp, Oxford, New York (2003) ISBN:90-5095-229-1

[27] Olsen, T., Mahler, T.: Identity management and data protection law: Risk, responsibility and compliance in 'circles of trust'. Computer Law & Security Report 23(4), 342–351 (2007)

[28] Matulevičius, R., Mayer, N., Mouratidis, H., Heymans, P., Genon, N.: Adapting secure tropos for security risk management in the early phases of information systems development. In: Bellahsène, Z., Léonard, M. (eds.) CAiSE 2008. LNCS, vol. 5074, pp. 541–555. Springer, Heidelberg (2008)

[29] Blackburn, P., van Benthem, J.: Modal logic: A semantic perspective. ETHICS 98, 501–517 (1988)

[30] Blackburn, P., de Rijke, M., Venema, Y.: Modal Logic. Cambridge University Press, Cambridge (2010) isbn:978-0-521-80200-0

[31] Bidoit, N., Cerrito, S., Thion, V.: A first step towards modeling semistructured data in hybrid multimodal logic. Journal of Applied Non-Classical Logics 14(4), 447–475 (2004)

[32] Areces, C., ten Cate, B.: Hybrid logics. In: Blackburn, P., Wolter, F., van Benthem, J. (eds.) Handbook of Modal Logics. Elsevier, Amsterdam (2006)

[33] Blackburn, P., Ten Cate, B.: Pure Extensions, Proof Rules, and Hybrid Axiomatics. Studia Logica 84, 277–322 (2006)

Privacy-Preserving Storage and Access of Medical Data through Pseudonymization and Encryption

Johannes Heurix[1] and Thomas Neubauer[2]

[1] SBA Research, Austria
jheurix@sba-research.org
[2] Vienna University of Technology
Institute of Software Technology and Interactive Systems, Austria
neubauer@ifs.tuwien.ac.at

Abstract. E-health allows better communication between health care providers and higher availability of medical data. However, the downside of interconnected systems is the increased probability of unauthorized access to highly sensitive records that could result in serious discrimination against the patient. This article provides an overview of actual privacy threats and presents a pseudonymization approach that preserves the patient's privacy and data confidentiality. It allows (direct care) primary use of medical records by authorized health care providers and privacy-preserving (non-direct care) secondary use by researchers. The solution also addresses the identifying nature of genetic data by extending the basic pseudonymization approach with queryable encryption.

Keywords: e-Health, Privacy, Pseudonymization.

1 E-Health and the Need for Privacy

Today's health care is driven by the goal of streamlining and optimizing processes in order to reduce costs without compromising the quality of patient treatment. E-health denotes the application of information and communication technologies (ICT) to support the medical workflows and to improve the communication between health care providers. Over the past years, interconnected systems, such as electronic health records (EHR), provide the technical infrastructure for facilitated document sharing by making them digitally available, having the potential to increase the quality of health care while keeping the costs at a controlled level [1]. However, facilitated access also means higher chance of misuse. Thus sensitive information such as HIV infection data or drug abuse histories must be adequately protected to prevent discrimination, such as denied insurance coverage. Even the sole probability of developing a serious illness may be sufficient to decide against health or live insurance coverage. A particular example of this form of prejudice is called genetic discrimination, the biased treatment of people due to gene mutations that may cause or increase the risk of an inherited disorder [4], [2]. There are numerous documented cases where the results of so-called

S. Furnell, C. Lambrinoudakis, and G. Pernul (Eds.): TrustBus 2011, LNCS 6863, pp. 186–197, 2011.

predictive genetic tests were disclosed to insurance companies resulting in denied insurance coverage, although genetic tests usually deliver uncertain probabilities instead of clear-cut predictions of developing a genetic disorder. Genetic discrimination is also an issue with job applications and employment, where employees were fired because of 'unfavorable' genetic tests and thus keeping them would be too 'risky'.

Although legal acts such as the Genetic Information Nondiscrimination Act (GINA) [3], the Health Insurance Portability and Accountability Act (HIPAA) [12], and the Directive 95/46/EC [5] by the EU exist, technical solutions are still required to prevent the disclosure of medical records to unauthorized persons. At the same time, the vast amounts of digitized data produced in today's health care environment should be available for secondary use, for non-direct care use of personal health information including (but not limited to) analysis and research, as well as quality and safety measurement [9]. Providing access to this rich source of information can help to expand knowledge about diseases and treatment and enhance the effectiveness and efficiency of health care, which in turn improves direct care for the individual patient. But considering reports on buying and selling of non-anonymized patient and health care provider data by the medical industry without the explicit consent from patients or physicians, making these data available poses a significant privacy risk. The effective primary and secondary use of medical records is a major challenge for developing appropriate privacy protection measures.

1.1 Anonymization and Encryption

Two techniques often mentioned when confidentiality and privacy of data is required are *anonymization* and *encryption*. Anonymization refers to removing the identifier from the medical data such that the records cannot be traced back to the corresponding patient [11]. Anonymization can be achieved by depersonalization, the removal of any patient-identifying information from the health records. Because perfect depersonalization, where the data subject is no longer identifiable at all circumstances, is practically impossible to achieve, the assumption can be relaxed to modifying the health data such that the corresponding patient can either not at all or only with a 'disproportionate amount of time, expense and labour' be identified (cf. [6]). A well-known technique of anonymization is k-anonymity [10] where identifying information is removed in such a way that each person cannot be distinguished from at least k-1 individuals by comparing the remaining data stored in the database. A particular downside of anonymization is the fact that it cannot be reversed, which means that anonymized health data cannot be used for direct care or primary use where the link between health data and corresponding patient obviously needs to be known by the health care providers. Anonymization also has its downsides in secondary use, where it is usually applied: As the patient cannot be identified any more, they cannot be contacted to ask for necessary further information or be directly informed of any results either, thus cannot immediately profit from advances in medical treatment. Anonymization may also be inadequate for securely storing genetic data due to their identifying nature. The other technique, data encryption, is usually employed when data confidentiality is required. By fully encrypting health data with a secret key only known to the patient, his or her privacy can be assured as well. Native data encryption is provided by many major database providers and prevents unauthorized disclosure of any sensitive data as long as the decryption key is kept secret and protected adequately. Unlike anonymization, full data encryption is obviously reversible, but the major problem is that secondary use of the records in research projects is entirely prevented, unless the patient explicitly decrypts the data, thus unconcealing his or her identity. Also considering the technical heterogeneous environment of health institutions, (authorized) sharing of encrypted records is also more complicated. Furthermore, encryption and decryption can be very time-consuming when large (monolithic) medical records are involved such as imaging data, in this case rendering data access operations quite tedious.

1.2   Pseudonymization as a Solution

Pseudonymization combines the strengths of anonymization and (full) document encryption: It achieves unlinkability by introducing specifiers (pseudonyms) which cannot be associated with the patient without knowing a certain secret. Other than plain anonymization, it is reversible. Therefore, with prior depersonalization of health records, it allows storing the records in an anonymized state, while this anonymity can be reversed by authorized persons having the knowledge of the secret key. While pseudonymization itself also relies on cryptography (when no cleartext mapping/linking list is involved), only metadata need to be encrypted, and thus the necessary cryptographic overhead can be considerably reduced, compared to simply fully encrypting the health documents.

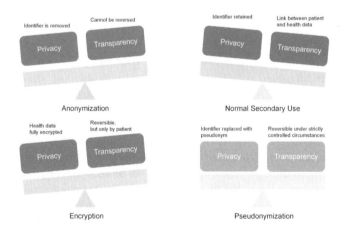

Fig. 1. Trade-off between Privacy and Transparency

Figure 1 represents the difficulty of keeping the patient's privacy and data usability as a trade-off between privacy and transparency: Both anonymization and encryption shift the emphasis on privacy, compromising transparency, while secondary use without anonymization or data encryption discloses the link between patient and health data, compromising patient's privacy. Pseudonymization however is able to keep the balance between privacy and transparency.

2   The PIPE Approach

We developed an approach denominated as 'Pseudonymization of Information for Privacy in E-Health' (PIPE) to provide a secured and privacy-preserving storage and retrieval of sensitive medical data [7]. The basic idea is that many medical records alone such as X-ray images (of frequent mishaps like broken legs) are insufficient to uniquely identify the patient after depersonalization. Therefore, this medical content is separated from identifying information (patient's name, address, ...) and both records are assigned randomly-selected pseudonyms, i.e., identification and health pseudonyms that form a 1:1 relation. These pseudonyms act as access tokens: knowing the correct pseudonyms allows to relink health records to the corresponding patients. The pseudonyms are protected by encryption with a user-specific secret key. We developed the approach with the following aspects in mind:

- Privacy-Preserving Storage: Unlike some other pseudonymization approaches where data are not pseudonymized until export, health data are already stored uncoupled from the identification record, i.e., the data are protected even against potential internal attackers having/gaining direct access to the database (e.g., administrator).
- Privacy-Preserving Secondary Use: The decoupled storage structure facilitates privacy-preserving secondary use, e.g., for research institutions without taking additional anonymization steps. Still, the capability for relinking the records for authorized users allows direct care primary use.
- Patient-Centric Authorization Model: In our approach, the patient is defined as data owner who retains full control over his health data at all times, i.e., the patient is the only person that is able to define access authorizations for trusted persons. In this context, *authorizations* and *access* do not refer to traditional access rights but to the ability to relink certain medical records to the patient and can be stated for just specific health records (e.g., for health care providers) or for the entirety of the patient's data (e.g., for close relatives).
- Secured Authentication: Because passwords are often too weak for dependable authentication, we utilize security tokens (i.e., micro controller smartcards with integrated crypto chips) for dependable authentication. The token acts as trusted user-owned cryptographic module.

- Cryptographic Standards: For simple implementation, we use standard cryptographic symmetric and asymmetric protocols (e.g., RSA and AES) which can be easily replaced should the need arise.

2.1 User Roles

The major roles in our pseudonymization scheme are the patients, health care providers, and trusted relatives:

- Patient: As data owner, the patient is the only person that is in full control over his or her health data and can add and delete owned data at his or her discretion. The patient can also grant data access authorizations for trusted health care providers and relatives. The patient retrieves his or her records by root pseudonyms which are created for and (initially[1]) only known to the patient.
- Health Care Provider: Authorizations for a health care provider involve access rights for specifically selected health records defined by the patient. The patient creates an authorization by creating and assigning a unique (shared) pseudonym to the particular health record to share with the health care provider. Combined with another new pseudonym assigned to the patient's identification record, the newly created pseudonyms form the access token which can be deleted when necessary. The pseudonym pair is known to both patient and health care provider, i.e., encrypted with both their keys. A health care provider can also be authorized to add a new health record for the patient. In this case, the health care provider is automatically granted access to the record in the future as well.
- Relative: In contrast to health care providers, a relative is granted access to the entirety of a patient's data records by sharing the secret information to decrypt the root pseudonyms. The relative is also automatically authorized to access any records stored in the future as well, either added by the patient himself/herself or by a trusted and authorized health care provider.

The pseudonymized data structure of PIPE provides two different 'views' depending on the granted authorizations (cf. Figure 2). The left side represents the data view for administrators and secondary users (unauthorized in terms of data confidentiality and privacy), or internal/external malicious users. Although the identification and health records are clearly visible for them, they are not able to identify the correct links between the pseudonymized health records and identification records. All they can do is try to guess. Authorized users however, i.e., the patient, authorized health care providers, and relatives, are able to 'see through' the pseudonymization and can re-establish the correct links. As shown on the right side, it becomes clear that the four highlighted medical records belong to the patient represented by the identification record in the middle.

---

[1] cf. Relative.

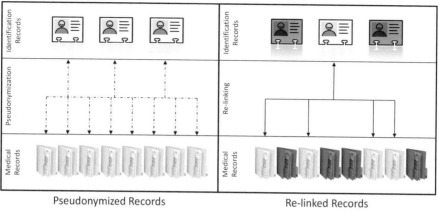

Pseudonymized Records

All persons and medical records are known, but non-authorized users cannot distinctly link the medical records to the individual persons represented by identification records.

Re-linked Records

Authorized users have the ability to identify the correct medical records that belong to a particular individual.

Fig. 2. Pseudonymized View for Authorized and Unauthorized Persons

2.2 Security Architecture

We built PIPE around a security architecture with three different layers each responsible for different aspects of the security framework (cf. Figure 3): The *authentication layer* is realized by the outer asymmetric keypair (outer private and public keys). The purpose of the first layer is to unambiguously identify the user, as the outer private key is only stored at the user's security token. With this outer private key, the next layer can be accessed by decrypting the inner private key which in turn allows decryption of the inner symmetric key. The inner asymmetric keypair and the inner symmetric key form the *authorization layer*. The inner symmetric key grants the user access to the final and innermost layer, the *pseudonymized data layer*. By decrypting the pseudonyms with the inner symmetric key, the user can finally relink the health record to the corresponding identification record.

In Figure 3, the health care provider on the right is authorized for a specific health record which is related to an identification record (dotted arrow) representing the patient in the center. This relation is mirrored by the relation between the identification and health pseudonyms, protected by encryption with the inner symmetric keys. Only users in the possession of the correct security tokens are able to pass each layer to finally decrypt this relation. The shared pseudonyms are encrypted with both the patient's and the health care provider's inner symmetric keys. The root pseudonyms are solely encrypted with the patient's inner symmetric key and therefore initially known to the patient only. Because of sharing the patient's inner private key with the relative who stores his version of this key encrypted with his inner symmetric key, the relative thus gains access to the root pseudonyms too.

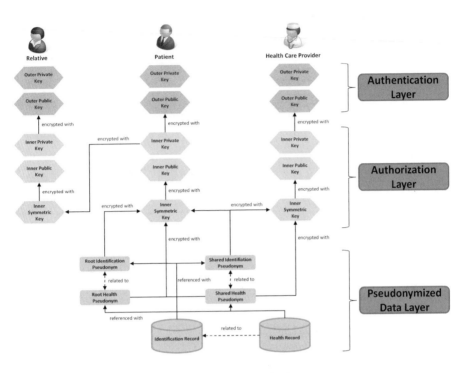

Fig. 3. Layered Security Architecture

2.3   Search within Pseudonymized Records

Because the encrypted pseudonyms do not (and must not) contain any semantic information on the data records they are referenced with, a query mechanism is required. We developed a simple keyword mechanism for that purpose. As arbitrary keywords are ill-suited for range queries and may reveal to much information that could compromise privacy, we allow only structured keywords that are constructed from pre-specified keyword templates. Depending on the actual application domain of the pseudonymization framework, the keyword templates may vary in type and range. For example, for the general e-health scenario, a preferably broad classification of diseases could be used. Standards like the International Statistical Classification of Diseases and Related Health Problems (ICD) or the Logical Observation Identifiers Names and Codes (LOINC) make ideal keyword templates. In addition to these standards, other general purpose templates such as document type (e.g., X-ray image, anamnesis, etc.) and date can complete a specific keyword. Privacy-preservation requires obscuring the relationship between keywords and pseudonyms too, wherefore the keywords' identifiers, like the pseudonyms, are encrypted with the inner symmetric keys and referenced with the encrypted pseudonyms.

3   Pseudonymization and Genetic Data

Like simple anonymization, plain pseudonymization for privacy preservation reaches its limits when genetic data are involved. In recent times, genetic testing has become increasingly popular for identifying genes inducing fatal diseases (predictive genetic testing) or testing individuals for drug responses (pharmacogenetics) [8]. Especially the results of predictive genetic tests must be handled with great care to prevent discrimination as explained earlier in this article. Predictive genetic testing usually involves the analysis of so-called Single Nucleotide Polymorphisms (SNPs), single-base differences at specific locations in the DNA sequence. Certain SNPs (or combinations of SNPs) are reported to be influential in causing a higher risk for certain illnesses. So by building an individual SNP map and comparing them with known profiles, a higher susceptibility to develop one of the categorized illnesses can thus be identified. Due to the identifying nature of genetic data, depersonalization is often not sufficient to hide the corresponding person: a specific X-ray image of a broken leg usually gets lost in the mass of images stored in a medical database, but depending on the size of a gene sample and the included SNPs (around 1 per 1000 base pairs), this gene string may uniquely identify the corresponding person. There are two ways to address this problem:

- Fragmentation: To reduce the information stored within a single data record, it can be fragmented and the data stored in separate records individually pseudonymized. This is appropriate for predictive genetic test results where usually only a very limited number of SNPs (and corresponding gene sequences) are analyzed. Predictive genetic tests are often issued in packages either suited for a certain group of persons (e.g., age 50+) or to check for a specific group of illnesses (e.g., cardiovascular diseases), involving different points of interests (POIs). By breaking up the individual results, patient-identifying profiling can be prevented.
- Encryption: In clinical research, especially basic research, gene sequences usually represent not single points of interest but rather areas, which means that the genetic data stored include much longer gene strings. Fragmentation could be too tedious here and would require a respectively large number of individual authorizations to cover a complete data set. In this case, full record description is more appropriate where each record is encrypted with its own data encryption key which is also shared when authorized.

For both scenarios, our basic pseudonymization scheme is no longer suitable: (i) Fragmentation requires that the information of the relationships between fragments is kept somewhere; the 1:1 pseudonym relationship is no longer suitable for hierarchical structures. (ii) Encryption of larger document content requires some mechanism to efficiently query within the encrypted record without fully decrypting it. The basic keyword scheme as described in Section 2.3 is no longer adequate to cover these issues.

3.1 Record Description Kit

To handle these new requirements, we developed a separate XML-based record description module or Record Description Kit[2], which allows processing of queries and updates over encrypted XML documents stored at untrusted servers by exploiting the structural semantics of XML records to return certain parts of the document without decrypting the whole record, and it uses the following mechanisms:

- Schema Labeling: An XML document is defined by a schema definition like an XML Schema or DTD. Each element, attribute, and text node of the XML document is assigned a unique label which encodes structural semantics of the items (path information), resulting in a schema-aware labeling scheme. This labeling schema allows querying for specific parts of the XML document and improves query efficiency because certain query parts can be processed without accessing the database
- Index Structure: In order to speed up frequently executed queries, index structures are created in an XPath-like syntax. These structures support typical queries such as for exact matches, range queries, or queries for structural information like 'all nodes on a specific path'.
- XML Document Storage Structure: XML documents are stored fragmented as key/value pairs, with labels as cryptographically hashed keys and the corresponding XML item as encrypted value. Fragmentation depends on the size of useful pieces of information within the document. Encryption and decryption can be done with standard symmetric cryptographic algorithms (e.g., AES). This ensures that the structure and content of the XML document is hidden from unauthorized viewers. Data stored in this form include index structures, metadata such as schema information, as well as the actual XML documents.

Queries are accepted in the form of (simple) XPath queries and translated to be checked against the labeling schema and index structures for the desired entry. If successful, the corresponding document fragment is retrieved from the database and decrypted.

3.2 Search within (Pseudonymized) Fragmented or Encrypted Records (Genetic Data)

Using the RDK, fragmentation and encryption can be supported as follows:

- Fragmentation: To support record fragmentation without encrypting the health records, the RDK can be used to create an XML-encoded 'inventory'

---

[2] The Record Description Kit was developed in close collaboration with our colleagues at the Data and Knowledge Engineering Group of the Johannes Kepler University in Linz, Austria, and is based on their Semantic-based Encrypted XML Document processing architecture SemCrypt
(http://www.dke.jku.at/research/projects/semcrypt.html)

or 'table of contents' listing all records the user is currently allowed to access. Data fragmentation needs to be done at a level such that the individual fragments do not allow patient profiling, but still provide useful information for clinical research. As usual, each fragment is assigned pseudonyms (depending on the number of authorizations) which are also kept in the XML document, along with suitable descriptions. Due to their encrypted state, arbitrary and more accurate record descriptions instead of high-level keywords can be stored without compromising confidentiality and privacy.

– Encryption: When fully encrypting the records, the RDK can be used to directly query within the encrypted record for certain parts of the document. Therefore, the record's information needs to be encoded in an XML-conforming data structure, like the Health Level 7 Clinical Document Architecture standard (HL7 CDA). This specification separates the document into a header and body part, where the header's elements are standardized for facilitated data interchange and the body can be arbitrarily defined, depending on the application domain. For genetic data, a specialized HL7 Clinical Genomics (HL7 CG) specification was developed, especially suited to fit the characteristics of genetic information including complete DNA sequences, SNPs, and individual alleles.

Although it seems redundant to pseudonymize fully encrypted records, pseudonymization still has its benefits. Consider the following scenario: Genetic data for clinical research are stored in a central database which is accessible by different research institutions and data contributed by multiple data providers (owners). The documents, which include larger amounts of genetic information, are only disclosed at a need-to-know basis to the research institutions by individual authorizations, and thus data disclosure can be strictly controlled. These authorizations include the encrypted and fragmented XML-encoded document including the labeling schema and index structures, as well as the document-specific cryptographic key required to decrypt the fragments; the dataset is referenced as usual with pseudonyms. While data confidentiality is no issue because of encryption, pseudonymization prevents the individual research institutions from learning which of the records where accesses by fellow researchers, which may be useful in competitive scenarios (e.g., patenting).

4   Formal and Practical Validation

We validated our approach both formally and practically: The formal validation involved the verification of the correctness of the PIPE pseudonymization protocol using the AVISPA tool (Automated Validation of Internet Security Protocols and Applications[3]), while the practical validation was conducted by developing a prototype, which has been implemented in a medium-sized firm offering predictive genetic testing. The AVISPA tool is a protocol verifier which provides implementations of different model-checking techniques in the form of multiple

---

[3] http://www.avispa-project.org

back-ends and requires the security protocol to be defined in the High Level Protocol Specification Language (HLPSL). We modeled each of the core pseudonymization workflows by defining the authorized users (patient, health care provider, relative), the server, and the database as individual roles and assigned them the corresponding knowledge (keys, pseudonyms, etc.). Assuming perfect cryptography and a Dolev-Yao attack scenario, the tool then checked whether an attacker was able to undermine the security goals, i.e, identify the correct pseudonyms and users (identifiers). At any state, the protocol was verified as secure, given that the attacker was provided with publicly available information only. For practical validation, we implemented a prototype to test our approach in a real-life scenario. Using this prototype, the firm pursued to fulfill several goals: (i) to comply with legal requirementsgenetic data need to be stored in an anonymized state; (ii) the data's confidentiality and privacy needs to be protected against attackers (especially insiders); (iii) secured data access should be possible for authorized external personal, and (iv) secondary use for internal statistics and research should be supported. The basic data entities which were decoupled included the patients (i.e., the test orderers) and the test results in the form of SNPs. In this closed scenario, the organization's administration department, managing the complete workflow, requires to know the relationship between test orderers and corresponding test results. Therefore the administration acts as data owner, while the lab has no authorization and thus no knowledge of the test orderers' identities either. We implemented the fragmentation scenario and tested two different cryptographic scenarios: In both scenarios, smart cards were used as authentication tokens. In the first scenario, all cryptographic operations were conducted within the smart cards, but in the second, the main cryptographic operations involved during accessing the authorization and pseudonymized data layer (cf. Figure 2) were executed on the host machines. The resulting performance differences were significant: While the limited calculation power of the smart cards resulted in data retrieval operations lasting several seconds, with host cryptography, the results were produced in well under a second, i.e., with neglectable overhead compared to non-pseudonymized records. Creating specialized index structures (cf. Section 3.1) improved the performance of smart card cryptography by reducing the individual encryption/decryption operations, but as expected never reached the speed of host cryptography.

5   Conclusion

Pseudonymization is a promising technique to fulfill the requirements of data storage and access for primary use as well as privacy-preserving secondary use, but in general requires a sufficiently large number of individuals and records to be effective. We also need to stress the fact that successful pseudonymization (as well as anonymization) requires reliable depersonalization, which can be quite difficult, if not impossible, for certain types of health data. Especially data involving genetic information need to be handled with special care due to the identifying nature. Therefore, we presented a pseudonymization approach that is suitable for pseudonymizing medical records. If required, the basic approach can be extended to handle queryable (selective) document encryption to handle genetic data. In this case, highly sensitive data fragments can be encrypted and still preserve query functionality, while depersonalized and large data, such as medical images, can be left unencrypted, but are still protected by pseudonymization.

Acknowledgements. This work was supported by grants of the Austrian Government's BRIDGE Research Initiative (contract 824884) and was performed at the research center Secure Business Austria funded by the Federal Ministry of Economy, Family and Youth of the Republic of Austria and by the City of Vienna.

References

1. Chaudry, B., Wang, J., Wu, S., Maglione, M., Mojica, W., Roth, E., Morton, S.C., Shekelle, P.G.: Systematic review: Impact of health information technology on quality, efficiency, and costs of medical care. Annals of Internal Medicine 144(10), 742–752 (2006)
2. Coalition of Genetic Fairness: Faces of genetic discrimination - How genetic discrimination affects real people (July 2004)
3. Congress of the United States of America: Genetic Information Nondiscrimination Act (2008)
4. Council for Responsible Genetics: Genetic discrimination (January 2001),
   http://www.councilforresponsiblegenetics.org/
   pageDocuments/2RSW5M2HJ2.pdf
5. European Union: Directive 95/46/EC of the European Parliament and of the Council of 24 October 1995 on the protection of individuals with regard to the processing of personal data and on the free movement of such data. Official Journal of the European Communities L 281, 31–50 (1995)
6. Fischer-Hübner, S.: IT-Security and Privacy: Design and use of privacy-enhancing security mechanisms. Springer, Berlin (2001)
7. Neubauer, T., Heurix, J.: A methodology for the pseudonymization of medical data. International Journal of Medical Informatics 80(3), 190–204 (2011)
8. Roses, A.D.: Pharmacogenetics and the practice of medicine. Nature 405, 857–865 (2000)
9. Safran, C., Bloomrosen, M., Hammond, W.E., Labkoff, S., Markel-Fox, S., Tang, P.C., Detmer, D.E.: Toward a national framework for the secondary use of health data: An american medical informatics association white paper. Journal of the American Medical Informatics Association 14, 1–9 (2007)
10. Sweeney, L.: k-Anonymity: A model for protecting privacy. International Journal on Uncertainty, Fuzziness and Knowledge-based Systems 10(5), 557–570 (2002)
11. Thomson, D., Bzdel, L., Golden-Biddle, K., Reay, T., Estabrooks, C.A.: Central questions of anonymization: A case study of secondary use of qualitative data. Forum Qualitative Social Research 6, 29 (2005)
12. United States Department of Health & Human Service: HIPAA Administrative Simplification: Enforcement; Final Rule. Federal Register / Rules and Regulations 71(32) (2006)

Correcting a Delegation Protocol for Grids

Benjamin Aziz

School of Computing
University of Portsmouth
Portsmouth PO1 3HE, United Kingdom
http://azizb.myweb.port.ac.uk/contact.html

Abstract. Delegation is one important aspect of large-scale distributed systems where many processes and operations run on behalf of system users and clients in order to achieve highly computational and resource intensive tasks. As such, delegation is often synonymous with the concept of trust, in that the delegator would expect some degree of reliability regarding the delegatee's ability and predictability to perform the delegated task. The delegation protocol itself is expected to maintain certain basic properties, such as integrity, traceability, accountability and the ability to determine delegation chains. In this paper, we give an overview of the vulnerabilities that one such delegation protocol exhibits, namely DToken, a lightweight protocol for Grid systems, as interesting examples of design mistakes. We also propose an alternative protocol, DToken II, which fixes such vulnerabilities.

Keywords: Delegation Protocols, Grid Systems, Security, Trust.

1 Introduction

Delegation is a concept that is usually mentioned in the context of trust, where generally a delegator would hold some trust in the ability and predictability of the delegatee in carrying out some task on behalf of the delegator or performing some behaviour related to the purpose of the delegation. There have been numerous definitions of what delegation is in the context of computing systems (e.g. [1, 2, 5, 18]). In Grid systems, a common mechanism used to achieve delegation is via *proxy certificates* [20]. However, proxy certificates have often been criticised in the past [20–22] for their weak performance, the lack of symmetric non-repudiation (only the identity of the delegator is preserved in the delegation) and the various security implications arising from the fresh generation of encryption key pairs at each delegation level.

Hence, DToken was proposed as a lightweight protocol [22] that could replace proxy certificates as a reliable and secure solution for the problem of delegation in large-scale Grid systems. Grid middleware systems, such as Globus[1] or GLite[2], adopt a model of the Grid often referred to as Virtual Organisations

---

[1] www.globus.org
[2] glite.web.cern.ch

S. Furnell, C. Lambrinoudakis, and G. Pernul (Eds.): TrustBus 2011, LNCS 6863, pp. 198–209, 2011.

(VOs), where in a VO, users from one organisation are permitted access and usage of resources such as computational power, storage and network bandwidth, belonging to another organisation under certain constraints. However, such cross-organisational provisioning of resources requires critical issues of trust and security to be managed in a reliable manner. One such issue is related to delegations by users to Grid *gateways* that allow the gateways to perform tasks on behalf of the users within the scope of the delegated permissions. DToken was designed to achieve such delegations in an integrity-preserving, accountable, traceable and determinisitic manner.

In this paper, we provide an overview of the results of a formal analysis that applied to the DToken protocol in [4] and that uncovered serious vulnerabilities in the protocol related to the above properties. We furthermore propose a second corrected version of the protocol, DToken II, which we claim fixes the vulnerabilities of the original version by changing slightly the specification of the protocol to allow agreement on the session identity number between the delegator and the delegatee, prevent the immature passing of permissions from the delegator to the delegatee and finally, use ordered lists instead of sets to pass information about delegation chains.

In the rest of the paper, we give an overview of the DToken protocol in the next Section 2 and discuss three essential properties that we expect to hold of this protocol, namely integrity, traceability and accountability, and deterministic delegation chains. In Section 3, we demonstrate that the protocol in fact suffers from vulnerabilities that undermine all of these desirable properties. In Section 4, we propose a new version of the protocol, DToken II, which implements fixes to the vulnerabilities in the original version. Finally, in Section 5, we discuss related work and conclude in Section 6.

2   The Delegation Protocol

We give an overview here of the DToken delegation protocol as was defined in [22]. The protocol comprises secure communications between a *Delegator*, *Dor*, and a *Delegatee*, *Dee*. The following sequence of messages describes the interactions in the protocol:

1. $Dor \rightarrow Dee : C_{Dor}, C_{Dee}, V_{fr}, V_{to}, TS, P_{Dor \rightarrow Dee}, DS_{Dor \rightarrow Dee0}, Sig_{Dor \rightarrow Dee}$
2. $Dee \rightarrow Dor : C_{Dor}, C_{Dee}, V_{fr}, V_{to}, TS, P_{Dor \rightarrow Dee}, DS_{Dor \rightarrow Dee}, Sig_{Dor \rightarrow Dee},$
$$Sig_{Dee \rightarrow Dor}, C_{Dor_{CAs}}$$

where,
C_{Dor}: Long-term public key identity certificate of *Dor*,
C_{Dee}: Long-term public key identity certificate of *Dee*,
V_{fr}: The starting validity date of the delegation,
V_{to}: The expiry date of the delegation,
TS: A timestamp representing the time the message is generated,

$P_{Dor \to Dee}$: The delegated permissions from Dor to Dee, which include the delegation policies,

$DS_{Dor \to Dee}$: A number representing the delegation session identifier,

$DS_{Dor \to Dee0}$: Initial empty value of $DS_{Dor \to Dee}$, which for simplicity is assumed to be $Null$,

$Sig_{Dor \to Dee}$: The signature of the delegation information in the first message signed by the private key of Dor, K_{Dor}, where

$$Sig_{Dor \to Dee} \overset{\text{def}}{=} \{\!| C_{Dor}, C_{Dee}, V_{fr}, V_{to}, TS, P_{Dor \to Dee}, DS_{Dor \to Dee0} |\!\}_{K_{Dor}},$$

$Sig_{Dee \to Dor}$: The signature of Dor's signature in the first message signed by the private key of Dee, K_{Dee}, where $Sig_{Dee \to Dor} \overset{\text{def}}{=} \{\!| Sig_{Dor \to Dee} |\!\}_{K_{Dee}}$, and

$C_{Dor_{CAs}}$: The list of subordinate CAs linking C_{Dor} to the trusted root authority.

Where we write $\{\!| M |\!\}_K$ to represent the signing of the message M by the private key K, which is also a syntactic sugar for applying an encryption $\{\!| - |\!\}_K$ to the hash of the message; i.e. $\{\!| M |\!\}_K \overset{\text{def}}{=} \{\!| hash(M) |\!\}_K$, such that $hash(-)$ is any of the MD5 or SHA hashing functions.

From this definition of the protocol, there are a few points to note as highlighted in [22]. In the first message, $DS_{Dor \to Dee}$ has an empty value, which we assume to be some default value like $Null$. The choice of the delegatee's decision to assign the delegation session identifier rather than the delegator was not explained by the designers of the protocol. Timestamps in both messages are neglected in our analysis, as these are often non-reliable means of sequencing events in distributed systems due to the problem of clock synchronisation.

The second message is referred to as the DToken (Delegation Token) from Dor to Dee, written as $DT_{Dor \to Dee}$, which represents the mutual delegation agreement between Dor and Dee. In this message, Dee will update the value for $DS_{Dor \to Dee}$ assigning it the current delegation session identifier. Furthermore, in between the two messages, Dee performs some verification tests to ensure that Dor is authorised to delegate permissions to Dee and to ensure that the security information Dor has sent in the first message is indeed valid. For example, Dee will ensure that the certificates are valid and can be traced up to the root of trust and that the token has not expired.

Another main assumption in the protocol is that all the communications between Dor and Dee are carried over Secure Sockets Layer (SSL)-based channels [11]. This means that Dor and Dee are sure of each others identities and the privacy of messages is guaranteed against external intruders. However, communication security does not imply that such external intruders cannot participate in the protocol like any other agents.

The protocol is claimed to form chains of delegation. Once the last delegatee in the delegation chain decides to stop delegating, it is assumed that it will execute the delegated permissions, $P_{Dor \to Dee}$, by applying them to a *Delegation Enforcement Point* (DEP), typically a service or a resource. The DEP will perform a couple of validation steps to check the integrity of the DToken containing the permissions and other DTokens forming the full delegation chain. In [22], the authors give an example of a delegation chain in Grid systems as shown in Figure 1.

Fig. 1. DToken Chained Delegation through a Gateway (cited from [22, Figure 5])

This chain consists of the user as the delegation root, who then delegates some permissions to run a job to a gateway (a computer on which the user can login). Then the gateway delegates the job to a job queueing system, which itself is the end of the delegation chain. The job queueing system will then execute the job on a file system (the DEP). One aspect of the communication between the job queueing system and the file system is that the DTokens generated in the previous communications are passed as a set. We demonstrate later how this aspect introduces a vulnerability in the protocol.

2.1 Protocol Properties

The DToken protocol was designed to achieve lightweight delegation focusing on traceability of the participants rather than their privacy (in contrast to protocols such as [20]), therefore, it should sustain a few properties related to its purposes and functionality.

DToken Integrity. This property refers to the success of a DEP in validating the integrity of a DToken. This implies that the two hash comparisons mentioned in Section 4 in [22] must always succeed.

Property 1 (DToken Integrity Validation). A DToken is said to be valid if the following equations are true:

$$hash(C_U, C_G, V_{fr}, V_{to}, TS, P_{U \to G}, DS_{U \to G}) = decrypt(Sig_{U \to G}, C_U)$$
$$hash(Sig_{U \to G}) = decrypt(Sig_{G \to U}, C_G)$$

Where $decrypt(\{\!|M|\!\}_{K_A}, C_A)$ is a decryption function that if applied to a message encrypted with the private key K_A of some agent A using the public certificate C_A for that agent, will yield back the plaintext M corresponding to the ciphertext.

The first of the above equations compares the hash of the delegation information to the decryption of the signature of the delegator. The success of this validation implies the consent of the delegator to the delegation. The second compares the hash of the delegator's signature with the decryption of the delegatee's signature. This second validation implies the consent of the delegatee to the delegation. In general, the success of both comparisons ensures that the DToken's integrity is preserved.

Traceability and Accountability. Traceability is defined in [22] as the ability of the delegatee to uniquely identify the identity of any of the previous delegators.

Accountability, on the other hand, is verifiable traceability where such identity is cryptographically identifiable. Accountability is also called non-repudiation. More specifically, we define non-repudiation as the property that neither the delegator nor the delegatee can deny their acceptance of the delegation at the point of permission execution. This implies further that the delegatee must not be able to use the delegated permissions before at least having signed the DToken containing those permissions initiated by the delegator.

We define the property of verifiable non-repudiation as follows, assuming *Perms* is the set of all permission.

Property 2 (Verifiable Non-repudiation). Given a delegator, *Dor*, and a delegatee, *Dee*, then we say that neither can deny the delegation if the following holds:
$$\forall P_{Dor \to Dee} \in Perms : use(Dee, P_{Dor \to Dee}) \Rightarrow$$
$$(signed(Dee, P_{Dor \to Dee}) \land signed(Dor, P_{Dor \to Dee})) \qquad \square$$

Where $use(Dee, P_{Dor \to Dee})$ is a predicate implying that *Dee is able to use* the permissions $P_{Dor \to Dee}$ it has received from the delegator *Dor*, and $signed(A, P_{A \to B})$ is another predicate meaning that the signature $Sig_{A \to B}$ exists and has been created by A. Hence, the above property says that it must hold that each time a delegatee is able to use some permissions, then those permissions must have been signed by both the delegator and the delegatee agents.

Deterministic Delegation Chains. The property of *deterministic delegation chains* implies the ability of determining the delegation chain ending at a DEP based on the set of DTokens received by that DEP. The property is deterministic since the delegation chain consists of a single trace of delegation events.

In order to define this property, we first need to establish what is meant by a delegation chain according to the DToken protocol, assuming *Agents* is the set of all possible agents that can participate in the protocol.

Definition 1 (Delegation Chains). *Given a set of DTokens, DT_{set}, then we name the set of all DToken chains that can be constructed from DT_{set} as DT_{chain}. Every element in DT_{chain} is a finite list, dc, where $|dc| > 1$ and such that for any two adjacent DToken elements, $a, b \in dc$, then the following holds:*
$$\exists Dor, Dee, H \in Agents : \quad (a = DT_{Dor \to Dee}) \land (b = DT_{Dee \to H}) \qquad \square$$

Hence, in a delegation chain, adjacent elements have common adjacent participating agents (i.e. *Dee*). Now, we can define the property of deterministic delegation chains as follows.

Property 3 (Deterministic Delegation Chains). Given a set of DTokens, DT_{set}, then a deterministic delegation chain implies that $|DT_{chain}| = 1$. $\qquad \square$

If however, $|DT_{chain}| > 1$, then a DEP validating the delegation path from a specific root delegator will not be able to determine the exact chain of delegations leading to itself.

3   Vulnerabilities of the Current Protocol

In [4], we carried out a verification of the DToken protocol using static analysis techniques based on abstract interpretation. The analysis revealed several vulnerabilities in the protocol, which we summarise in the following sections. The assumption we made regarding the nature of the intruder was that the intruder was just another protocol participant (same assumptions made in [22]) who has a well-known certified identity who is only able to divert the protocol via messages that make sense to other participants. The use of secure communications in the protocol prevented external intruders from interfering with the protocol messages. This assumption yields our intruder less powerful than Dolev-Yao's *most powerful attacker* [8, 10], since for example, we do not assume that the intruder is capable of listening passively to communications among other participants or injecting data into the exchanged messages without participating in a protocol session.

3.1   Non-matching Hash Validation

The first vulnerability we discovered was in the case of a single delegation step, i.e. where there is one delegator, *Dor*, and one delegatee, *Dee*, though it is also applicable to the more general case of n delegation steps. The vulnerability is simply an incorrect specification of the protocol that prevents the integrity of a DToken from being validated. This is caused by the fact that the delegator (*Dor*) agent always signs a *Null* value for the delegation session identifier, which is $DS_{Dor \rightarrow Dee0}$ in Message 1. This is, in Message 2., assigned a different value by the delegatee (*Dee*), which is the value of the identifier $DS_{Dor \rightarrow Dee}$. In the protocol of Section 2, this is equivalent to the first integrity check:

$$hash(C_{Dor}, C_{Dee}, V_{fr}, V_{to}, TS, P_{Dor \rightarrow Dee}, DS_{Dor \rightarrow Dee}) =$$
$$decrypt(\{C_{Dor}, C_{Dee}, V_{fr}, V_{to}, TS, P_{Dor \rightarrow Dee}, DS_{Dor \rightarrow Dee0}\}|_{K_{Dor}}, C_{Dor})$$

Applying the decryption of the signature, we further simplify the equation to:

$$hash(C_{Dor}, C_{Dee}, V_{fr}, V_{to}, TS, P_{Dor \rightarrow Dee}, DS_{Dor \rightarrow Dee}) =$$
$$hash(C_{Dor}, C_{Dee}, V_{fr}, V_{to}, TS, P_{Dor \rightarrow Dee}, DS_{Dor \rightarrow Dee0})$$

which clearly does not hold, due to the difference in the value of $DS_{Dor \rightarrow Dee}$ in both messages. This reveals a lack of agreement on the delegation session identifier values as assigned by the delegator and the delegatee, and it is a significant result as it undermines the claims in [22] of the ability of the DEP to validate the integrity property of any DTokens it receives and further brings in to question some of the evaluation results presented for the case of chained delegations, since any such chains could not possibly have been successfully validated since the first DToken validation will always fail.

3.2 Delegation Repudiation

The second vulnerability that we uncovered was that delegations in the DToken protocol can be repudiated. This is relevant to the case of a delegation where the delegatee attempts to execute permissions received from the delegator on a DEP. For example, in the case of a Grid system, the delegator could be the user U and the delegatee the gateway G. G then attempts to execute permissions received from U say on a file system. The case assumes that both U and DEP play their normal roles in an honest manner, whereas G is playing a man-in-the-middle role where in addition to being able to run its normal protocol behaviour (delegatee for U and user of DEP), it is also running extra code that attempts to subvert the protocol. A "robust" protocol, hence, would be expected to withstand such subversive behaviour.

Assuming that U delegates to G and G attempts to execute the delegated permissions on the DEP, the attack occurs with the following run of messages from two sessions:

1. $U \rightarrow G : C_U, C_G, V_{fr}, V_{to}, TS, P_{U \rightarrow G}, DS_{U \rightarrow G0}, Sig_{U \rightarrow G}$

1′. $G \rightarrow G : C_G, C_G, V_{fr}, V_{to}, TS, P_{U \rightarrow G}, DS_{U \rightarrow G0}, Sig_{G \rightarrow G}$

2′. $G \rightarrow G : C_G, C_G, V_{fr}, V_{to}, TS, P_{U \rightarrow G}, DS_{U \rightarrow G}, Sig_{G \rightarrow G}, |\{Sig_{G \rightarrow G}\}|_{K_G}, C_{G_{CAs}}$

In the first session, the user U attempts to delegate some permissions $P_{U \rightarrow G}$ in Message 1 to G. This session is left incomplete by G, and so it does not sign anything (i.e. there is no Message 2 for the first session). In the second session, G simply delegates the received permissions to itself in order to create a syntactically valid but semantically dummy DToken. The DEP will successfully validate (on the condition that the integrity validation vulnerability of the previous section is fixed) the token as it is syntactically correct and will assume that G has delegated the permissions to itself. Therefore, the delegation that occurred in the first session can easily be repudiated by the delegatee.

The vulnerability works because it is possible, with the above run of messages, to show that:

$$\exists P_{U \rightarrow G} \in Perms : use(G, P_{U \rightarrow G}) \Rightarrow \neg(signed(G, P_{U \rightarrow G}) \wedge signed(U, P_{U \rightarrow G}))$$

As a result, the right hand side of the implication will always be false in either of the two sessions. In the first session, G does not sign the delegation token and so can repudiate the delegation, and in the second session, U has not signed the delegation, and so it can repudiate the delegation as well. The main reason behind this vulnerability is that the delegatee always receives permissions prematurely from the delegator, therefore, it is able to subvert its part on signing the DToken, whereas it is too late for the delegator to sign those permissions in the second session.

One argument against the validity of such a vulnerability is that the local policies at the DEP should be able to prevent G from using $P_{U \rightarrow G}$. However, we consider this argument to be weak as it associates the robustness of the protocol with the expressivity of the DEP policies. There are simply no guarantees that the DEP will enforce such policies, specifically in scenarios where the anonymity of the agents is required or where the DEP is a stateless Web service.

3.3 Non-deterministic Delegation Chains

This case is an interesting one since it did not feature in the original design of the DToken protocol presented in [22] and it assumes the presence of four agents, two of which are playing men-in-the-middle roles, though the vulnerability also applies to the general case of $n \geq 4$ number of agents. The original protocol of [22] assumes in several occasions[3] that the protocol is indeed able to form deterministic delegation chains. This is true in the specific case where the number of participating agents is less than or equal three. However, in the case of four agents, the possibility of internal circular delegations arises. In order to explain this, consider the following example.

Example 1. Assume agents A, B, C and D with the following scenario of delegation: *A delegates to B, B delegates to C, C delegates to A, A delegates to C and C delegates to D.* This scenario results in D receiving the following set of DTokens: $\{DT_{A \rightarrow B}, DT_{B \rightarrow C}, DT_{C \rightarrow A}, DT_{A \rightarrow C}, DT_{C \rightarrow D}\}$

However, due to the presence of the delegation cycle - C delegates to A and A delegates to C-, D is able to form the following chain using the same set of tokens: *A delegates to C, C delegates to A, A delegates to B, B delegates to C and C delegates to D.* This is clearly different chain from the actual one above. The implication of this is that D will not be able to *determine* the exact set of delegations leading to itself.   □

From our analysis in [4], we were able to show that $|DT_{chain}| > 1$ in the case of four agents or more participating in the protocol. Since delegation is a form of trust, this vulnerability breaks the trust chain and does not preserve the deterministic delegation chain property of Section 2. Chains of trust are common in many sensitive scenarios, such as in the case of digital forensics evidence preservation, where Chains of Custody (CoC) require that every step in the handling of a criminal evidence is well documented and its integrity can be proven for the evidence to be acceptable in a court. Hence, the CoC (*A delegates to B, B delegates to C, C delegates to A, A delegates to C and C delegates to D*) may be trusted in a court, whereas the CoC (*A delegates to C, C delegates to A, A delegates to B, B delegates to C and C delegates to D*) may not.

Technically, this vulnerability arises from the fact that DTokens are passed as a set, rather than as a list as is expected from the definition of delegation chains in Property 3. A set has no notion of ordering or indeed multiplicity. A richer structure, like lists, is needed when grouping and passing DTokens, such that some reasoning on their temporal ordering can be achieved.

---

[3] See, for example, Verification 3 of page 7 and Section 5 of page 8.

4   DToken II: The Corrected Version

We now propose a new version of the DToken protocol, which we believe does not suffer from any of the above vulnerabilities in the original protocol. The protocol consists of the following steps:

1. $Dor \rightarrow Dee : RfD_{Dor}$
2. $Dee \rightarrow Dor : \{\!|DS_{Dor \rightarrow Dee}, RfD_{Dor}\!|\}_{K_{Dee}}$
3. $Dor \rightarrow Dee : C_{Dor}, C_{Dee}, V_{fr}, V_{to}, TS, P_{Dor \rightarrow Dee}, DS_{Dor \rightarrow Dee}, Sig_{Dor \rightarrow Dee}$
4. $Dee \rightarrow Dor : C_{Dor}, C_{Dee}, V_{fr}, V_{to}, TS, P_{Dor \rightarrow Dee}, DS_{Dor \rightarrow Dee}, Sig_{Dor \rightarrow Dee},$
   $\qquad\qquad Sig_{Dee \rightarrow Dor}, C_{Dor_{CAs}}$

In this corrected version, the delegator commences the protocol by sending a *request for delegation* message RfD_{Dor}. This messages can be considered as a negotiation message, which may include description of the delegated permissions or any other delegation information. If the delegatee accepts the request, it will reply by proposing the delegation session identifier signed with its signature along with the original request from the delegator. Next, we discuss the three properties we introduced in Section 2.1 in light of this new protocol.

4.1   DToken Integrity Validation

One suggestion to fix the vulnerability of non-matching hash validation in the current protocol is to simply allow the delegator to choose the session identifier instead of the delegatee. In this way, the delegator will agree on the same value of the identifier as the one chosen by the delegatee. Hence, in DToken II, both messages 3 and 4 (corresponding to messages 1 and 2 in the original protocol) use the same value for delegation session identifier, $DS_{Dor \rightarrow Dee}$, therefore both validation steps of Property 1 involving the comparison of the hashes of the two signatures will succeed, since they both are applied to the same value of $DS_{Dor \rightarrow Dee}$.

4.2   Verifiable Non-repudiation

Fixing the vulnerability of delegation repudiation in the original protol, the delegator should only send the permissions to the delegatee *after* the latter has agreed (by signing the delegation information) to participate in the delegation session. In this way, the delegatee has no means of denying its participation in the protocol. Also, a monitoring service should be introduced to the architecture to record the signatures and provide evidence whenever required.

   To be able to prove Property 2 holds, the definition of RfD_{Dor} in Message 1 of the new protocol will need to include some reference to $P_{Dor \rightarrow Dee}$. Once this is signed in Message 2 by the delegatee, the latter cannot repudiate its acceptance of the session, even though this is proven outside the structure of the DToken itself (i.e. within RfD_{Dor}). This is because the implication in Property 2 will hold true. Additionally, since the delegatee has signed the session identifier also in Message 2, the delegator can now prove the association between the delegated permissions and the delegation session through this identifier.

4.3 Deterministic Delegation Chains

Finally, in order to achieve deterministic delegation chains, we propose that DTokens be passed in a *list* structure as opposed to the *set* structure as it was done in the original protocol, when performing second and further level delegations. Let's consider the same example we discussed in Section 3.3. The set of DTokens passed will be a list $[DT_{A\to B}, DT_{B\to C}, DT_{C\to A}, DT_{A\to C}, DT_{C\to D}]$, which is unique, i.e. adding new elements or changing the ordering sequence of elements will result in a new list (chain). From a practical point of view, this implies that in the case of the original design of Figure 1, we propose that the job queueing system passes the list [DTU $\to$ G; DTG $\to$ JQS] instead of {DTU $\to$ G, DTG $\to$ JQS}. This will ensure that DTokens are ordered in their temporal sequencing and so non-determinism does not arise when building chains.

5 Related Work

The use of tokens for achieving delegation in distributed systems is a common technique that has been used in many popular systems throughout the years, such as for example, Kerberos [14]. A recent taxonomy of delegation methods has recently been published in [15], where various types of delegation tokens and credentials are discussed. Further uses of delegation tokens in collaborative applications include healthcare [13], identity management in service-oriented architectures [23] and in the context of Web-based social networking [16].

Literature provides several protocols for achieving delegation. In [7], the security implications when adopting delegation solutions in Grids are considered. These implications are discussed in the scope of two delegation schemes for Grids; delegation chaining and call-back delegations. Another research work closely related to the DToken protocol is the hierarchical delegation tokens architecture and protocols proposed by Ding and Petersen [9]. In this work, the authors propose a number of delegation protocols based on the Schnorr signature scheme [17], which are either key-based, identity-based or a combination of the two.

The work in [4] is not the first case where formal analysis techniques have been applied to delegation protocols. In [3], the authors verify the delegation scheme in the SESAME protocol, a compatible extension version of Kerberos [14], using the Coq theorem prover [6]. In [19], the authors provide a formalisation of the security of proxy signature schemes and analyse one such scheme, namely the Kim, Park and Won scheme [12].

6 Conclusion and Future Work

We presented in this paper an overview of the vulnerabilities that were formally proven in [4] to exist in the DToken protocol [22]; a lightweight delegation protocol for Grid systems. As a result our conclusion regarding the protocol is that it is not suitable for delegations in scenarios where the delegated permissions refer to stateless Web services or require the anonymity of the participants. Also, it is limited by its lack of an essential feature in delegations, i.e. deterministic delegation chains, which are essential when chains of trust are to be preserved, for example in cases where forensic evidence on the usage of Grid resources must be maintained over the chain of custody handling the evidence. We also presented DToken II, an alternative protocol, which include fixes to the above vulnerabilities. In the future, we plan to formally verify the new DToken II protocol to analyse its behaviour against the three properties described in this paper.

References

1. Atluri, V., Warner, J.: Supporting conditional delegation in secure workflow management systems. In: Proceedings of the Tenth ACM Symposium on Access Control Models and Technologies, SACMAT 2005, pp. 49–58. ACM, New York (2005)
2. Aura, T.: On the structure of delegation networks. In: Proceedings of the 11th IEEE Workshop on Computer Security Foundations, pp. 14–26. IEEE Computer Society, Washington, DC, USA (1998)
3. Ayadi, M., Bolignano, D.: On the formal verification of delegation in SESAME. In: Proceedings of the 12th Annual Conference on Computer Assurance (COMPASS 1997), pp. 23–34. IEEE Computer Society, Los Alamitos (1997)
4. Aziz, B., Hamilton, G.: Verifying a delegation protocol for grid systems. Future Generation Computer Systems: The International Journal of Grid Computing and eScience 27(5), 476–485 (2011)
5. Barka, E., Sandhu, R.: Framework for role-based delegation models. In: Proceedings of the 16th Annual Computer Security Applications Conference, ACSAC 2000, pp. 168–176. IEEE Computer Society, Washington, DC, USA (2000)
6. Bertot, Y., Castéran, P.: Coq'Art: The Calculus of Inductive Constructions. Springer, Heidelberg (2004)
7. Broadfoot, P., Lowe, G.: Architectures for Secure Delegation within Grids. Tech. Rep. PGR-RR-03-19, Oxford University Computing Laboratory (2003)
8. Cervesato, I.: The dolev-yao intruder is the most powerful attacker. In: Halpern, J. (ed.) Proceedings of the 16th Annual Symposium on Logic in Computer Science, pp. 246–265. IEEE Computer Society Press, Boston (2001)
9. Ding, Y., Petersen, H.: A New Approach for Delegation using Hierarchical Delegation Tokens. Tech. Rep. TR-95-5-E, University of Technology Chemnitz-Zwickau (1995)
10. Dolev, D., Yao, A.: On the security of public key protocols. In: Proceedings of the 22nd Annual Symposium on Foundations of Computer Science, pp. 350–357 (October 1981)
11. Group, T.L.S.W.: The ssl protocol version 3.0 (November 1996)
12. Kim, S., Park, S., Won, D.: Proxy signatures, revisited. In: Han, Y., Quing, S. (eds.) ICICS 1997. LNCS, vol. 1334, pp. 223–232. Springer, Heidelberg (1997)
13. Masi, M., Maurer, R.: On the usage of SAML delegate assertions in an healthcare scenario with federated communities. Tech. rep., Dipartimento di Sistemi e Informatica, Univ. Firenze (2010)

14. Miller, S.P., Neuman, C., Schiller, J.I., Saltzer, J.H.: Kerberos authentication and authorization system - project athena technical plan. Tech. Rep. Section E.2.1, MIT, USA (October 1987)
15. Pham, Q., Reid, J., McCullagh, A., Dawson, E.: On a Taxonomy of Delegation. Challenges for Security, Privacy and Trust 29(5), 565–579 (2010)
16. Schiffman, J., Zhang, X., Gibbs, S.: Dauth: Fine-grained authorization delegation for distributed web application consumers. In: IEEE International Workshop on Policies for Distributed Systems and Networks, pp. 95–102 (2010)
17. Schnorr, C.P.: Effecient Signature Generation by Smart Cards. Journal of Cryptology 4, 161–174 (1991)
18. Stein, L.A.: Delegation is inheritance. SIGPLAN Not. 22, 138–146 (1987)
19. Tan, Z., Liu, Z.: Provably secure delegation-by-certification proxy signature schemes. In: InfoSecu 2004: Proceedings of the 3rd International Conference on Information Security, pp. 38–43. ACM, New York (2004)
20. Tuecke, S., Welch, V., Engert, D., Pearlman, L., Thompson, M.: Internet x.509 public key infrastructure (pki): Proxy certificate profile. RFC 3820 (June 2004)
21. Welch, V., Foster, I., Kesselman, C., Mulmo, O., Pearlman, L., Gawor, J., Meder, S., Siebenlist, F.: X.509 proxy certificates for dynamic delegation. In: Proceedings of the 3rd Annual PKI Research and Development Workshop (2004)
22. Yang, E.Y., Matthews, B.: Dtoken: A lightweight and traceable delegation architecture for distributed systems. In: SRDS 2009: Proceedings of the 2009 28th IEEE International Symposium on Reliable Distributed Systems, pp. 107–116. IEEE Computer Society, Washington, DC, USA (2009)
23. Zhang, Y., Chen, J.L.: A Delegation Solution for Universal Identity Management in SOA. IEEE Transactions on Services Computing 99 (2010)

Risk Assessment for Mobile Devices

Thomas Ledermüller[1,3] and Nathan L. Clarke[1,2]

[1] Centre for Security, Communications and Network Research,
University of Plymouth, Plymouth, UK
[2] School of Computer and Information Science, Edith Cowan University,
Perth, Western Australia
[3] Upper Austria University of Applied Sciences, Hagenberg, Austria
nclarke@plymouth.ac.uk

Abstract. With the market penetration of mobile phones and the trend towards
the adoption of more sophisticated services, the risks posed by such devices, for
the individual and the enterprise, has increased considerably. Risk assessment
(RA) is an established approach with organisations for understanding and
mitigating information security threats. However, it is also a time consuming
process requiring an experienced analyst. Within mobile devices, the interested
stakeholders range from administrators to the general public and an approach is
therefore required that can establish RA in a fast, user convenient and effective
manner. The proposed method utilises a number of approaches to minimise the
effort required from the end-user, taking the different security requirements of
various services into account and ensuring a level of flexibility that will enable
all categories of user (from novice to expert) to engage with the process.

Keywords: Information security, risk assessment, mobile phone, smart phone,
end-user risk assessment, computing, IT.

1 Introduction

Mobile phones (the single most popular category of mobile devices) have a market
penetration of 119% in the developed world [1]. The technology has become
ubiquitous with people increasingly reliant upon the services it provides. No longer is
the device simply for telephony or text messaging, but rather a whole host of
applications that enable the user to complete a variety of actions form banking to
accessing corporate networks. This increasing range of functionality and the access to
personal/corporate information they provide is becoming more and more the focus of
attackers [2-3].

As such the risk posed by mobile devices has increased. Indeed, a number
of surveys, such as the Computer Crime and Abuse Survey [4] indicate that 42.2% of
respondents experienced laptop/mobile device theft – 6% of which reported loss of
intellectual property due to the loss. Current approaches to RA tend to treat the mobile
device in its entirety, without looking at the actual functions and information they
store. Whilst this was appropriate when devices had little functionality, the level of
sophistication of current mobile devices and services, requires a re-evaluation [5].

S. Furnell, C. Lambrinoudakis, and G. Pernul (Eds.): TrustBus 2011, LNCS 6863, pp. 210–221, 2011.
© Springer-Verlag Berlin Heidelberg 2011

Whilst current RA methodologies could simply be extended to facilitate mobile devices, this is a rather narrow perspective to take – as only enterprise organizations will have the expertise, time and money to fund such an assessment. Mobile devices are not merely an enterprise-level technology, indeed all aspects of society use mobile devices – albeit to varying degrees. Nevertheless, an approach to RA is required that is able to access all levels of society and provide the robustness and flexibility to enable enterprise organizations to also benefit.

As no such existing methodology could be identified, the focus of this paper is to present a novel methodology that enables users with differing levels of knowledge about information security to understand and to assess the risks related to their mobile device. As well as providing a mechanism for informing users about the risks, the approach also provides detailed risk information regarding individual application and service usage. Such information could be directly used by security countermeasures to provide a more granular perspective on the problem [6]. In this manner, the device would assess the risk of access prior to deploying potentially inconvenient and intrusive security measures. For example, why enforce a 12-character password when the user simply wants to play a game on the device. Should they wish to access the users bank account, such a mechanism would be far more applicable. This paper develops the concept first proposed by [7].

The paper is begins with a review of the current RA approaches in section 2. In order to reduce the complexity of RA processes, Section 3 discusses the process of identification and categorization of applications. The risk calculation method is described in section 4 and the corresponding process is shown in the following section. Section 6 describes the developed prototype and preliminary end-user evaluation. Finally, the conclusion and future work is presented.

2 Classic Risk Assessment

RA is a well-established mechanism within information security for ensuring a commensurate level of security is provided given the risks. As such, various information security standards such as, ISO/IEC 27000 standards and the National Institute of Standards and Technologies Special Publication 800 Series were developed. Also various RA methodologies like for example OCTAVE(-S) [8], CRAMM [9], MEHARI[10] have also been designed to meet specific requirements.

All analyzed RA approaches treat mobile/smart phones as a single entity and make heavy use of workshops and interviews to identify assets, threats and vulnerabilities. The worth of an asset, the likelihood of a threat and the severity of vulnerabilities is mainly assessed through a qualitative rating scheme using different scales. As these ratings are subjective, knowledge in the area of information security and about the used assessment approach is imperative, in order to get realistic ratings. Furthermore, all methodologies are complex and time consuming. As the intended methodology shall be usable even by novice or average end-user, existing methodologies are not appropriate. The methodology must be fast in execution, options must be limited and yet comprehensive [11].

3 Categorisation

To individually risk assess mobile applications would be a time consuming and never-ending task. For example, the number of applications in Apple's App Store has increased more than fivefold within one year (207,639 – May 2010) [12]. Moreover, this fails to take into account bespoke organizational applications that might exist. Therefore, in order to support end-users, reduce the loading yet provide a meaningful assessment, the approach has proposed a categorization (which can also be referred to as assets in RA nomenclature). Based on the identified mobile phone usage trends and the market offer (Blackberry App World, Apple App Store, Android Market, Nokia Ovi Store and HTC Apps) the following asset categories have been developed:

Table 1. Asset categories

Network access - communication:	
Voice communication	Messaging
Network access - data network:	
E-mail	Web access
Personal information (online synchronized)	Bluetooth/IR
Network access - data network - applications:	
Maps & Navigation	Social networking
News & Information	E-banking
E-learning	E-health
Remote access	Ticketing/Shopping
Utilities, Personalization, Games, Entertainment	Books and libraries
Business applications (3rd party applications)	Business applications – in-house developments
Music/Audio/Video, Photography	
(Control) of device/Stored data:	
Physical device	Offline applications/Utilities
Data synchronization with PC	Documents
Multimedia data stored on device	Configurations and other
Password storage	Personal information

The determination of risk within the methodology is based upon the standard formula; risk is calculated from the multiplication of the asset value, threats and vulnerability. The worth of an asset can result from various dimensions. It can be estimated in terms of money, but also as impact in terms of CIA. Derived from previous RA methodologies, seven dimensions for the estimation of the value of an asset are defined. These asset value categories **Error! Reference source not found.**are the same, whether a mobile device is used in a private or a corporate environment; however, the terminology has been modified to ensure it is appropriate for the particular audience.

Table 2. Asset value categories

Private context	Corporate context
Impact of Disruption	Loss of availability
Impact on personal privacy	Breach of commercial confidentiality
Impact of data corruption	Loss of data integrity
Impact of embarrassment	Loss of reputation
Financial loss	Financial loss
Legal liability	Legal liability
Impact on personal safety	Impact on personal safety

Compared to the traditional computer environment (servers, clients, network components, etc.) little research and real world data exists concerning the likelihood of threats and the severity of vulnerabilities within a mobile context. Therefore a set of generic threats categories was developed. The proposed categorization of threats was generated based [2], [9],[13], [14]:

Table 3. Threat categories

Unauthorized information access	Denial-of-service
Unauthorised use of a service, an application	Malicious content Unauthorized collection of user data
Communications Technical failure of device	Theft/Loss/Damage by insiders/outsiders
Unsolicited information	Repudiation
Communications interception (including active and passive interception)	

The level of vulnerability is determined in terms of the thoroughness of the design process itself. To identify those, a list of questions were developed (see Annex A) based on the SANS top software errors (http://www.sans.org/top25-software-errors/) was developed. An except is illustrated in Table 4.

Table 4. Excerpt of vulnerability questions

TRUE	Are credentials transmitted via an encrypted channel?
TRUE	Is 3rd party encryption used for storage of data on the device?
FALSE	Are there any encryption algorithms used which are no longer considered as secure?
TRUE	Is there a procedure in place to ensure regular updates of the application?
FALSE	Claims the application per default access to data stored on the phone, which are not necessary (e.g. Game - access to call history)

4 Risk Calculation Scheme

Based on the developed categories, which are the input parameters for the proposed RA method, the risk calculation scheme, which consists of the following 6 steps works in the following way.

— RA_Step 1 – Evaluation of asset value categories
— RA_Step 2 – Calculation of a single asset value
— RA_Step 3 – Evaluation of threats
— RA_Step 4 – Calculation of a single threat value
— RA_Step 5 – Answer vulnerability questions.
— RA_Step 6 – Calculation of risk level

During the first step the asset value categories for an asset are evaluated in terms of potential consequences using a scale from 0 – not applicable, to 8 – critical. These values are used in the second step to calculate a single asset value. The procedure is the same for the threats in step three and four. The threat categories are evaluated (0 – not applicable to 5 – almost certain). To determine the vulnerability level the questions listed in Annex A are answered. Taking the asset value and the threat rating a temporary risk level is calculated using the matrix provided in Table 5.

Table 5. Temporary Risk Matrix

		Asset value							
		1	2	3	4	5	6	7	8
Threat level	1	1	1	2	3	4	5	6	7
	2	1	1	2	3	4	5	6	7
	3	1	2	3	4	5	6	7	8
	4	2	3	4	5	6	7	8	8
	5	2	3	4	5	6	7	8	8

The outcome can be in-, decreased or stay unaltered based on the determined vulnerability level. As little data about vulnerabilities and threats are available, the asset value has the highest impact on the resulting risk level. To show the performance an exemplary RA result is provided in Table 6, combining the output of RA-Step 2, RA-Step 4 and RA-Step5 to a single risk level per asset.

Table 6. RA-Step 6 -Risk Assessment Results

Asset category	Asset value	Threat level	Risk temp	Vulnerability level	Risk level
E-Mail (corporate)	8	4	8	2	8
E-banking	7	5	8	1	7

Table 6. (*continued*)

E-health	8	4	8	2	8
Remote access (corporate)	7	5	8	1	7
Remote access (private)	6	5	7	1	6
Voice communication	6	3	6	1	5
Stored business documents	6	3	6	3	7
Physical device	6	2	5	0	5
Personal information (online synchronized)	4	3	4	2	4
E-Mail (private)	4	3	4	2	4
Social networking	4	3	4	1	3
Messaging	3	3	3	2	4
Personal information	4	2	3	2	3
Web access (browser)	2	4	3	3	4
Stored documents	3	1	2	2	2
Maps & Navigation	2	1	1	3	2
News client	1	1	1	1	1
Utilities	1	1	1	2	1

5   Mobile Device Risk Assessment (MDRA)

The process consists of three main stages, which are shown in Fig 1. MDRA is designed to operate in the following contexts:

- Private User
- Corporate User
- Hybrid mode of private and corporate usage

It is envisaged these contexts incorporate the principal stakeholders that interact with mobile devices. This distinction is important as there may be different security requirements and threat levels in the different contexts. An example to illustrate this is that the confidentiality requirement with regard to a private e-mail account is likely to be lower than compared to a corporate e-mail account. It is also important to ensure corporate IT administrators have the ability to control the risks associated to company information and this responsibility is not left to the user.

Various stakeholders exist within this process. End-users and corporate organisations have an obvious requirement for the system. Network operators also have an important role to play. Misuse of services on mobile networks cost operators a tremendous amount of money (i.e. telephony fraud).

The first stage of the process relies upon the network operator to undertake the RA process for each category and define default risk scores. This alleviates the workload from the individual user and also provides a mechanism for informed and educated responses to be given. The default values for all asset categories are then set (O_Phase 1). Should a finer level of assessment need to be made for a particular asset (rather than asset category) this can also be established (O_Phase 2). The second stage is executed by the organization, should the device been used to access or store company information. If it is simply a personal device, this stage is not necessary. Under the C_Phases, the company has the opportunity for defining which applications it has control of and undertaking the necessary RA process. (C_Phase 1). After the company has conducted their RA they can store their RA settings.

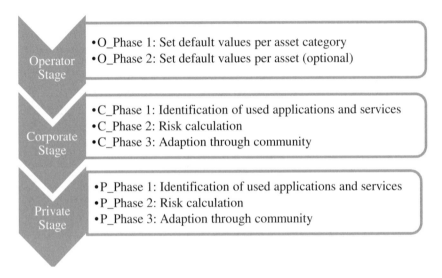

Fig. 1. Stage overview

The user of the device executes the last stage. Similar to the corporate stage, the installed applications and services are determined automatically and the risk level is calculated. In situations where the smart phone is used in a mixed (personal and corporate) context, only the applications that do not belong to the organization can be modified by the user. A private end-user starting the MDRA for the first time only has to choose his knowledge level – all other steps are automated.

P_Phase 3 is an essential phase. In order to keep the system up to date over time, the default values must be updated regularly. In order to integrate and automate the update a relative majority-voting scheme is proposed; where any alteration or modification of risk, made by a user, is transmitted to central storage by the network operator. Based on the knowledge level, chosen by the private end-user, different types of values, as shown in Table 7, can be edited. As soon as sufficient risk scores for a particular asset/application are available, the default value is replaced by the majority decision. The priority of the risk scores, assigned by the different parties involved, is shown in Table 8. It is also necessary with majority voting that a separation between private and corporate context exists. As such data is also stored centrally, the network operator has oversight and control if necessary to mitigate against any attacks against majority-voting systems. With wide adoption, risk estimation is moved away from the default values towards a community decision system.

Table 7. Community decision - editable RA input parameters

Knowledge level	Input paramters		
	Asset value	Threat	Vulnerability
Novice user	✓	⊘	⊘
Average user	✓	✓	⊘
Security expert	✓	✓	✓

Table 8. Priority of risk scores

Priority	Private context	Corporate context
1	Settings of user	Imported corporate settings
2	Community decision (majority voting data)	
3	Settings assigned through operator – O_Phase 2	
4	Default values inherited from corresponding asset category	

6 Evaluation

In order to evaluate the performance of the proposed methodology and to gather feedback a proof of concept prototype was developed. The prototype screens, which are shown in Figure 2 and 3, are a subset that was used to conduct a preliminary physical trial with thirteen participants. The participants were grouped into "novice user" (4 participants), "average user" (5 participants) and "security expert" (4 participants). Most participants were extensive application users, (based upon their own assessment), but few of them had ever considered installing applications to improve their security level.

This first screen shows the default view. It provides a list of installed applications and the automatically calculated risk level. The applications are assorted descending based on their risk level. In order to have a look on the input parameters, which were used for the risk calculation, the user simply selects the desired applications by touching it on the screen.

On the second screen the user can chose to have a closer look at the e-banking application "Money Transfer". On the resulting screen the values, which are assigned to the seven asset value categories, are shown in descending order. If the user wants to, this can be altered here. Furthermore, the asset value categories descriptions of threats, which may come with this application, are listed. But they cannot be changed. In order to change the threat rating, it is assumed that a certain level of information security knowledge is required. Therefore this can only be done in the advanced view.

Fig. 2. MDRA Prototype (a) Default Screen (b) Individual Application

Fig. 3. MDRA Advanced Screenshot

The user can change the view to "advanced". Compared to the base view from the first screen all input parameter values (asset value, threat and vulnerability rating) are shown on this screen. In order to change these values, the same procedure as before can be executed. Select the desired application by touching it on the screen. In contrary to the base view the user can change all values (asset value categories, threat and vulnerability rating)

After the walkthrough most participants, also the novice users, agreed that there is valuable information stored upon their mobile devices. Not all of the participants understood the way the risk was calculated the first time. The whole risk calculation process and the combination of asset, threat and vulnerability rating was especially challenging for novice users. Keeping that in mind the limitation of assessment options is an important concept. A novice user stated that too many options would prevent him from using such an application; however, the participants categorized as security experts preferred the more detailed view.

The walkthrough showed that novice users tend to use such an application in a passive way, which means they would use it as an information source without changing values. With an increasing knowledge level (average user and security experts) the participants tend to want to use such an application in an active way. This is important, as the automated update of the assigned values through adaption by the users is a vital concept of the proposed methodology.

Some participants identified that it would be a helpful feature to integrate the rating directly in the various application stores in order to have a look at the rating prior the installation of a particular application.

Providing information like security guidelines for a secure smart phone and application usage would also be appreciated. Taking this further one of the participants, who belonged to the group "security expert", stated that it would be an interesting feature to directly provide company guidelines and policies about mobile phone usage on the smart phone. Providing information directly where it is needed is supportive with regard to secure handling and can raise the user's awareness.

The walkthrough showed that people are interested in learning more about the risks they are facing. Half of the participants stated that they would use such a system, whereby the novice users tended to use the system in a passive way (as an information source). The average users and especially the security experts tend more towards an active usage (changing values). A further evaluation, using a larger group of participants is imperative, including a comparison between the risk estimation outcome of novice users and experts.

7 Conclusions

The main goal of this research was to develop a methodology, which enables mobile device users with differing knowledge levels to assess and understand their level of risk connected to their handset behavior. The second objective was to devise an approach that understood the risks associated with various actions and applications. Through those risk outputs, further research can be conducted on developing security countermeasures that do not simply provide a one-fits-all approach but tailors the response with the associated risk.

The largest assumption of this research is the focus upon the network operator and their need to undertaken the in the first instance RA, in order to establish the default values. Whilst there are some strong reasons for them to do so, other options do exist – security vendors themselves could be interested stakeholders that would provide the application and associated risk scores.

Future work needs to focus on the usability of such an approach and a wider comparison of novice user and security experts concerning the risk estimation with a fully operational prototype and full end-user evaluation. Whilst much discussion can be placed on the subjectivity of risk scores, MDRA provides the robustness and flexibility to suit a wide population basis in a user-friendly manner.

References

1. ITU Key Global Telecom Indicators for the World Telecommunication Service Sector, `http://www.itu.int/ITU-D/ict/statistics/at_glance/KeyTelecom.html`
2. Dagon, D., Martin, T., Starner, T.: Mobile phones as computing devices: the viruses are coming! IEEE Pervasive Computing 3(4), 11–15 (2004)
3. Ziemann, F.: http://www.pcwelt.de/news/Trojanische-Spiele-Mobile-Malware-in-sechs-Monaten-verdoppelt-351574.html
4. Richardson, R.: CSI Computer Crime and Security Survey. Computer Security Institute (2009), `http://www.gocsi.com`
5. Verkasalo, H.: Analysis of Smartphone User Behavior. In: 2010 Ninth International Conference on Mobile Business and 2010 Ninth Global Mobility Roundtable (ICMB-GMR), pp. 258–263 (2010)
6. Clarke, N.L., Furnell, S.M.: Advanced User Authentication for Mobile Devices. Computers & Security 26(2), 109–119 (2007)
7. Clarke, N.L.: Advanced User Authentication for Mobile Devices. PhD Thesis. University of Plymouth, United Kingdom (2004)
8. Carnegie Mellon University, `http://www.cert.org/octave/download/intro.html`
9. Insight Consulting, `http://dtps.unipi.gr/files/notes/2009-2010/eksamino_5/politikes_kai_diaxeirish_asfaleias/egxeiridio_cramm.pdf`
10. Clusif, http://www.clusif.asso.fr/fr/production/ouvrages/pdf/MEHARI-2010-Overview.pdf
11. Clarke, N.L., Karatzouni, S., Furnell, S.M.: Towards a Flexible, Multi-Level Security Framework for Mobile Devices. In: Proceedings of The 10th Security Conference, Las Vegas (2010)
12. Statista, `http://de.statista.com/statistik/daten/studie/157934/umfrage/anzahl-der-apps-im-itunes-app-store-seit-2008/`
13. Microsoft, `http://msdn.microsoft.com/en-us/library/ee823878%28CS.20%29.aspx`
14. Fried, S.: Mobile Device Security - A Comprehensive Guide to Securing Your Information in a Moving World. Auerbach Publications, Boca Raton (2010)

Annex A

TRUE	Are credentials transmitted via an encrypted channel?
TRUE	Is there a mechanism in place, so that the user can be sure to talk with the correct server (X.509 certificates for example)?
TRUE	Are all sensitive data transmitted via an encrypted channel?
TRUE	Is 3rd party encryption used for storage of data on the device?
FALSE	Are there any encryption algorithms used which are no longer considered as secure?
FALSE	Are there any encryption keys used which key length is too short?
FALSE	Are there any hashing algorithms used which are no longer considered as secure?
FALSE	Are there any hashing algorithms used which output length is too short?
FALSE	Are there any signing algorithms used which are no longer considered as secure?
FALSE	Are there any signing keys used which key length is too short?
FALSE	Are there any user data collected (and sent to a central server), without noticing the user in advance or at all?
TRUE	Is an authentication mechanism in place, to prevent unauthorized usage?
TRUE	Is an authorization mechanism in place, to prevent unauthorized usage of particular features?
TRUE	Is a bug reporting procedure in place, enabling user to report bugs and security issues?
TRUE	Is there a procedure in place to ensure regular updates of the application?
FALSE	Claims the application per default access to data stored on the phone, which are obviously not necessary (Game - access to personal data (phone numbers, calendar, etc.))?
FALSE	Are any input data processed without prior sanitation?
TRUE	Is the Up/Download of files with dangerous type restricted?
	Are any internal software information leaked through error messages?
TRUE	Implements the application handling of unusual/error conditions?
FALSE	Are any updates installed without integrity checks?
FALSE	Are there any known vulnerabilities/exploits, which are not fixed by now?
TRUE	Are the privileges of the application set to the minimum required per default?
TRUE	Are there any indications for a secure software development process like: security requirements, internal/external review, automated code review, abuses cases, risk analysis, penetration testing?
TRUE	Does the application logging (e. g. login, security events), in order to provide data for post incident analysis?

Author Index